ON THE RECORD

YTECHNIC

ON THE RECORD

Surveillance, Computers and Privacy –
The Inside Story

DUNCAN CAMPBELL
AND STEVE CONNOR

MICHAEL JOSEPH
LONDON

First published in Great Britain by Michael Joseph Ltd
27 Wright's Lane, Kensington, London W8
1986

British Library Cataloguing in Publication Data

Campbell, Duncan
On the record: surveillance, computers and
privacy: the inside story.
1. Privacy, Right of — Great Britain   2. Computers
— Access control   3. Public records — Great
Britain — Access control
I. Title   II. Connor, Steve
323.44'83   JC596.2.G7

ISBN 0 7181 2575 4 (hardback)
ISBN 0 7181 2576 2 (paperback)

Printed in Great Britain by Billing and Sons
Ltd, Worcester

Contents

Acknowledgements

We are grateful to many colleagues, friends and confidants, some of whom must unfortunately remain anonymous, for information and assistance in putting this book together, and for help, advice, criticism and guidance. In particular, we thank Stuart Anderson, Alan Burkitt, Alan Campbell, Claire Demuth, Paul Gordon, Julian Jaccotet, Gary Murray, Fred Pearce, Dan Re'em, Richard Sharpe, Joe Sim, Andy Thomas and Steve Walker. Tony Meredith, research assistant to Paddy Ashdown MP, provided valuable research material. Lynda Bransbury's information and criticism made a substantial difference to the accuracy and originality of our accounts of the major central government computer systems. Dr Chris Pounder was originally to have participated as a third co-author of this book, but moved to the GLC to work on police monitoring, and published his researches there. We are grateful to the Home Office for supplying detailed and unpublished information about the Police National Computer and about Home Office police computer policy. Duncan Campbell's assistant, Patrick Forbes, carried out much essential final research. We are obliged to Richard Kinsey and Robert Baldwin for supplying a copy of the job specification for an area constable in the Lothian and Borders Constabulary from their book, *Police Powers and Politics* (Quartet, 1982); and to the Data Protection Registrar, Eric Howe, for general discussion of the Data Protection Act, and for commenting on and correcting factual material in the last chapter of the book. As usual, all statements of opinion are our own, and should not be considered to have been endorsed by Mr Howe or anyone else whom we have thanked. Any mistakes that remain, too, are our responsibility.

Plates, Tables and Figures

Plates (between pages 128 and 129)

Tables

Figures

'The Area Constable should ...

Secure the services of at least one observer in every street, not a paid professional informant, but someone who knows the inhabitants and is inquisitive enough to find out what is going on and who is willing to pass on such information ...

Make himself known to local officials, ... housing department, social workers, gas and electricity board officials, or anyone who has legitimate access to private houses and premises and is in a position to give information ...

Cultivate shopkeepers, tradesmen and garage proprietors who are always a good source of information ...

His effectiveness ... will be judged by the amount of information he feeds to records of local crime intelligence.'

From the job specification for police area constables (confidential)

Introduction

Which large computers have details of your personal life on the record? What does the Police National Computer say about your 'association with organisations'? What suspicions about your sexual life, family relations or friends may have been put in a databank by government investigators who are checking your entitlement to financial benefits? What hidden dossier about your pattern of foreign travel may be updated, or details of your political views displayed, each time you present a computerised passport when travelling? Will National Insurance 'Numbercards' become part of a national identity-card system?

Why, in some areas, should as many as one in five British adults, most without criminal records, be the subject of police local intelligence files? In accordance with instructions such as those on the previous page, local intelligence gathered by area ('community') constables has been used to put millions of names onto intelligence indexes – which are increasingly held on computer. Under the 1984 Data Protection Act, members of the public have no right to see, check, challenge or correct such information if it is said to be held for 'the prevention or detection of crime' and disclosure would be likely to prejudice that purpose. The information may, however, be disclosed to any third party for the same purpose. Information may also be secretly supplied to police or Inland Revenue files from any confidential source – and no record or registration of such disclosure need be made. And whose names are contained in nearly two million Special Branch and MI5 files – and why?

Faced with these threats, some people say that they have 'nothing to hide'. They have 'done nothing wrong'. They ask, by implication, why others should fear to have information about their private lives exposed to public or official gaze. But such questioners cannot be serious. Information in government or police records is often inaccurate. Even if it is correct, it may have been obtained unfairly or unlawfully. It may be handled dishonestly or incompetently. It may have been provided for a different purpose from that to which it is later put. Few people would wish to grant others the untrammelled right to view their personal tax or medical records, to know the results of a means-test inspection, or to discover the black spots of family history – especially if such information might be erroneous, incomplete, even falsified. If information of this kind is systematically processed and distributed by computer, the damage done by improperly handled or revealed data may be worsened.

Personal privacy – in the context of this book, personal *information* privacy – gives the individual the right to some control over government or private activities which may affect his or her interests. There is nothing illegitimate about that. To suggest that individuals should not have some rights to control how personal information about them is used is to assume that agencies and organisations handling personal information are always benignly motivated, unprejudiced, even-handed in objectives, and staffed at every level by individuals of impeccable care, total honesty and scrupulous performance.

Such bodies do not exist. There are ample reasons for the ordinary person not to grant unqualified trust to those who seek or require personal information. Conflicts of interest between individual and state are real, necessary and unavoidable. Given the disparity of power and resources between individual and state when such conflicts arise, the right to privacy is one of the few defences an ordinary person has. Privacy is fundamental to personal integrity. It is an essential right, enshrined in international treaties on human rights to which the United Kingdom is signatory.

This book, we hope, explains why some people become scared to say what they think, or to ask for what they want or need. They fear that openly to criticise government or authority, or to challenge decisions, or to advertise needs, will result in files being opened; in information being passed; and that they may then suffer for it. Better to remain silent, they suspect. We should like to be able to say that such fears are ill founded. This book explains why we cannot do that.

Knowledge of official surveillance, and of unjustifiable trafficking in personal information, has what has been called in international courts a 'chilling' effect on people's willingness to exercise their rights or speak their minds. The dangers of unregulated databanks and information trafficking range from the simple harassment of being on unwanted mailing lists through to the systematic exclusion of certain strands of (lawful) opinion from public life. With that loss of civil liberty may go employment and other rights. By the late 1990s, government central computer databanks, bringing together all kinds of personal information, will exist in all but name. But even before that point is reached, privacy and liberties have already long been in danger.

When registration of personal databanks under the Data Protection Act became compulsory (shortly before this book was published), it was expected that between 200,000 and 600,000 databanks would be registered. Most are in the private sector. Many are relatively small – containing a few hundreds or thousands of entries. The register, to be published in 1987, may itself contain as many as half a million pages of information. Describing the entire spectrum of such databanks in this book would be neither reasonable nor practicable. It would also be premature, as well as unnecessary.

This book is about the major databanks which hold personal records on a large proportion of the general population. Most, but not all, such databanks are in the public sector, belonging to central government departments and the police. We look at how they were established and how they are being linked. Since most computer databanks started life as manual card indexes or filing systems, we have looked also at the manual predecessors to today's automatic systems – and at those of today's manual filing systems which may become major privacy-threatening databanks of the 1990s.

We start by explaining the legal right to privacy and how it has been implemented. The Data Protection Act has brought some statutory recognition for individual rights to information privacy. But the creation of the first-ever British privacy law has taken decades – a battle against a civil service and successive

administrations wholly uninterested in legislating. Even as the
new law was passed, ministers in Mrs Thatcher's government
remained resolutely opposed to the creation of an independent and effective body to protect privacy. Reluctantly, they
granted the Data Protection Registrar a measure of independence.

Despite its inadequacy – as we shall show – to deal even
with the existing problems of giant manual or computerised
databanks, the law will soon have to confront the new challenge of 'clever systems'. These are advanced computers – the
so-called 'fifth generation' – which can scan TV images or
photographs and identify faces or other features of a picture;
or which can interpret, understand and record human speech.
They include 'thinking' computers which learn in the same
way that humans do, adapting their behaviour to deal with
new situations or information that may be encountered. They
also include 'expert' computers, which can be used equally for
medical diagnosis or for tracking down 'target' social groups.
Expert computers will use the information held in linked
databanks to make decisions according to rules devised by
machines rather than by humans.

These new developments create the potential for highly
sophisticated automatic surveillance. The plummeting cost of
storing and processing computer data means that, during the
1980s and 1990s, there will be more and more such data
recorded on such diverse personal matters as foreign travel
(through new immigration computers and machine-readable
passports), telephone use (through itemised billing) and financial affairs (through the increasing use of credit and electronic
funds transfer (EFT) in the 'cashless society').

Control and intimidation of the entire population does not
require a wholly technocratic society. Civil and political
liberties are won – and lost – at the margins; it is how the
minority speak out and act, and how they are treated, that
determines issues of freedom for the majority. A telescreen or
telephone tap in every home is neither a necessary nor an
effective means for an elite to keep a population under control.
But large computer databanks are particularly suited to this
task. A computer's unique ability is rapidly to arrange data, to
identify exceptions, to distinguish dissenters, to isolate those

who are different. Legal or extra-legal sanctions can be used to discriminate against the non-conforming, or to punish unorthodoxy or dissent.

On the Record reveals a startling spectrum of threats to privacy posed by personal records on computer. They range from damaging and distressing minor information 'leaks' to the inequitable political power that major information databanks grant to an increasingly harsh and authoritarian public administration. The first chapter describes the recent history of the privacy issue in Britain. Chapter 2 explains the technology and programming of computer databases. We describe how 'clever systems' will pose new problems for a legal profession that has still to adapt to the present level of technology. Chapter 3 analyses existing and new threats to information privacy from public and private databanks, and reveals how many people have been or will be damaged by the improper use, inaccuracy, leakage or other abuses of personal information.

The next three chapters deal with the computer networks and information systems of central government. The central index which the Department of Health and Social Security is establishing at Newcastle will be a complete, computerised register of the entire adult population. It will hold full personal information, usually including details of employers, family, household and other circumstances. The information on this register may be, as now, freely available to the police and several other government departments. Both the DHSS and the Inland Revenue already operate a host of major computer databanks, holding the records of a lifetime – which, over the next 15 years, will be welded together. Once these databanks are established, expert computers can be used to identify the targets of future government social policies.

The treatment of confidential personal health information is the subject of Chapter 5. As every sector of the health service, from general practitioners to regional hospital administrations, puts personal information on computer, the threat to privacy grows with the increasing availability of such information. The medical professions are worried. New medical computer arrangements also mean that children now enter local and national computer records at birth, and never leave.

Chapter 6 focuses on travel and communications, and in

particular on the Home Office immigration services and the Customs and Excise. Automatic passport-reading machines will soon be linked to Home Office computers to supervise entry to and departure from the British Isles, checking on 'suspect' Britons and monitoring the movements of immigrants. The privacy of home life will soon be threatened by British Telecom plans to revamp the telephone system, creating computer records of who phones whom. The early computerisation of other government records, ranging from the postal-code system to TV licences, has already had an impact on personal privacy.

Police 'local intelligence' computer systems are described in Chapter 7. Such systems – which routinely hold large volumes of unsubstantiated and often derogatory information about anyone 'coming to notice' of the police – are slowly being welded into a nationwide network. The Police National Computer (PNC), all of whose special features have never before been fully described in a book, is detailed in Chapter 8. The PNC is, perhaps, the most powerful, rapidly accessible national computer network in Britain. It has repeatedly been abused to extract unauthorised information.

Chapters 9 and 10 describe the computer networks of the Special Branch and Security Service. The Special Branch anticipated that, by 1985, they would have 1.4 million names on file. MI5 has also developed its own huge, secret computer network, linked to other intelligence departments. In Northern Ireland, the effectiveness of computers in use by the security forces may have been overstressed – but nevertheless half the population of the North is on file.

The final chapter describes the weaknesses of the 1984 Data Protection Act in relation to public and private information gathering and trading. The Act resembles previous British equal rights or civil liberties legislation. The government has done its best to limit its effect, to leave enforcement agencies weak, and make the law as a whole sufficiently vague for court judgements to finish off such little protection as might remain to protect the average citizen.

With the year 1984 past, there may be a trend to regard George Orwell's warnings as dishonoured and disproven. But they remain as a true reminder about the nature of

administration. Like Big Brother, the designers of the surveillance cameras, national central indexes, police local intelligence systems, computer networks and loophole-ridden laws
usually claim to be acting wholeheartedly in the interests of
public welfare.

We know they are not. We hope you will read the facts and
agree.

DUNCAN CAMPBELL
STEVE CONNOR
DECEMBER 1985

1 The Politics of Information Privacy

British public opinion has long avowed concern for personal privacy – and, in particular, its protection from encroachment by centralised systems of surveillance and supervision, such as data processing machinery. Electronic computers – impersonal, mechanical, often incomprehensible and certainly quite unlovable – are consequently a centrepiece of popular demonology.

But public interest in privacy is matched and more than countered by official lack of interest. The key problem about computers and databanks is the nature of administration. The power of computers to convert fiction to totalitarian fact is in the hands of the administrators – administrators who should be accountable to both electors and elected, but seldom are, though official possession of personal information can confer the opportunity to govern in detail the lives and actions of masses.

For that reason, we concentrate primarily in this account on official databanks and on the handling of information by public agencies and organisations. From welfare to health, from taxation to policing, it is government agencies who are the collectors, distributors and users of the most sensitive of personal information. It is these agencies who have at their disposal, also, the most exclusive and effective means of social control. The record shows that society has been best protected from autocratic excesses not by the altruism or honesty of administrators but by their incompetence.

A similar conclusion was reached in 1978 by the government's own Data Protection Committee, which spent over two years examining in depth the threats which computers might pose to personal privacy. The committee's chair, Sir Norman Lindop, recalls:[1]

> We did not fear that Orwell's 1984 was just around the corner, but we did feel that some pretty frightening developments could come about quite quickly and without most people being aware of what was happening.

'In the view of most of us who have looked at the subject in some detail,' Lindop has added, 'the greatest threat, if threat there be, does not come from the private sector, from the entrepreneurial sector, it comes from the public sector.'[2]

Years before the scale of personal data on official computer had reached its present level, public concern on the issue was clear. In 1971, a Royal Commission on Privacy examined public attitudes to the subject through a wide-ranging national-opinion survey. They found that 'protecting people's privacy' was the social issue rated most important throughout the population. They also discovered that, among a wide range of potential threats to privacy outlined in their survey, none attracted more public concern, fear or hostility than the putative creation of a central computer, the collation of all personal data and files in a national databank.

Every group polled regarded such a databank as the most disturbing example of intrusion on privacy that the Royal Commission's survey team could cite – more disturbing, for example, than unsolicited sex manuals in the mail, spying neighbours or breaches of personal privacy by the news media. All but 7 per cent of the population considered the establishment of an open official databank a serious breach of privacy; and 90 per cent of the population wished the creation of a central computer to be prohibited by law. But – regardless of popular fears or the warnings of the Lindop committee that such a central computer should not come about by stealth – it is now in the process of creation.

Many extensive works have been written about the meaning of privacy. It is a social and political idea, which needs legal form to have effect and to be enforced. In fact, it is extraordinarily difficult to define privacy, particularly in relation to the handling of information. The type of personal information which the subject may desire the right to control will vary from country to country, and across age, class, sex, race and other barriers. Personality, temperament and culture each plays a role. Whether the handling of personal information affects privacy depends much less on the information itself than on *who* may have and use that information, which items of information are correlated, and what use is to be made of the information.

In Britain, the age of a woman is usually held to be particularly sensitive. It is not so in other European societies. Details of personal taxation and financial affairs, the secrecy of which is revered in the United Kingdom, are openly accessible to any enquirer in Sweden. Details of personal (and corporate) land and house ownership are wholly secret in England and Wales, but wholly public in Scotland. And so on. Some types of data are universally regarded as sensitive – information stored about personal health, sexual life and religious belief comes in this category. But the sensitivity with which information about criminal convictions is regarded can depend entirely on the individual's situation – on, for example, which social groupings he or she belongs to, or on a temporary concern such as facing an employment interview. Some male youths may wear convictions like a badge of pride, or regard them as a mere nuisance and think nothing of discussing them or having them known; while middle-class women may regard a single shoplifting conviction as an unending source of stress and shame.

'Data protection' is something of a misnomer, although we are stuck with it. In the 1984 Data Protection Act, data is given (otherwise inaccurately) to mean machine-readable information such as that stored on magnetic or paper tape, magnetic discs, and so on; while 'information' is human-readable, i.e., sheets of paper. The distinction between the two is anyway eroding, as optical character recognition (OCR) equipment has given computers the facility to read most ordinary printed text (such as this page) as efficiently as most humans. It is not the data, however, that needs to be protected, other than in the orthodox sense of security; it is the use to which it may be put that needs to be controlled.

'Information privacy' is often thought to be a more meaning-
ful term. A useful definition which we would endorse is 'the
claim of individuals, groups and institutions to determine for
themselves when, how and what information about them is
communicated to others'.

Britain's data protection laws were finally enacted not
through the good intentions of government, but in consequence of the European Convention on Human Rights,
which came into force in 1953, under the auspices of the
Council of Europe (embracing 21 non-Soviet bloc European
states). Although, throughout history, human societies and
civilisations have adopted legal codes requiring respect for the
rights and liberties of the citizen, the idea of an internationally
enforceable human rights code is relatively modern. Since the
Second World War there has developed a body of international
law – and accompanying regulatory and enforcement institutions – concerned with human rights. The British government, it may be noted in passing, has had more cases brought
against it in the European Court of Human Rights than any
other member of the Council of Europe. The British government's attitude in respect of human rights, as the following
account amply illustrates, has been both dilatory and negligent.

The starting point for recent human rights legislation is the
1948 United Nations Universal Declaration on Human Rights,
which called for 'respect for human rights and fundamental
freedoms for all, without distinction as to race, sex or religion'.
Regional treaties on human rights – such as the European
Convention – then followed. Article 8 of the European Convention deals with the right to privacy, and it is this article that has
ultimately led to the British data protection law:

1. Everyone has the right to respect for his private and family life,
his home and correspondence.

2. There shall be no interference by a public authority with the
exercise of this right except such as in accordance with the law
and is necessary in a democratic society in the interests of
national security, public safety or the economic well-being of the
country, for the prevention of disorder or crime, for the protection
of health or morals, or for the protection of the rights and freedom
of others.

When the Data Protection Act finally comes into effect, late in

1987, it will have been over 20 years since the issue was first raised in Britain as a matter of serious parliamentary and public concern. In the interim, legislation has been postponed, delayed and sidestepped via a bewildering collection of standard Whitehall dodges – one departmental committee report, one Royal Commission, two draft bills, three Private Members' bills (dismantled), three White Papers, four conveniently disruptive general elections, and official 'consultation' exercises almost beyond number. The two decades of non-legislation on privacy are as impressive a textbook achievement of Whitehall delaying tactics as one might hope not to find.

Privacy, in legislative terms, is a Home Office matter. With a few honourable exceptions, no one senior in the Home Office, be they civil servants or ministers – of either party – has ever given a damn about personal privacy. The process of giving British citizens the right to privacy began by accident, as an attempt to head off an MP's private bill on the legal 'Right to Privacy'. It has only now been enshrined in law because British international trading interests in information technology might otherwise have been damaged.

During the two decades of inaction, the Home Office first excluded all government activities from being considered as threats to privacy. Forced to broaden the issue, they ruled that Home Office interests, which in fact pose the major threat to privacy – police, immigration and national-security activities – should be wholly exempt from scrutiny. Finally driven to the point of near legislation, they nominated a Home Office official as a suitable protector of privacy against the abuse of personal information. Dragged by Parliament and public opinion far enough to give the Data Protection Registrar some measure of independence, they robustly fought to ensure that the Registrar had few duties, no powers to speak of and a staff as small as conceivable. To acknowledge that a little useful protection for privacy may yet have come from this process is not to minimise the determined and forthright avoidance of the issue successively displayed by Home Secretaries James Callaghan, Reginald Maudling, Merlyn Rees, William Whitelaw and Leon Brittan.

In February 1967 Alex Lyon MP introduced a Right of Privacy

Bill. It failed to get a second reading. But at the same time, the National Council for Civil Liberties (NCCL) launched a privacy campaign; and Justice, the British section of the International Commission of Jurists, started to draft potential legislation. A more serious threat, from the government point of view, arose in January 1970 in the form of a Right to Privacy Bill introduced by Brian Walden MP. Walden's bill was adapted from the draft by Justice, who had just published a report on privacy and the law. The Walden bill recommended a general, enforceable right to privacy. It attracted widespread support.

Neither government nor Home Office cared in the slightest for this proposal; they reached quickly for one of the regular Whitehall standbys – a Royal Commission. Walden was cajoled into withdrawing his bill during its second reading, so that the commission might deliberate. The Younger Commission on Privacy was appointed in May 1970, but central government activities were excluded from its terms of reference. The scope of Sir Kenneth Younger's investigations included computers, but the inquiry was charged only to:

> Consider whether legislation is needed to give further protection to the individual citizen and to commercial and industrial interests against intrusions into privacy by *private persons and organisations, or by companies* ... [our emphasis].

Although 'many of the anxieties which had led to the demand for the creation of a legal right of privacy concerned the activities of Government departments and other public agencies', government was to be excluded from examination or consideration. Home Secretary James Callaghan ruled that government was already 'accountable directly or indirectly to the electorate' for their activities. So far as computers were concerned, the government 'was considering the possibility of working out a code of practice' for the use of government-owned computers. (Nothing happened.)

Younger reported in July 1972,[3] recommending, *inter alia*, legislation on technical surveillance ('bugging') devices and the rapid creation of a 'standing commission' to keep under review the gathering and handling of personal information on computer. This issue had attracted more concern than any other (see page 20). The Home Office offered no action, but announced a new consultative exercise in order to 'take public reaction and the views of those interested in this matter into account before announcing our conclusions'. A White Paper would be proffered 'in due course'. A general election conveniently intervened before any further action was needed.

Some of Younger's recommendations were adopted in the Consumer Credit Act of 1974, which now gives everyone the right to check, challenge and correct any credit references that may be held on them. (The provision came into effect in May 1978.) Such limited measures did not seem unduly threatening to Whitehall. By 1974, four years had passed since the Walden bill, and government action on computers and privacy had successfully been avoided.

The incoming Labour administration promised an early White Paper on the issue – no later than the summer of 1974. By January 1975, the White Paper remained unpublished. Home Office ministers had found 'a need to re-examine certain parts [of it]'. It was eventually published in December 1975, eighteen months late. A supplement listed central government computers then in use. That it ever emerged at all owed a great deal to Alex Lyon, then a newly appointed Home Office junior minister, who as a member of the Younger commission had signed a minority report recommending stronger protection for personal privacy. To assist in drafting the White Paper, Lyon brought into the Home Office the distinguished barrister Paul Sieghart, who was chair of the executive committee of Justice and a determined and impressive privacy campaigner. Sieghart had worked on the drafting of Walden's bill, and was subsequently appointed to the Data Protection Committee.

The 1975 Home Office White Paper was drafted in less than the usually vague terms. *Computers and Privacy* warned that:[4]

> The time has come when those who use computers to handle personal information, however responsible they are, can no longer remain the sole judges of whether their own systems adequately safeguard privacy.

A Data Protection Committee was to be appointed forthwith, with the intention that it should lead directly to legislation for an independent Data Protection Authority. In February 1976, Sir Kenneth Younger was appointed to lead the new committee, but he died shortly afterwards. His place was taken by the then director of Hatfield Polytechnic, Sir Norman Lindop. The Lindop committee started work in July 1976. Curiously, one of the committee appointees – a senior IBM manager – was said to have been a past employee of MI5.[5] The Data Protection Committee reported in June 1978; six further months elapsed before the government published the report.[6] The Lindop report described how an independent, statutory Data Protection Authority should be set up; and recommended a range of codes of practice, legally enforceable, to govern the handling of personal data in different areas of concern.

By 1979, over eight years had passed since the Walden bill, with legislative action successfully avoided. But Lindop offered the Home Office clear recommendations for early legislation, to which the government had earlier said it was committed. The Home Office offered no action, however, but announced a new consultative exercise so that 'interested bodies' might offer their comments on the report. In effect, all the people whom Lindop had just consulted were to be consulted again. In January 1979, Home Office junior minister Lord Boston stated that 13 government departments would soon be consulting over 200 such bodies, seeking their views. Home Secretary Merlyn Rees explained that this process might take some time as he did 'not think it appropriate to impose a rigid time limit upon consultation'. In the event, the new consultations eventually took nearly two years to complete. The Home Office studied the responses, co-ordinated them, and considered their view. By the time the responses had been fully examined, and a suitable view formed, a general election had conveniently intervened. The new government had no policy, a clean slate, and plenty of time to start re-thinking the issue from the beginning.

The new incumbents at the Home Office were, from the departmental point of view, commendably uninterested in information privacy. They wanted legislation on it like they wanted a hole in the head. But in their first report of the new Parliament, the House of Commons Home Affairs Committee decided to examine the Home Office's remarkable record in delaying and obstructing legislation[7] – and in particular the way in which Royal Commissions and sundry committee reports had been employed as a substitute for action. Over the preceding decade, Home Office responsibilities had been considered by more than 40 Royal Commissions and other committees, and examined in seventeen House of Commons reports. But almost nothing had happened as a result. The first issue the House of Commons chose to examine in its inquiry was the history of privacy legislation and the department's treatment of the Lindop report.

After receiving a 'disturbing impression of the Department's response', the Home Affairs Committee reported that the Home Office could only be described as 'dilatory and complacent'. The committee spent a particularly arduous day in July 1980 trying to get intelligible information from Home Office witnesses. Home Office Deputy Secretary Ralph Shuffrey was repeatedly asked when legislation would come; repeatedly he answered that it was 'under consideration', no more. When it was pointed out that a special Council of Europe Convention on data protection would soon be in effect, Shuffrey suggested that this provided good reason for further delay:

> It is not necessarily a good idea to have a policy cut and dried before the convention is ready for signature ...

The Home Affairs Committee pointed out that many prospective signatories to the convention had determined their data protection policy and legislated years previously. By 1980, at least eleven major western nations had data protection legislation. Shuffrey also rejected the complaint that British industry was losing business because of the lack of legislation. The Home Office, he said, knew of 'few, if any, examples of loss of business arising from the non-implementation of Lindop'. The Home Office didn't know because it hadn't cared to find out. Furious business managers and Conservative MPs rapidly disabused the Home Office of Shuffrey's complacent view.[8] Two months later, the Cabinet Office produced a formal report warning of the economic costs of being debarred from international data processing business.

Despite British delaying tactics in Strasbourg (Mr Shuffrey called it '[action] to ensure that the draft Convention is phrased in the most sensible terms'), the Council of Europe's Committee of Ministers approved the Convention in October 1980. Styled the *Convention for the Protection of Individuals with regard to Automatic Processing of Data*, the new agreement was opened for signature at the start of 1981. The Convention requires each signatory to have data protection legislation, and not to transfer personal data to or from countries lacking such legislation. It prescribes a basic right to individual privacy, in terms broadly similar to the British data protection principles (see page 32). One of the conditions with which member states of the Council of Europe have to comply is the appointment of authorities to supervise the operation of data protection laws. Britain signed the Convention in May 1981 – but could not ratify it until data protection legislation had been passed.

The Home Office was cornered. Consumer groups, civil rights bodies, medical and other professions, computer operators and users, trade unionists, the information technology industry and other government departments now shared an interest in early legislation. The Home Office promised an early statement. None came until March 1981, when Home Secretary William Whitelaw conceded that legislation 'in principle' would have to come 'when an opportunity offers'. It would be the 'minimum' necessary to comply with the Convention. But, first, there would be a White Paper, so that the government's views could be discussed and appropriate groups consulted yet again.

Junior minister Timothy Raison explained in September 1981 that, contrary to the practice in every other country in the world which had appointed an independent data protection authority or ombudsperson, in Britain the Home Office itself would be a suitable body to supervise the operation of data protection laws, as 'we shall be accountable to parliamentary and public scrutiny in a way which would not apply to a non-accountable body'.

A new statutory body would only be unaccountable to Parliament if the Home Office made it non-accountable. However, it fell to Sir Norman Lindop to reconvene his Data Protection Committee and report on the absurdity of this proposal and commentary. 'We could not envisage any department of government satisfying the criteria of independence and impartiality,' he considered, adding that 'the Home Office can hardly be held to be impartial or disinterested in the area of personal information'.[9] Citing the department's direct responsibility for the Metropolitan Police (and Special Branch), immigration, national security, prison and probation services, he pointed out that the Home Office was 'necessarily deeply involved with some of the most sensitive areas of personal data collection and handling in the public sector'.

By the start of 1982, 12 years had passed since the Walden bill, 15 years since the issue had been first raised; the European Convention was a year old – and all government action had been successfully avoided. Labour MP Michael Meacher proposed a private member's Data Protection Bill. Like its predecessors, it did not reach a second reading. But a remarkable accident of fate now forced political commitment and a timescale for action onto a reluctant Home Office.

The *Sun* newspaper embarked on an exercise in breaching Meacher's personal privacy by hiring private detectives to see how much information they could gather on his personal life. Hedging their bets, they knew the exercise would either yield embarrassing data on his personal life (a good *Sun* story) or alternatively illustrate how even innocuous information could be gathered to the detriment of the citizen (a good shock-horror story). They got the latter (see page 79). When the *Sun*'s probe into Meacher's personal life was raised in Parliament, the Prime Minister responded with unusual sympathy and characteristic impetuousness. 'I share your distaste,' Mrs Thatcher told the questioners, adding that legislation was 'urgent'. It was, she pronounced, the government's intention to legislate on data protection in the next session of Parliament. This was the first that stunned and dismayed Home Office officials had heard of it.

Now the promised White Paper had actually to be written. It emerged hastily two months later. After years of effort, and a thousand pages of previous reports and White Papers, the Home Office proposals covered scarcely six pages. The new law, the Home Office then said, would be the 'minimum additional burden that is consistent with proper protection'. Their proposal to put a Home Office official in charge of data protection had quickly been laughed out of court. There would be an independent Registrar. But the Registry would be small: a staff of 20, and 'less once the Register is established'. Consequently, the Registrar's ability to police personal information privacy would be made impossible as he would 'not have the resources to supervise the operation of data systems in detail'. Manual files and records were to be excluded from the register. There would be no binding codes of practice.

The White Paper on 'proposals for legislation', published in April 1982, stated that the purpose of legislation would be:[10]

> [to] ensure that the United Kingdom's substantial international trade in information, and its key role as a crossroads on the international data highway, are not compromised ... without legislation, firms may be at a disadvantage compared with those based in countries which have data protection legislation.

The White Paper had presented the forthcoming bill as a measure which would provide protection for privacy. But the proposed register was, and remains, subject to many defects. Databanks used for national security purposes would not be registered. Many other government and police files would or could be exempt from subject access. Anyone who had registered a databank, and thereby advertised compliance with the principle that 'personal data held for any purpose or purposes shall not be used or disclosed in any manner incompatible with that purpose', was, however, to be able to 'make information available to the authorities ... [and would] not be required to register such disclosures of information'. The White Paper stated that such 'derogation' from normal practice (i.e., the absence of normal protection) was permissible for 'protecting state security, public safety, the monetary interests of the state, or the suppression of criminal offences'. But the strong qualifying words which appear in the European Convention, namely that such alterations must be on the grounds that they are 'a *necessary* measure in a democratic society' (our emphasis), were omitted.

The Data Protection Committee described the permission to transfer data without proper registration as a 'palpable fraud on the public'. At a conference to discuss the bill, Paul Sieghart put the matter succinctly. He regretted that:[11]

the British statute book [would be] disfigured by a public and official register of users of computerised data systems which purports to tell the truth, but will in fact tell lies.

But the exemptions remained in the Act as eventually passed (see pages 304–6).[12] The relevant section (Section 28) makes the Act a charter for the abuse of privacy and the abandonment of protection, in areas in which it matters most.

The bill was published in December 1982. It set out the data protection principles, which are listed in Table 1 (overleaf). The purpose of the bill was to do the 'minimum necessary' to enable Britain to ratify the European data protection convention. Manual records were excluded, but computerised records of almost every description had to be registered; failure to register was to be a criminal offence. The Registrar was nevertheless given few formal powers and duties. The bill had failed to make the statute book when a general election was called in 1983. Before that time, the government had estimated that registration would take at least two years, meaning that a new Act could not take effect until 1985.

Despite the collapse of the 1982 Data Protection Bill because of the election, the argument was over. A new bill, presented quickly by the returning government in June 1983, was described as 'simplified'. Computer information held solely for payroll and accounting purposes was excluded. In a move to further weaken the bill – which the Home Office were pleased to describe as 'easing the Registrar's workload [and enabling] him to devote more of his resources to the general oversight of data protection' – the Registrar lost powers to enter premises to check on the conduct of databank operators. The new bill required him to apply to a circuit judge for this purpose.

The bill faced renewed, fierce and well-deserved criticism, particularly from such powerful professional lobbies as the British Medical Association (BMA). The BMA described it as 'a load of holes joined together'. The major features criticised were the total exclusion of manual records, the vaguely drafted definitions and terms of reference, and above all the numerous and very widespread exemptions. It was rather doubtful, according to both the National Council of Civil Liberties and Conservative Lawyers, that the bill even achieved its objective

Table 1
The data protection principles

1. The information to be contained in personal data shall be obtained, and personal data shall be processed, fairly and lawfully.

2. Personal data shall be held only for one or more specified and lawful purposes.

3. Personal data held for any purpose or purposes shall not be used or disclosed in any manner incompatible with that purpose or those purposes.

4. Personal data held for any purpose shall be adequate, relevant and not excessive in relation to that purpose or those purposes.

5. Personal data shall be accurate and, where necessary, kept up to date.

6. Personal data held for any purpose or purposes shall not be kept for longer than is necessary for that purpose or those purposes.

7. An individual shall be entitled –

    (a) at reasonable intervals and without undue delay or expense –
      (i) to be informed by any data user whether he holds personal data of which that individual is the subject; and
      (ii) to access to any such data held by a data user; and
    (b) where appropriate, to have such data corrected or erased.

8.* Appropriate security measures shall be taken against unauthorised access to, or alteration, disclosure or destruction of, personal data and against accidental loss or destruction of personal data.

* Applies only to computer bureaux.

of enabling Britain to ratify the European Convention. The vagueness of its terms created considerable doubt as to how the bill would apply to computer applications such as word processing systems. The weak position of the Registrar was attacked, and there was renewed pressure for an independent authority, as Lindop had recommended. But if there was one thing the Home Office would not do, it was to accept any part of any of Lindop's suggestions. Because of this hostility, all reference to codes of practice was excluded.

During examination in the House of Commons, the exemption provisions continued to attract the greatest criticism. The Home Secretary proposed to grant to himself, rather than the Registrar, powers to create special regulations for data on religious belief, political opinions, physical or mental health, or sexual life. He would take further powers to determine the extent of subject access to health and social work records. And in one small but sweeping section, the Home Secretary was granted power to exempt from subject access any material the disclosure of which was already restricted or prohibited by an existing enactment. Since all information handled by the government is prohibited from unauthorised disclosure under the Official Secrets Acts, this section (Section 34 (2)) allows the complete exclusion of the whole or any part of any government databank from subject access, if the department does not wish to authorise disclosure. For such access to be obtained regulations would have to be drafted and laid before Parliament. But in the last resort, the government can rule – and might yet decree – that despite the Act there should be no subject access to any of its databanks.

As the bill was debated, the Home Office refused to give way on these provisions. Ministers also refused to appoint an advisory committee to help the Registrar – even though a suggestion to this effect had been made in their own 1982 White Paper. The White Paper had given a cautious endorsement to the codes of practice proposals, but this too was now rejected; it was, after all, a Lindop heresy. The government was forced to drop a proposal which would have wholly exempted from subject access all personal data held for the 'control of immigration'. Such a provision was completely contrary to the letter, as well as the spirit, of the European Convention. There was no permission under the Convention to 'derogate' (make exclusions) in respect of immigration records when they did not involve crime, taxation or national security.

A more remarkable example of the unfitness of the Home Office to supervise data protection would be hard to find. The sole department concerned in the control of immigration had sought *carte blanche* to continue to gather personal information on possible unlawful immigrants secretly from other departments and public agencies. The move was intended to protect the system whereby the Home Office encouraged local offices of other departments, particularly those concerned with health and social security, to provide details of their clients, for immigration checks (see page 112). Naturally, the victims of this process were usually Asian or West Indian blacks, many of whom, although not subject to immigration control, were nonetheless checked and harassed. Critics pointed out that this exemption was unnecessary to deal with criminal offences concerned with illegal immigration. But for the sake of Home Office convenience and prejudice, the bill lumped persons subject to immigration control together with criminals.

The Home Office argued that immigration fell within the meaning of 'protecting the rights and freedoms of others', which they evidently took to mean their right and freedom to keep other people out of the country. But the immigration exemption was dropped after four months' debate. Had the Home Office succeeded in its self-interested intentions, the bill would have failed even to achieve its primary (commercial) objective – the ratification of the European Convention. Another major concession for the privacy of patients' records was won by the BMA and the powerful medical lobby. An independent agreement was reached between the DHSS, the Association of Chief Police Officers and the BMA that medical data should not be disclosed except by a doctor, and only in extreme circumstances without the consent of the patient. The increasingly tortuous Act was again modified to allow the Secretary of State to exempt some categories of data from the exemptions to the non-disclosure provisions. In plain English, this meant that health information could not normally be passed to police, tax or security authorities without the disclosure being admitted.

Finally, the Home Office introduced amendments requiring the Registrar to investigate (non-trivial) complaints brought to attention (he had previously been given no duty to do this), and to promote the adoption of codes of practice. During its final reading in June 1984, the Labour Party chose to support the bill.

The Data Protection Act received the Royal Assent in July 1984. Mr Eric Howe, the Deputy Director of the National Computing Centre in Manchester and chair of the National Computer Users' Forum, was selected as the first Data Protection Registrar, at a salary of £35,000 a year – equivalent to a Deputy Secretary in the civil service. It took less than a year for him to discover that the Home Office's concept of fewer than 20 staff and a diminishing workload was an hilarious underestimate. In August 1985, the Registry was given an establishment of nearly 50 staff, with a starting budget of £1.2 million. There might be over half a million register entries, many times the number originally estimated before the bill became law. Complaints about the alleged misuse of computer data started arriving during 1985 – even though the Act would not take effect for another two years.

Some public servants made an auspiciously early start with the Act, seeking its aid in situations it did not and was never intended to cover. Even before the bill was passed – after years of fighting it – some Whitehall officials started using its terms as an excuse for *more* secrecy, in order to withhold public records from disclosure.[13] By the beginning of 1985, voluntary advice agencies began reporting that officials in many public services – gas, electricity, and local authorities – were citing the Act in refusing to disclose personal data to advice agency workers who were acting on behalf of their clients. This new attention to personal privacy would have been commendable, were it not that the new law – even if the information *is* held on computer, and the Act *were* in force – does not restrict the authorised transfer of data in these situations; and that the officials' real intent, perhaps, was to protect their own privacy at work from the public and their representatives.

Offices for the Data Protection Registry were established in 1985 in Wilmslow, Cheshire. The two-year transitional period for the Act to take effect began with the opening of registration of data users in November 1985. The initial registration period ended on 11 May 1986. It is now an offence to operate a databank holding personal information unless you have registered, and are acting in accordance with the data protection principles or your register entry. Each user has to pay £22 for a three-year registration period. The register, itself stored on computer by the Datasolve bureau, at a cost of about £2.5 million, will be published via libraries or Viewdata (Prestel) services.

The subject access provisions, finally granting individuals the right to check and correct personal information held on computer (subject, of course, to the numerous exemptions), take effect on 11 November 1987. For better or worse, the Home Office's long battle against privacy legislation ended with the 1984 Act. But the war was far from over.

Most people now know that computers store personal medical information, tax and financial details, social security and employment records, police criminal records and other intelligence. But very few outside the departments directly concerned are aware that several very large government computer complexes are being expanded and interconnected, which will result in the linkage of important but hitherto distinct record systems. Linkages between different computer databanks already exist – but so far they have been partial. Computer systems such as those run by the police or MI5 now have both the technological potential and the legal authority to extract personal information from all other official databanks.

Orwell's fictional design for the year 1984 was not completed on time or to its original specification. But many key elements of technocratic autocracy are available today. Government departments and agencies now hold one and a half *billion* personal computer records. By the year 2000, public sector databanks will probably store more than 600 gigabytes (about one hundred thousand million words) of personal information, accessible from a hundred thousand computer terminals; no one will be excluded. Every day, a new government office is computerised. Central government will remain the largest holder and processor of personal information for the foreseeable future, followed closely by other public agencies such as the police service.

For the individual, there is a balance of advantage and risk. Much information is held for the ostensible benefit of the person named on a computer record (the data subject), for example to provide appropriate health care or to grant correct welfare benefits. But many databanks are concerned almost entirely with information of which the holding is at worst to the disadvantage of the individual concerned and at best intended to strengthen the hand of authority. These databanks include the information files of the police and security services. The terms of the Data Protection Act were largely designed by the Home Office, which sponsors or controls those same agencies. The most sensitive personal data are often held by agencies which are the least regulated.

Successive governments have found it difficult to grasp or tolerate the idea that citizens might need independent protection and some statutory rights for their defence against the authorities. Opposition to libertarian measures guaranteeing individual rights still remains entrenched in the Home Office.

An American specialist on privacy, attorney John Shattuck of the American Civil Liberties Union, warned during the 1970s' US debate on privacy and freedom of information that:

> Power may come out of the barrel of a gun, but far more power comes out of a computer or databank, particularly if the information in it relates to people who do not know that it has been collected or cannot challenge its accuracy or use.

Shattuck was analysing the conflict between the need to collect personal information to support essential social services and the danger that such information, in another guise, transferred elsewhere without consent, provides an insidious and powerful means of exerting social control. Trust in institutions should not be unconditional.

In the mid-seventies the Lindop committee took evidence – or at least attempted to take evidence – from the Metropolitan Police. At the start of a hearing its three witnesses were asked by Sir Norman Lindop if they minded their evidence being tape recorded so as to assist the committee's clerks. They certainly did mind. They went on to tell Lindop that his committee – appointed on the authority of the Home Secretary himself – was untrustworthy. Lindop then asked why they, alone of all the witnesses to the committee (including three Chief Constables and many senior civil servants), had objected to the tape recording.

'I'm sorry to say this, Sir Norman,' responded the Assistant Commissioner of the Metropolitan Police, 'but there are members of your committee whose loyalty we cannot take for granted.' In the words of one participant, the police demonstrated 'a remarkable paranoia' in seeing 'danger in a group of almost boringly respectable middle-aged establishment figures'. If these senior officers of the Metropolitan Police thought an official and distinguished Home Office Committee disloyal by their remarkable lights, then who was not? Who in society would not qualify for Special Branch surveillance of the most punitive sort at the hands of these men?

The Data Protection Committee was infuriated, and Sir Norman Lindop wrote in protest to the Home Secretary, who was, after all, also ultimately responsible for the Metropolitan Police. The protest was of little avail; Rees, an unusually unprepossessing, weak and unimaginative holder of the Home Secretaryship, was evidently as unable to call the police to order as he was uninterested in the committee's work.

These incidents, as Fred Martin, one of its members later observed, should have enabled the committee to spot the 'writing on the wall' and realise that the official commitment to wide-ranging data protection legislation was suspect. Martin, Glasgow University's Professor of Social Administration, suggested that part of the reason for the eventual disregard of the Lindop committee's work was the Thatcher government's whimsical attitude to public-interest organisations:[14]

> The incoming government was committed to the destruction of what it was pleased to call 'quangos'. How useful to manufacture a name like this, a slightly comic, slightly ominous name which enables you cheerfully to demolish some useless, some harmless, but some quite valuable and constructive bodies. How could they contemplate setting up a Data Protection Authority which could be immediately identified as another quango?

The Data Protection Act, Martin predicted accurately, would 'ensure that there is no embarrassment to government activities'. He added his own epitaph to the work of the Data Protection Committee:

> The fact that the report has been so effectively neutralised is a striking testimony not only to political indifference, but to the ease with which some powerful interests can take advantage of that indifference to ensure that their own domain remains inviolate.

2 Inside a Databank

This book is about databanks, but it is not – much – about computers as such. The machines on their own do not threaten civil liberties – although it is important to remember that certain types of technology, particularly that developed for specialised military purposes, are first created to meet requirements of a political or administrative sort. Some sophisticated developments in the use of computers, such as pattern and voice recognition, are of obvious value in police and intelligence applications, and it is usual to find that such organisations have taken the early research lead in these areas.

With some qualifications, what happens inside a computer is irrelevant to the present discussion. What matters is the uses to which the computer is put. Broadly, computers will do anything they are told to do with information that they receive, providing the instructions they are given are unambiguous. To understand the nature of a database – or, less formally, a databank – requires nothing beyond ordinary understanding and familiar images. Once the image of a computer as a variation on a clerk holding a card-index box is established, it is possible simply to establish what a computer can do that *is* different. The distinctive features of a computer are its ability to store large quantities of data; to operate very, very quickly; and to do so with a remarkable degree of accuracy. Computers are servile creatures, whose operations are wholly determined by and are in essence predictable from the stored instructions – usually known as software or programs – with which they have been provided.

Compared to card indexes and clerks, computers are extremely small, and cheap. Let us envisage a basic personal card index which contains a name, address and about a hundred words on each 'data subject'. It is a large index, covering no fewer than five million people, stored on cards six inches by four. To store and access these card-index boxes requires the space of a standard tennis court. The boxes themselves occupy five rows each forty feet long, six feet high and eighteen inches deep.

But in 1984, we might have bought a computer disc-storage system which could hold all this data, for less than £100,000. The discs are coated in magnetic material, spin at very high speed while reading and writing heads (similar in principle to those found in tape recorders) move in and out to look at or change ('write') data onto concentric circles, or 'tracks' on the disc.

A disc-storage system is the size of a wardrobe – six feet tall, and about four feet square. One particular disc-storage system, which is not unusual in its capacity, is called the IBIS 5000 and stores, in the jargon, 5 gigabytes of computer data. The byte is the yardstick, the basic measure of such data. One thousand bytes are a kilobyte (KB), one million bytes are a megabyte (MB), and a thousand million bytes are a gigabyte (GB). Technology has not quite advanced to the point where there is a need to identify a unit of data storage of a million million bytes, although that time will come.

A byte is a quantity – 8 smaller 'bits' – of binary electronic data. But for our purposes, a byte can be regarded as more or less the same thing as a single letter or digit on a written page. This book has been written on a computer. The page you are looking at, while being written, used up about 2700 bytes of the computer's disc store. The whole of this chapter is about 40 kilobytes. The entire text of *On the Record* uses about 840 kilobytes of disc storage. (This is slightly larger than the total number of letters, since extra storage space is needed by the computer to remember where paragraphs start, and so on.)

In the manual card index, information is found in specified places on each card. The name of the data subject is at the top, together with a reference number we have given her or him. Below that comes the address and telephone number, followed by the names of her or his two best friends and any pets, followed by other information. According to the regulations governing the work of the tennis-court card-index clerks, only certain predetermined sorts of information can be recorded on the cards, and each must be written on a prescribed line of the card. The cards are indexed in alphabetical order.

Most computer databanks follow essentially the same pattern. Each index card is replaced by an electronic *record*, stored on a disc. In order to operate the disc store, a computer processor performs most of the work of the scurrying Dickensian clerks, and a new breed of clerks – called terminal operators – take their place, equipped with visual display units (VDUs). To look at a particular record, the terminal operator types in the name of the person concerned on a keyboard, just as the clerk would go to the appropriate index box to extract the card. The record may even *look* like an index card – to all intents and purposes, it records the same information, and handles it in the same way.

This type of computer operation is called an *on-line* system, a term appearing occasionally in later chapters. Broadly, it means that the computer more or less immediately processes the information and gives the answer. Some types of enquiries – for example, the production of statistics from the database – would not be handled on-line. A written instruction would be sent to the computer centre; and a boxful of printout returned the following day. Enquiries which may generate a large volume of information or printout are less suitable for on-line operations.

So what difference does the computer make? Suppose that a detective arrives with news of a particularly foul murder. The police do not know who did it, but a reliable informant has told them that he lives in a house called Chestnuts, has a pet called Cripps, and will be fleeing to Bolivia in two days' time. Could the card index be checked, they ask, for people answering to this description? To check each of the five million index cards would take a single clerk about two normal working years. Every card must be looked at to see if the house is called Chestnuts; and, if so, is the pet called Cripps? To find the villain within the 48-hour time limit would require more than 80 clerks continuously working side by side. But there isn't room for that number to work together on the tennis court. The villain will be languishing in the hot Bolivian sun well before the search for his identity is finished.

But the computer can perform the same exhaustive search extremely quickly. The central processor can extract information from the disc store and check it against the informant's tipoff, at the rate of 3 megabytes per second. All the information in the databank can be searched in less than half an hour.

But computers are capable of performing this sort of information trawling in another way, enhancing their effectiveness by a further order of magnitude, by means of free text retrieval (FTR) – a system whose potency scares many people who are concerned about personal information privacy. An alternative system, called Contents Addressable File Store (CAFS), creates a similar facility, by changing the physical nature of the computer (hardware) rather than altering its stored instructions (software).

FTR makes searching for random items of information much faster. A search taking half an hour is a very long time indeed by computer standards. The use of such time on a large installation is also costly. In the example given above, the search took so long because the known information was not indexed. On the other hand, had the detective arrived with news that the murderer was called Bill Bloggs and asked for his address, the computer would have come up with the reply within a few thousandths of a second (because the computer's records, like the tennis-court cards, are indexed by name).

To make searching a database more efficient, more than one element may be indexed. If the clerks at the tennis court had frequently been asked for information about people who had particular pets, or who lived in particular towns, they might find it convenient to create cross-reference indexes – yet further sets of cards, this time organised in alphabetical order of pet name or town name. The new card-index boxes occupy another two tennis courts, and twice as many clerks have to be employed to keep the cross-reference index cards up to date. Naturally, the computer can do this too, a great deal faster. If our original computer databank was also indexed by house name, for example, then obtaining a list of all those on record living in houses called Chestnuts would take no longer than finding the man called Bloggs. The search to see which of these had a dog called Cripps would be over within a second.

Suppose, however, that we want to perform the same

operation on *unstructured* data like the text of this chapter. Free text retrieval can do that for us. This book – or thousands of other potential data sources like it – could be fed into a database, without predefining any structure or context for the data concerned, and *every substantive word of every record would be indexed*. So every occurrence of any data item – whether it be in a newspaper report, a criminal records file, a report from an informant, the electoral register – can rapidly be located. The characteristic of free text storage is that there is no need to define *in advance* what data will be entered or to define any structure within which the given data will appear.

Had our tennis-court card index been put into a database which was searched by FTR, the record on the man with the dog called Cripps could have been located in a few tenths of a second – as fast as if we had known his name to start with. But FTR has a disadvantage. Because every significant word (other than common words like 'the', 'of' or 'for') in an FTR databank is indexed unless the user chooses otherwise, a lot of extra space is required. Instead of one of those wardrobe-sized IBIS disc stores, we should probably need three, for the same amount of basic data stored. The computer processor would also have to be larger, since as well as answering the terminal operators' enquiries, it would have to maintain the many indexes, keeping them up to date as new data was entered, deleted, amended, or moved around the storage system. For this reason, the extra expense of operating an FTR system is only met by those organisations – such as the Special Branch – who expect many of their enquiries of the computer database to be of the unstructured, unpredictable kind.

Another aspect of FTR and other advanced databases is the ability to provide a dictionary, thesaurus or 'concordance' of equivalent or similar terms or phrases. Different people putting data into the system may use different terms or descriptions for the same attribute – for example, by describing eye colour variously as 'blue-grey', 'grey' or 'blue-green'; or light brown hair as 'fair' or just 'brown'. Such dictionary systems may also make allowance for such things as phonetically equivalent or near-equivalent names – for example, by treating Smythe, Smith, Smiths and Schmitt as the same when searching the database. The Police National Computer (PNC) uses a particularly extensive system of this kind, called Soundex, when searching its criminal names or wanted/ missing persons indexes.

When making an enquiry of an FTR databank the usual practice is to specify various words, names or attributes, and the ways in which they might occur together. Suppose that the separate paragraphs of this chapter form some of the many records in a large databank which uses FTR. A detective arrives with news that a reliable informant has phoned to say that a man called Young and, of all people, a vicar or a priest, whose name is unknown, plan to murder a man known as Sandy. Typed on the VDU screen, the enquiry could look something like this:

FIND: Young + (vicar, priest) + Sandy

This is an instruction to the FTR software to look for any record which contains the name Young, refers to a vicar or a priest and to someone called Sandy. There is no point in looking at everybody called Young – there would be too many. But someone who is called Young *and* who is associated with a priest or vicar *and* with a man called Sandy, might be a very good bet indeed.

The FTR system searches and replies twenty seconds later: have a look at page 25 of *On the Record*. There you find closely associated: a man called Younger (a possible equivalent for Young); a minister (which is synonymous with vicar in the Church of Scotland); and a man called Alex (which, like Alexander, is synonymous with Sandy). If that paragraph (record) did not so obviously indicate a quite different relationship between Kenneth Younger and Alex Lyon than that of intending murderer and victim, our detective might become rather excited. He realises that he might have misheard some of the names on the phone. This Younger could probably be the very villain for whom he is looking. Other checks are carried out, but Younger doesn't appear to have a current criminal record. No matter, since an extremely serious criminal offence is in the offing. A search warrant for his last-known address is obtained and the Tactical Firearms Unit breaks in with sledgehammers at 4.00 a.m. the next morning. It is deeply unfortunate for police and the aggrieved new occupants of the address alike that there was no time to check other records on Younger (for example, the next paragraph), and discover that the eminent Sir Kenneth was not only an unlikely prospective murderer, but had been more than ten years in the grave.

Most of the computer systems described in this book use data in the relatively simple, cardbox-analogue fashion described above.

Information may also be stored on computer in an *unstructured* way. The text of this chapter, for example, written on a word processor, is – in the data sense – unstructured. (It is *semantically* highly structured as English language writing, but computers cannot yet interpret the series of characters which it comprises on the level of comprehensible *language*.) The word processor software knows where the beginning and end of this chapter is – and that is about all it can know. This book contains significant personal data about Sir Norman Lindop, but neither the computer hardware nor its word processing software has any idea where in the text this data might be found, or whether it is there at all. Its capabilities are as limited as those of the authors – it can plod through every line, every group of bytes, to see if any of them are called Lindop, then shout that it's found something about him.

Structured records, in contrast, are retrieved directly by reference to predetermined variables, such as name, address, national health number, national insurance number or vehicle registration. Sometimes even this limited degree of automation makes possible processes which are otherwise unworkable. A good example of this is the way in which new machine-readable passports and computer terminals will make it possible for immigration-control officers to check their 'suspect index' (a blacklist book which cannot normally be consulted in the short time available to check a UK passport holder). As Chapter 6 explains, such checks on UK citizens were more or less infeasible by manual methods.

To take another example, police criminal records or vehicle registration details were effectively maintained on card indexes even before computerisation, and could be quite rapidly searched. But the inclusion of vehicle registrations on the PNC now makes possible the special kind of enquiry, described above, which asks: is there an estate car with P and R in the registration, owned by someone in the Bristol area, coloured fawn or khaki? Like finding the man with the pet called Cripps, before the PNC was established, this question could not have been answered in a reasonable time. This facility is generally called a *multi-factor search* of the databank concerned; it is a general (and time-consuming) search for an unindexed item or items of information.

For another example of the privacy-threatening use of a computer, suppose that Jenny Bloggs puts a lonely-hearts advertisement in a magazine, appending just her first name and telephone number to the characterisation of her desired partner. She does not wish her inquisitive neighbours to know her sexual preferences, or unsuitable partners to find her address if she rejects them on the phone. Jenny has nothing sinister to hide, just privacy to protect. Of course, her name, address and telephone number is available in the public telephone directory. But the phone book is indexed only by name, not by number; a manual search for her name and address by looking for a single number among millions would be almost impossible. Her privacy is well protected in this situation, as those who have information indexed by tele-phone number – British Telecom customer-accounts staff – are not authorised to release details of their customers' identities in response to an enquiry from the public about a number. But place the information in the telephone directory on a suitable computer database and her address could be available in seconds. Now the neighbours are hostile, as they don't share Jenny's warm feelings towards short men who were born in Greenland. And too many undesirable local male lonely hearts are ringing her doorbell day and night. The Data Protection Act cannot deal with this kind of issue, since it foolishly does not direct itself towards *applications* – the use to which data is put – but concentrates on the data *per se*.

Free text retrieval gave the Lindop committee great cause for concern. Noting that 'an unstructured file places virtually no constraints on the quantities or types of data which may be stored', they commented that 'FTR systems will clearly present special problems of definition and control.'[1] In an FTR system, there can be no way of regulating the use of information collected and recorded by reference to the structure or nature of the information. Preventing abuse of information privacy in an FTR system is only possible if the use of the system, and the intent of each enquiry, is tested each time the system is used. To this sort of problem, the 1984 Data Protection Act is blind.

When the Lindop committee sought to examine the Metropolitan Police Special Branch computer system, they felt rather less than reassured. Deducing, accurately, that the system used free text retrieval, they warned that it introduced 'a new dimension of unease. We have commented (elsewhere) on the exceptional risks inherent in such systems.'[2]

The Metropolitan Police Special Branch and 'C Department' uses a powerful, effective and large-scale FTR system called Status; within government and public agencies, Status is currently used almost exclusively for intelligence purposes and in systems generally exempt from subject access. Status and other FTR systems are also used in intelligence computers of the Home Office immigration service (IVAN) and of the Customs and Excise (CEDRIC); and those of the Lothian and Borders, Humberside and Kent police forces.

When records of this type are computerised, it is common to hear official apologias along the lines of: 'This new computer won't store any information different from that which we have been putting on manual index cards for years and years.' (This dialogue generally continues with further remarks to the effect: 'We haven't had any substantiated complaints about privacy problems before, you know. And the new computer will obviously make the performance of our tasks more efficient, which is self-evidently a jolly good thing and in the public interest too.')

The argument that most computer databanks are born the daughters of manual card-index or filing systems is almost always true; that fact alone should have made it obvious that the Data Protection Act should have covered major manual systems. In the near future, a wholly manual personal-information index is likely to become a very rare creature. But mixed systems, with computer records and manual files interlinked, will predominate, blurring the effect of the new law. Indeed, the very terms of the Data Protection Act encourage some users to keep – or even create – certain

manual indexes, in order to remain exempt from registration
and/or subject access.

The government position, in instructing the Lindop committee and subsequently in drafting the Data Protection Act, has
always been that manual records should be excluded from
legislation. But Lindop took a different view. There are, it is
argued, few firm boundaries between manual and computerised systems; any computer input undergoes at least some
initial manual processing. The government case for concentrating only on computers was put in the 1975 *Computers and
Privacy* White Paper:[3]

> Computers facilitate the maintenance of extensive record systems
> and the retention of data in those systems.
>
> They can make data quickly and easily available from many distant
> points.
>
> They make it possible for data to be transferred quickly from one
> information system to another.
>
> They make it possible for data to be combined in ways which
> might not otherwise be practicable.
>
> Because the data are stored, processed and often transmitted in a
> form which is not directly intelligible, few people may know what
> is in the records, or what is happening to them.

The additional danger to privacy from computers arises from
the relatively low cost of assembling, sorting and combining,
retrieving and transferring massive databanks. No data handling task accomplished by computer is ultimately infeasible, if
near-infinite time is available; in the case of manual records
privacy is well protected by the disproportionate effort that
may be required to retrieve some types of information. But, as
we will see, a law that fails to cover both manual and automatic
records makes a mockery of privacy.

The power of computers to handle and analyse large quantities of personal data has – until recently – been constrained
by technical limitations on the absorption of information.
Written information is not generally 'machine-readable'; somehow, by human or automatic means, it has to be converted into
a form in which it can be handled and analysed. Until recently,

this meant that a human operator had to type information onto paper tape or punched cards, magnetic tape or discs, or directly into a computer's memory store. But optical character recognition (OCR) equipment is already in widespread use, and its use is increasing. Database operators can now feed a newspaper, magazine or ordinary typed report page by page into a scanner; the computer reads the page, using relatively advanced software; no further typing is needed. OCR is the harbinger of new systems which will influence information privacy.

The discussion above showed how computerisation, then indexing, and finally free text retrieval applied to the tennis-court card-index system might dramatically alter the uses to which stored information could be put. This first phase of databank development has provided cheap computer storage. The next generations of computers will bring enormously cheaper computer intelligence. These clever systems will create new possibilities and new threats. They are qualitatively different from and have a potency far beyond even that of FTR. Most clever systems are still in the experimental stage. They include:

Optical pattern recognition systems – scanners which can look at live scenes, photographs or text, read numberplates, identify faces, observe and analyse motion, codify and identify fingerprints or rapidly turn written text into computer data.

Speech recognition systems – which can turn ordinary, continuous speech into machine-readable text, then process it.

'Artificial intelligence' or expert systems – which no longer process data according to unchanging, prewritten rules; they change the program and the rules as they operate. They may look for patterns in non-visual, non-spoken data; they can 'target'. *expands further on in Chapter*

Many projects of this type have been developed under a £350 million scheme called Alvey, and funded by the Department of Trade and Industry to boost British information and computer technology research. Alvey's interests include speech technology – speech recognition and synthesis; software engineering; and 'intelligent knowledge-based systems' – more colloquially, 'thinking' computers, which examine and manipulate concepts and ideas rather than numbers and data.

Already there have been applications of clever systems. Chapter 8 reveals details of the development of a computer-controlled vehicle-numberplate scanner. The system uses advanced pattern-recognition technologies. Positioned strategically on the M1 motorway, the scanner could monitor thousands of vehicles each hour – and check them off against lists of suspect vehicles (including those under surveillance) on the Police National Computer. In 1985, researchers from Sheffield and Manchester universities announced another type of computerised traffic scanner, able automatically to 'see' and count the number of vehicles in a street. Also in 1985, the Metropolitan Police installed the first of a new generation of computer scanners which have the potential almost entirely to replace human experts in the remarkably complex task of fingerprint coding and identification.

In the field of voice recognition, computers are becoming fully capable of analysing and comprehending continuous human speech. Many simple voice-recognition computers are already widely available for purchase, but their facilities, vocabulary and applications are limited. Other such systems have found some rudimentary security use, for example in Northern Ireland, where police officers have experimented in recording vehicle registration numbers for security checks by speaking the numbers into an IBM computer. But it is the engineering of speech-recognition systems that are capable of continuously understanding a whole range of voices, accents and dialogues which will herald a new and frightening era in technological surveillance. Instead of being a limited and difficult exercise, the surveillance and monitoring of voice communications (mainly through telephone tapping) will become as simple and as widespread as the surveillance of data and telegraph traffic is now. For many years, international intelligence agencies such as Britain's GCHQ have employed massive computers to sift through and harvest information of interest from all those international communications that are currently 'machine-readable'; they have not yet been able to treat human speech with the same facility, but they will become able to do so.

Computer software is undergoing similar radical developments in 'artificial intelligence' or machine 'thinking'. Some new programs are heuristic, meaning that they enable the computer to make deductions and *change its program as a result*. For example, suppose this book is held in a storage system. We ask: what is this book about? This question, normally, is meaningless to a computer – it does not speak English; though it could tell you how many times the word 'computer' appears in the text, perhaps faster than you could blink. A suitable expert system could at least attempt the task.

Several proposed expert systems are discussed in this book. It may be worth noting in advance that some such systems have been designed to enforce discriminatory aspects of public administration, such as the control of immigration or the aggressive policing of social security claimants. During 1981, an Imperial College scientist, Professor Robert Kowalski, worked on a 'logic programming' system (called Prolog), with which he in effect computerised the British Nationality Act, as a demonstration to the Home Office. Kowalski showed that the Act 'can be translated into [computer] rules intelligible to an educated person'.[4] In Chapter 4, we describe an Alvey 'technology demonstrator' project proposed by computer manufacturers ICL to the Department of Health and Social Security for an expert system to help track down suspected fraudulent social security claims. The computer would start by being told what patterns to look for, and select claimant targets accordingly. As time passed, the expert system would test alternative patterns for identifying fraud, and adapt its pattern-recognition knowledge and processing routines in order to maximise whatever criteria was defined as 'success'. It was said that, with increasing computer expertise, potentially fraudulent claims and claimants would be 'targeted'.

It may appear that the immediate effect of such computer operations is to intensify discrimination in the pursuit of prescribed political objectives. It need not be so. It is the attitude of administrators, not the nature of computer systems, which creates the threat to privacy and equality. In the case of the DHSS, for example, the same computers, the same basic data and the same software could be used to target the enormous number of claimants who are not given all the benefits they need and to which they are entitled. Such a system would clearly benefit rather than threaten the subjects of DHSS databanks. It would enhance the declared purpose of the social security system, to provide an assured minimum quality of life for those out of work or in special need. But the proposed intelligent computer for fraudhunting within the DHSS supports the covert political objective of making life on the dole as harsh as politically tolerable, in order to depress wage levels throughout the economy. The cleverer the computer, the wider and more accurate its spread of data, the better servant it is to such objectives.

The law has been very slow in attempting to deal with the personal privacy problems of computer databanks. It may take another decade for the deficiencies in the present data protection laws to be agreed and, it is hoped, corrected. By that time, the clever systems described here will be in routine use. The 'sixth generation' of computer systems and beyond – whose nature and dangers we can anticipate no better than Lindop's team could foresee today's clever systems – will be on their way. Information privacy problems will not end after the Data Protection Act takes effect. They will have only just begun.

3   The Threat

In delaying and diverting privacy legislation, the authoritarian argument has always been that there is little to worry about, scant evidence of abuse and no tide of public concern to meet. 'There have been few reported instances in this country of information held on computer being misused so as to threaten the personal privacy of individuals,' claimed the 1982 White Paper on data protection.[1] Therefore, it was argued, there was not a serious problem. Urgent or powerful legislation was not required. But this argument is a *non sequitur* – and its premises are in any case ill founded.

The portfolio of case histories on the abuse of information privacy may not bulge copiously, but it is ample. Past studies have brought together comprehensive and highly disturbing evidence of privacy violations.[2] Many more instances are mentioned in the book. But an accumulation of individual accounts of misfortune, however widespread or impressive, is not necessarily the point. However good such research might be, it can only illustrate the surface of a very deep problem. The case-history approach to privacy problems (with which part of this chapter is concerned) is entirely valid, but it is neither the only nor the primary means by which the arguments should be addressed. There are dozens of reasons why the nature and extent of individual case histories reported are a very poor guide to the extent of the problem.

Most invasions or breaches of personal privacy are by their very nature secret. They affect individuals in isolation – individuals who may well lack the educational skills, the articulacy or the determination to realise or find out what events have influenced their lives. Breaches of privacy often come to light, if at all, years afterwards; and in the absence of any right to know, or a regulatory body with powers of enquiry, the victims – even if they suspect something – will not be able to have their suspicions allayed or substantiated. <u>Most people affected will never know or even suspect the cause of their disadvantage.</u> Breaches of personal privacy, by definition, affect individuals rather than organisations or institutions. Consequently, they are seldom communicated widely. Even if they do discover them, victims will find few sympathetic ears. Indeed, if sensitive or damaging personal information has been wrongfully communicated, even to draw attention to the issue may well be to worsen the damage already caused.

The fact that Britain has hitherto lacked any general legal means of protecting privacy, or methods by which the aggrieved can seek redress, is a major deterrent to the reporting of privacy violations. People will not bother to draw attention to such events if there is 'no point'. There is acute public awareness, for example, that the police are not interested in, or unwilling or unlikely successfully to investigate and prosecute, certain kinds of crimes, such as ordinary assaults, domestic burglaries and thefts, domestic crimes, some driving offences, and so on. Consequently, the occurrence of such crimes is significantly under-reported. The unreported crimes happen, of course, but their nature and extent can only be determined by the investment of effort.

No such effort has been made on privacy issues. Indeed, both Sir Kenneth Younger and Sir Norman Lindop went out of their way to point out that it was not the job of their committees to find real cases of abuse, and that they had not been asked to look for them. Younger reported:

> We are not able to estimate the extent to which personal profiles are being compiled in the private sector ... nor how many cases of unauthorised access are taking place.

Lindop told an NCCL conference in 1979, 'We did not discover evidence of gross abuse ... we did not consider it our main job to carry out an investigative function searching for abuse.' Somewhat lamely, he added, 'That we did not discover it is not necessarily conclusive evidence that it does not exist.'

The problem of under-reporting will, in part, be solved by

the creation of the Data Protection Registry. Indeed, the Registrar started receiving complaints, in small numbers, immediately on appointment. Even without advertisement, and despite the substantial delay before the Registrar's enforcement powers will take effect, word had got around that there was at least somewhere to direct complaints.

The lack of official concern for privacy is in itself an aspect of the imbalance of power in British society between individual and institution – the very problem which personal privacy protection should redress. Politicians' general attitude towards the issue is disappointing, but unsurprising. Like so many civil liberties issues, what was popular in opposition suddenly becomes intractable when the party concerned wins power.

It is worth noting in passing that the Data Protection Bill was considered by Parliament in the same period as another major Home Office measure, the 1984 Police and Criminal Evidence Act (PACE). PACE granted the police sweeping new powers. One particularly controversial section, Clause 10, was to allow general searches of third-party professional records for any evidence of a crime – a power impinging directly on the privacy of computer records among others. At no time in the passage of the bill was it suggested that the case for new powers should be explicitly justified by the police, by providing case histories of serious problems. Theoretical arguments and hypothetical and contrived examples of potential difficulties were acceptable. No greater proof of the need to legislate should be required when privacy is at risk.

At one end of the spectrum of threats to privacy are the inherent dangers posed by large computers, including the central databank of both administrative and popular fiction. Other threats include the ill-considered linkage of different records, either directly or by means of standard personal identification numbers – which themselves create special dangers. Many problems flow from the quality or character of information which may have been transacted or recorded. Information in an official file may have been collected or inserted by underhand or improper means, or without consent; the information may be unnecessary for or irrelevant to

the purpose for which it is collected; or it may be false,
inaccurate, out of date, misleading or incomplete.

The threat of personal damage from such data becomes real
when inadequate physical security measures, or poor safeguards against staff misbehaviour, permit unauthorised parties access to confidential data; or when information given for
one purpose is transferred to be used for an entirely different
purpose, without the knowledge or consent of the data
subject. But the mere requirement for the citizen to give
personal information can be oppressive. So can the uses to
which it is normally put by some public institutions or private
employers. There are many situations where good security
and full adherence to formal regulations – including the
provisions of the Data Protection Act – are irrelevant to the
protection of human rights.

The first danger lies in the accumulation of very large
quantities of data. Such information stores are by their nature
the most heavily used. Consequently, erroneous data may
propagate more widely; and the opportunities for unauthorised or improper insertion or extraction of information are
multiplied.

As mentioned earlier, such databanks are predominantly,
but not exclusively, to be found in the public sector – these are
examined in depth in the remainder of the book. In this
chapter we briefly examine two organisations in the private
sector where threats may arise because of the sheer scale of
data accumulation. These are the computerising of the national electoral register and its merging with much other
marketing and socioeconometric data for profiling purposes.

The largest and most striking direct-mail database is run by a
Nottingham-based organisation, CCN. The installation uses
twin Amdahl 5860 computers with 60 gigabytes of on-line data
stored. It contains 43 million names and home addresses, and
is comparable in scale to the Police National Computer. The
basic data is extracted annually from the electoral register
(except for the London Borough of Greenwich, which refuses
to sell the register to commercial companies for this purpose).
This information is combined with mailing lists bought
from other organisations, or managed on behalf of clients.
Local census statistics are used to classify each housing

area on a socioeconomic base, assessing income levels, 'lifestyle', housing occupation, average age and family pattern, housing tenure and ethnic characteristics. A competing organisation, the United Association for the Protection of Trade (UAPT), offers similar services to its 10,000 terminal users.

The database is organised by postcode districts, and then subdivided into records on individual households. In the Post Office postcode system, each successive letter or number of the code indicates an increasingly smaller geographical subdivision. The smallest sub-area, which is allocated a unique postcode, is one part of a mail delivery walk, which might contain a single office block, or 20–30 houses. The postcode system is described as an 'extremely efficient address management device. [Postcodes] can be used to define target areas, and for a variety of other marketing purposes ...' Also recorded are credit data, obtained from county court judgements.

The CCN 'Nationwide Consumer File' database has thus merged, in a single, comprehensive national information store, all the particulars which individuals have supplied separately to other data users for the quite distinct purposes of registering to vote, obtaining certain goods, complying with the census law, and so forth. The CCN direct-mail databank uses a system called ACORN (A Classification Of Residential Neighbourhoods) to identify, it is claimed, household types 'in terms of their lifestyle and consumer spending habits'. Other analyses performed on electoral data indicate whether a household is likely to consist of a family or single young people, whether the householders have recently moved, where young voters are, whether an area is multi-ethnic.

Mailing lists can be compiled using any selection criteria. The data provided could be very specific – for example, a list of 'all young people aged 17–21, who are registered to vote, who live in new council estates, within an inner-city London borough, and who have appeared on mailing lists connected with record magazines or record promotion'. Or it could identify all families called Jones living in agricultural accommodation in south Devon or west Wiltshire against whom there has been an adverse county-court judgement.

CCN claim, correctly, that their analysis services can be 'precisely targeted'. Other mailing-list organisations have sold less comprehensive but more damaging information. A Conservative MP, Harvey Spellor, said in 1984 that he had been offered for sale mailing lists of subscribers to *Gay News* and of people who had purchased expensive jewellery.[3]

CCN's computer will automatically check, provide postcodes for and cross reference to all new personal data supplied to the system. One special facility of the network is to identify neighbours of a particular customer up to any given distance from their homes. This facility may be used automatically to write personalised letters to neighbours of someone who has bought particular goods or services, inviting them to do the same (and, by implication, treating their original customers as though they had agreed to provide sales demonstrations free to the company concerned).

Although CCN say that the information they sell is primarily for advertising purposes, their services are widely used by private detectives and other information-gathering agencies. All the data on the CCN databank can be supplied over the Viewdata network, and information on each individual household may be examined or updated from remote terminals by customers who subscribe to this service. The company offers to sell household names, selected geographically and using the ACORN system, for £45 per thousand; identifying recent house-movers or young voters for £5 more. Follow-up lists of the same category of names are a mere £5 a thousand. Non-advertising customers, such as private detective agencies, may purchase data on an individual basis, to obtain a profile of any person or household in whom they may be interested. A CCN brochure says that the Viewdata connection will give 60,000 terminals 'instant access to the 40 million postcoded names at home addresses held by CCN. As these are constantly updated as circumstances change, you can rely on their accuracy at all times.'

Government departments have also merged postcode and other records, thereby damaging many people's privacy. Postcodes and addresses were cross-linked to television licence records by the Bristol computers at the National TV Licensing and Records Office (NTVLRO). The resulting file was used automatically to generate letters to every household not listed as having a licence. The initial letters enquired about television ownership. These were followed by more mailings, one of which included a threat of visits by TV licence inspectors. Only one of these mailings seriously allowed for the possibility that the recipient did not actually possess a television set. Householders who did not own a TV – or who held a valid licence the details of which NTVLRO did not hold correctly – had an absolute legal right to refuse to respond to an inspector, or to ignore the harassing welter of unwanted computer mail.

Direct-mail databanks have also begun to make a disturbing impact on the democratic process itself. Political campaigning techniques which use direct-mail facilities have been imported to Britain from the United States, where, in 1980, political lobbyists of the far right were delighted at their success in promoting the election of Ronald Reagan as President. In recent elections in Britain (1983) and the United States, political parties of the right have made effective use of personal databanks. Lists of party supporters and of prospective financial backers have been assembled and cross-referenced by computer. A third target group consists of voters in marginal seats who have not revealed definite party allegiances. Analytical programs are used to direct suitable 'personalised' information and mailings to these selected groups.

The direct-mail technique relies on computers to sort and merge mailing lists, compiled or bought in, of voters likely to support (in this case) Conservative policies. Mailshots then canvass for votes, recruit help in constituencies or solicit financial donations. By obtaining mailing lists of better-off cunsumers, Conservative Party political managers can efficiently solicit much greater financial support.

Such techniques can also be used to promote single-issue campaigns, or to attack opponents for electoral office. Before himself being elected in 1983, Edward Leigh MP advocated that selected MPs be made 'targets' for de-election. This technique (and attitude to democracy) has also been borrowed from the USA's 'New Right'. In their 'de-election' campaigns, New Right groups have used computers to attack liberal US Senators or members of the Democratic Party. Mailshots have been used to broadcast selected criticism and innuendo about the politicians concerned, chiefly to marginal voters. Ironically, one of the first successes in this campaign was the defeat in 1980 of the distinguished Idaho Senator Frank Church, who had been in the vanguard of the post-Watergate investigations of US intelligence agencies. In committee reports following Watergate, Church had expressed serious concern about the potency of surveillance and information-gathering technology – particularly that used by the US National Security Agency. Senator Church warned that the power of technology 'at any time could be turned around on the American people ... the capacity is there to make tyranny total'.

A novel source of large volumes of sensitive personal data has begun to be created, as banks and financial institutions launch networks of electronic 'cashless' terminals which customers can use to pay for goods and services at shopping outlets. The terminals read a credit or banking card 'wiped' through a magnetic reader. The transaction is then checked and authorised by a central banking services computer, after which details of the sale are automatically transferred to customers' accounts on credit-card or bank computers. Because neither cheques nor cash are handled in this system, it is known as electronic funds transfer at the point of sale – abbreviated inelegantly to EFTPOS.

Several major British EFTPOS systems have already been announced. In August 1985, British Telecom Enterprises launched the first EFTPOS network, called Teletran. In 1986, Barclays Bank started a second national network by installing over one thousand EFTPOS terminals. The Barclays system is linked to the Visa credit card (including Barclaycard and Trustcard), which has some 10 million UK users. Other banks have also conducted pilot experiments with EFTPOS. But the cashless society boom is expected to begin in earnest in 1988, when the London central clearing banks EFTPOS system, developed in conjunction with IBM and British Telecom's national network organisation, is unveiled.

By the 1990s, there are expected to be up to 250,000 EFTPOS terminals installed throughout Britain. They will generate electronically, automatically and in machine-readable form an immense quantity of personal financial data. As cashcards and credit cards come to dominate retail transactions, the significance of the data flowing from EFTPOS terminals will grow; tapped by the authorities or the unauthorised, such data would chart moment by moment personal movements as well as giving a remarkable, although not complete, profile of lifestyle.

While banks have a reputation for high standards of confidentiality, there is evidence of occasional improper information transfers, as well as leakage. In 1979, for instance, Barclays Bank was reported regularly to have passed details of customers' financial standing to an insurance sales force.[4] The sales force concerned worked for an in-house insurance company, Barclay Life. The banks hope that, by 1991, EFTPOS networks will handle over 500 million transactions every year – it is hard to believe that, in the early stages at least, there will not be dangers of information leaking.

Personal financial data is also handled by extensive existing bank networks which link the major banks' own computer systems. The main UK networks are BACS (Bankers Automated Clearing System), and CHAPS (the Clearing House Automated Payment System), which began operating in 1984. An international network, SWIFT (Society for Worldwide International Financial Transfers), provides similar services at the international level – linking national banking networks such as Britain's CHAPS, and CHIPS and SAGITAIRE, the American and French equivalents. All these networks encrypt data being transmitted between computing centres and terminals.

By 1985, there were over 450 central government computer installations in use or on order for 'general and administrative' purposes (excluding micro-computers). Although most of these computers hold personal information, the general public need only be concerned with a small number of installations – albeit the largest computers of all. These major government computer centres are listed in Table 2 (overleaf). Figure 1 (page 66) illustrates how the databanks they contain interact, by routine or occasional links, electronic and otherwise. The diagram covers both 'machine-readable' information and orthodox printed records.

Table 2
Major existing or planned databanks holding personal information

Data user, computer system/databank	Site	Computer(s)	No. of Records	No. of Terminals
DHSS				
General Index (to become the Central Index, 1988)	Washington	ICL 2982 (2)	54 m	140
Local Office Project (LOP)	Livingston, Peterborough, Bristol	ICL 39/80 (3 per centre)	54 m	25,000
National Insurance Contributions System (NICS)	Newcastle	ICL 2980 (2)	52 m	120
Pensions, Widows Benefit	Newcastle	ICL 2980	10 m	50
Child Benefit, Maternity Grants	Newcastle, Washington	ICL 2988 ICL 2982	7 m	20
North Fylde Central Office (Family Income Supplement, Disablement allowances, War Pensions, etc)	North Fylde North Fylde	Honeywell PS6 ICL 2966 (2)	2.5 m	141
National Unemployment Benefit System (NUBS)	Livingston, Reading	ICL 2966 (5) ICL 2966 (7)	4.5 m 4.5 m	44 38
Department of Employment				
Terminal Retrieval and Enquiry Service (TRES); local office networks for NUBS system	Unemployment Benefit Offices (900)	Honeywell DPS6 (900)	(as for NUBS)	10,500
JUVOS (Joint Unemployment, Vacancy, and Operating Statistics)	Runcorn	ICL 2966	3.5 m	400
Inland Revenue				
COP (Computerisation of PAYE taxation);	Telford, Peterborough, Llanishen, West Byfleet,	}	28 m 3.5 m	· 17,000 [COP] 8,000 [CODA]

(*Continued in next column*)

Data user, computer system/databank	Site	Computer(s)	No. of Records	No. of Terminals
CODA (Computer-isation of Schedule D assessment) (Full system to be in operation by 1988)	Livingstone, Wythenshawe, Wentworth, Exeter, Netherton, Faverdale, London, East Kilbride	ICL 2988 and ICL 39/80 'Estriel' (at least 14 computers)	1.1 m [employers]	
Centre 1 (PAYE for Scotland) (including tracing service)	East Kilbride	ICL 2966 + CAFS store	3.7 m	Not 'on line'
Sub-contractors (the 'Lump')	Liverpool	ICL 2966	500,000	Not 'on line'
Mortgage and life assurance policy holders (LAPR, MIRAS)	Liverpool	ICL 2966	n/a	n/a
Tax collection	Cumbernauld	ICL 2982 (2)	2.1 m 0.6 m [employers]	140
	Shipley	ICL 2982 (2)	2.1 m 0.6 m [employers]	140

DHSS/Office of Population Census and Surveys (OPCS)

NHS Central Register	Southport	Manual records	50 m	—

National Health Service*

Regional Health Authorities District Health Authorities Family Practitioner Committees Hospitals General Practitioners	Over 50 major sites and 300 major record systems in use	Various computers and manual records	At least 80 million personal records	

OPCS[†]

Census data	Titchfield	ICL 2966 (2)	1000 m	—

General Register Office[†]

Census (Scotland); Register of Births, Deaths, Marriages	Edinburgh	ICL 2955	10.3 m 4.2 m	12
NHS Central Register (Scotland)	Edinburgh	ICL 2955	4.25 m	37

Data user, computer system/databank	Site	Computer(s)	No. of Records	No. of Terminals
Security Service (MI5)				
Joint Computer Bureau (JCB)	Mayfair	ICL 2980 (2)** ICL 2960 + mini- computers	2 m	200
Scottish Office				
Scottish Criminal Records Office (SCRO)	Glasgow	Honeywell DPS8	1.4 m	300
Home Office (*See also* Tables 4 to 10, Chapter 6)				
Police National Computer (PNC)	Hendon	Burroughs 7700 (3) Burroughs 7800 Burroughs 5900 (3)	52 m	1500
IVAN (Immigration Service Intelligence and Investigation Unit)	Harmonds- worth	Prime 9750	300,000	At least 3
INDECS (Immi- gration and Nationality Dept Electronic Computer System)	Bootle	ICL 2966 DEC PDP11/34 (4)	1.5 m	14
Passport Office – passport files	Passport Offices (6)	Not yet selected	15 m 8,000 [Special Files]	n/a
Metropolitan Police				
C Department computer (including Special Branch)	Victoria	CTL 8050 (8)	1.5 m	75
Fingerprints system	Victoria	Ampex (2)	3.2 m	26
Police forces++				
Local 'collator' or criminal inform- ation systems	Various	Various	1–2 m approx (each)	1000 approx (total)
Customs and Excise				
CEDRIC (Customs and Excise Depart- ment Reference and Information Computer)	Shoeburyness	Honeywell DPS8	110,000	25
VAT collection	Southend	ICL 2966 (2)	1.5 m	240

Data user, computer system/databank	Site	Computer(s)	No. of Records	No. of Terminals
Department of Transport				
Driver and Vehicle Licensing Centre (DVLC)	Swansea	IBM 3083 (2)	33 m vehicles 37 m drivers	1000 500
Department of Education and Science				
Further Education Statistical Record/ Universities Statistical Record (UCCA)	Darlington	ICL 2966	2.2 m	Not 'on-line'
	Cheltenham	Honeywell DPS 8	337,000	Not 'on line'
Post Office				
TV Licensing and Records Office (TVLRO)	Bristol, Bootle	Burroughs B1000 (2)	18.6 m licence holders 20,000 dealers (+ postcode index)	174
British Telecom (CSS system)	Various	IBM 3081 (32) (or equivalent)	20 m	More than 60,000
Private population registers				
CCN adult population register (electoral register, save for London Borough of Greenwich)	Nottingham	Amdahl 4/74	43 m	7000
UAPT adult population register (as CCN)	Croydon	Burroughs A15	4.2 m 1.7 m [organisations]	10,500

Note: The estimated number of personal records is quoted where exact figures have been withheld by government.

* See Table 3 (page 128) for further details of National Health Service computing. No exact figures can be given for the number of computers, terminals, or personal records within the Health Service because of the diversity of computer systems in use.

† Most Census records held by OPCS and the General Register Office do not identify individuals directly.

** New computers believed ordered, 1984.

†† The nature and extent of criminal information computerisation varies widely from force to force. An 'average' police force might have about 100,000 nominal records on computer, and 100 terminals connected to the computer. Some are much larger. Others have no plans to computerise such information in the near future.

n/a: Not available.

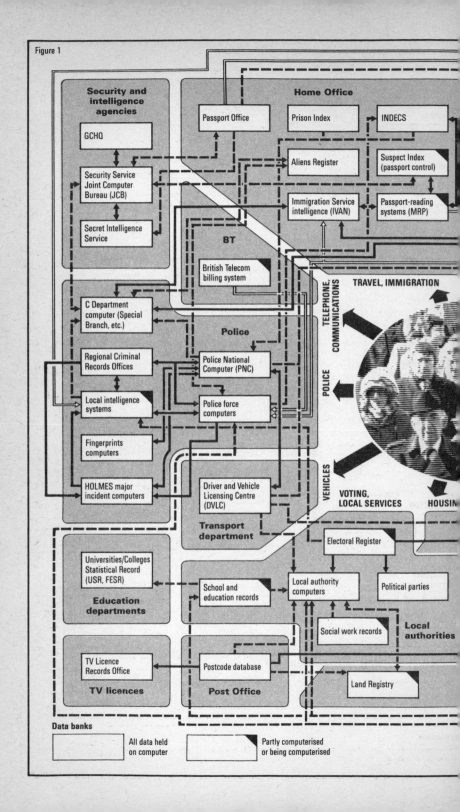

Figure 1

Security and intelligence agencies
- GCHQ
- Security Service Joint Computer Bureau (JCB)
- Secret Intelligence Service

Home Office
- Passport Office
- Prison Index
- INDECS
- Aliens Register
- Suspect Index (passport control)
- Immigration Service intelligence (IVAN)
- Passport-reading systems (MRP)

BT
- British Telecom billing system

Police
- C Department computer (Special Branch, etc.)
- Regional Criminal Records Offices
- Local intelligence systems
- Fingerprints computers
- HOLMES major incident computers
- Police National Computer (PNC)
- Police force computers

Transport department
- Driver and Vehicle Licensing Centre (DVLC)

Education departments
- Universities/Colleges Statistical Record (USR, FESR)
- School and education records

Local authorities
- Electoral Register
- Local authority computers
- Political parties
- Social work records
- Land Registry

TV licences
- TV Licence Records Office

Post Office
- Postcode database

TELEPHONE, COMMUNICATIONS

TRAVEL, IMMIGRATION

POLICE

VEHICLES

VOTING, LOCAL SERVICES

HOUSING

Data banks

All data held on computer

Partly computerised or being computerised

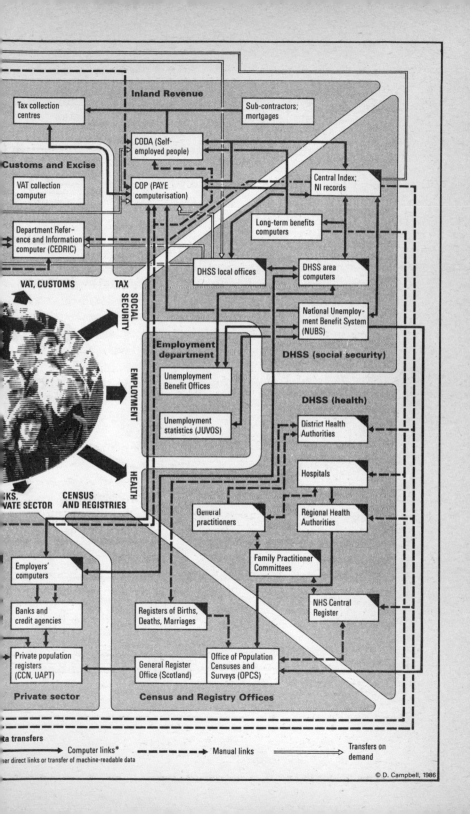

Inland Revenue

Tax collection centres

Sub-contractors; mortgages

CODA (Self-employed people)

Customs and Excise

VAT collection computer

COP (PAYE computerisation)

Central Index; NI records

Department Reference and Information computer (CEDRIC)

Long-term benefits computers

VAT, CUSTOMS TAX

SOCIAL SECURITY

DHSS local offices

DHSS area computers

National Unemployment Benefit System (NUBS)

Employment department

EMPLOYMENT

Unemployment Benefit Offices

DHSS (social security)

DHSS (health)

District Health Authorities

Unemployment statistics (JUVOS)

Hospitals

HEALTH

KS, VATE SECTOR

CENSUS AND REGISTRIES

General practitioners

Regional Health Authorities

Family Practitioner Committees

Employers' computers

Banks and credit agencies

NHS Central Register

Registers of Births, Deaths, Marriages

Private population registers (CCN, UAPT)

General Register Office (Scotland)

Office of Population Censuses and Surveys (OPCS)

Private sector

Census and Registry Offices

ta transfers

Computer links*

Manual links

Transfers on demand

er direct links or transfer of machine-readable data

© D. Campbell, 1986

As Figure 1 (page 66) illustrates, only a few more links are needed to match the description of the central databank which aroused such popular fears in the national privacy survey for the Younger commission (see page 20). In fact, a full-scale national databank was proposed as early as 1973 by LAMSAC, an organisation of British local authority administrative specialists. A few years later, it emerged that the Home Office had simultaneously but secretly been studying a similar proposal.

LAMSAC (Local Authorities' Management Services and Computer Committee) wanted almost every type of confidential personal information amalgamated into the central computer, with virtually all official bodies authorised to read and input information. Their proposed databank would have covered name, sex, marital status, electoral number, credit ratings, car ownership, nationality or immigration status, library records, occupation and income, educational achievement, medical and mental histories, and social security and welfare records. In the LAMSAC proposal, tidy-minded bureaucratic thinking was combined with a lack of appreciation of the practical technological limits to projects of this magnitude; the fault was then compounded by disregard for the implications of such a system for the privacy of personal information.

LAMSAC's only proviso for controlling the use of data was that the 'contributor and extractor of data should agree on the legitimate uses to which "their" data can be put'; there was no mention of any right of the individual concerned to have a view on the matter! In each local authority area, the planners envisaged, there would be an average of 280 access terminals. They reckoned that, by 1984, there would be 500,000 computer terminals in use across the country for this and similar systems.[5]

This proposal, fortunately, never got further than its quality merited. But the Home Office has also studied, even if it did not implement, the means of creating a central databank. This has never been admitted in the UK. In March 1975, staff of the US Senate's Government Operations Committee investigated privacy and the protection of personal information in Europe, consulting British officials in the course of their research. The committee reported that, in the UK:[6]

Computerisation at the national and local government levels is rapidly increasing ... under the direction of a central computer agency in the Home Office, the technical feasibility for linking several data systems and record compatibility and standardisation is being developed. This capability, if exploited, runs counter to a long tradition of keeping separate the personal information systems being maintained by major functional agencies.

The committee's researchers noted that law-enforcement agencies alone in the UK had adopted the type of extensive record linkages which were employed 'as a matter of course' in European continental countries. 'The British [Home Office] may dismiss the privacy debate as inapplicable,' the Senate report concluded. But they warned that it would be merely a matter of time before such issues as record linkage and the use of UPIs (see below) created significant public concern in Britain.

Evidence of more recent official desires or plans to establish a central databank is slim. Government departments have learned from the succession of disasters they experienced while establishing major computer systems during the 1970s. The Swansea Driver and Vehicle Licensing Centre (DVLC) has always been hopelessly inadequate for its task; the Inland Revenue's planned nine-computer national network never progressed beyond Centre 1; the Ministry of Defence hoped to set up a national bureau network that also stopped after the first centre, Bureau West, had been built. These are perhaps the most striking examples; major failures of this kind may not be repeated. But as we explain in Chapter 4, the DHSS has already stumbled repeatedly as it tries to engineer a new titanic of this kind, its computer-based 'Operational Strategy'.

Closely related to any discussion of record linkage is the question of whether at some stage the government might see fit to adopt or even legislate to provide standardised personal identity numbers (PINs), to replace the present multitude of different codes and numbers which each person has in relation to health matters, national insurance, banks and credit, and so on. The adoption, nationally, of PINs (which may then be known as Universal Personal Identifiers, UPIs) is held to be likely to promote data processing efficiency through the standardisation of records. The benefits of such a system are debatable; but there is no question about the dangers that such standard identification numbers create for the privacy of records (by facilitating both access and widespread linkage). These dangers are a matter of frequent public and professional comment. Overseas data protection regulations often stipulate special safeguards on the use of such identity codes.

A UPI is necessarily unique, unlike an individual's name, and permanent, unlike an address. It can unambiguously establish identity amongst millions of files and records. Although UPIs are widely used overseas (in the form of national identity cards and social security numbers), in Britain any proposal of this nature has so far been judged unacceptable or unnecessary. We can and do have national numbers, but in the past individuals have had more than one number, and those numbers have been incompatible between different systems. A major danger, however, is that a UPI may be created by stealth rather than by design. The Lindop committee warned:[7]

> If a particular number were adopted as the standard identifier in the public sector, private sector users might find it convenient to adopt the number themselves. Over time, people could be required to quote the same number in most of their transactions with public and private sector organisations.

In countries where UPIs already exist their use is invariably controversial. Sweden has used UPIs since 1947. A unique ten-digit number is given to every member of the population at birth and every new resident from abroad. The Swedish UPI code includes the person's date of birth, place of birth and gender. It is the index to a national population register, which is in general use. In the absence of privacy protection laws, such a system would be extremely vulnerable to abuse.

In 1974, the French government caused a public outcry when it announced its intention to set up a computerised national population register called Safari, involving the issue of a UPI. Safari was to link criminal, medical, social security, tax and other records. But Safari was so controversial that the government was forced to postpone the project and appoint a commission of inquiry. The commission's recommendations later formed the basis of France's data protection law; the Safari plan was abandoned.

Public disquiet in the United States has also been roused by the possibility that the Social Security Number (SSN) might become a UPI. In 1974, therefore, legislation made it unlawful to refuse benefit or privilege to any individual who refused to disclose his or her social security number.

British government behaviour has been directed towards the promotion of administrative convenience rather than the safeguarding of individual privacy. There is no official population register in Britain and government officials assured the Lindop committee that there were no plans to introduce such a system. This situation changed when, early in 1986, the Department of the Environment proposed introducing a community population register, to replace the present rating system. Moreover, new national identity numbers have been evolving stealthily since 1974, when two major computers and record systems were linked – the Police National Computer and the Driver and Vehicle Licensing Centre in Swansea. In effect a new law was created that year which requires all Britain's registered vehicle owners (over 30 million) to notify the police of any change in address – on pain of a £50 fine for non-compliance. Changes to the particulars of registered vehicle owners are communicated to the PNC more quickly than they are used to update the DVLC's own master files at Swansea. Information is also supplied to the Inland Revenue and Customs and Excise authorities.

Driving licence particulars are not automatically passed to the PNC. But the particulars, including addresses, are available to the police, and the law requires that the address given on a driving licence be kept up to date – although this information is excessive to the DVLC's requirements. (Full adult licences are normally issued to be valid until the subject is aged 60, and there is no need for the DVLC to be able to keep track of licence holders through a lifetime's changes of address, unless those licence holders have come to notice for other reasons – in which case their addresses are almost certain to have been gleaned by other means.)

The computerisation of driving licences also marked the introduction of the new 'driver number', which furtively added the holder's date of birth to the particulars shown on the licence. This was done in code so that drivers might not be aware that this was on display. But it was there, scrambled, for anyone who knew the coding system to read. (The code is a simple rearranging of the six date digits, adding 5 for a woman.) The reason for attaching this to the new licences has never been given (earlier driving licences did not specify date of birth). The driver number may well have been intended to assist police or other identification checks – intensifying the already prevalent use of driving licences as general identity cards. It may have been intended that the encoded date of birth could provide police with a simple check that the bearer was also the legitimate holder of the licence (by asking for the bearer's date of birth). The provision of the date of birth would also greatly facilitate identification in subsequent checks on police records.

A particularly cynical aspect of the change was the inclusion of a small tear-off strip on the licence on which the date of birth was printed in the ordinary fashion. A caption beside the date said: 'If the date is correct, you may remove it by cutting along the dotted line.' But despite this misleading invitation, the date of birth remained encoded in the driver number.

Criminal records do not provide the basis of a national identity system, since numbers identifying these records are held for only a minority of the population. Ominously, however, in December 1980 the Scotland Yard national Criminal Records Office (CRO) was restructured and renamed the National Identification Bureau (NIB). It moved from the control of Scotland Yard to become a national 'common police service' under the aegis of the Home Office. The apparent object of the change was 'to create a national system which would be more efficient and at the same time release staff previously employed in local criminal record offices for operational police duties'.

Although events such as those described above have not led to the creation of a UPI, a number of evolutionary developments involving the National Insurance (NI) number point at this identifier as being a likely eventual candidate for a UPI. These features, which are explored at more length elsewhere, are:

The issuing in 1985 of NI-based identity cards – 'Number-cards' (see Chapter 4, especially page 117).

The cross-linking of DHSS, Inland Revenue and Department of Employment records using the NI number, both overtly and covertly (pages 92 and 109).

The adoption of the NI number by the Security Service (MI5) as a key personal identifier (page 284).

Surveying this field, the Lindop committee warned that the establishment of a UPI 'would pose dangers for data protection'. The committee recommended that 'if a UPI is ever contemplated, special legislation for it should be laid before Parliament; it should not be permitted to evolve informally'.[8]

The idea of issuing national identity cards is raised periodically, usually by politicians of the authoritarian right – but is met with little enthusiasm. Despite endorsement of such a system by political mavericks like Manchester Chief Constable John Anderton, operational police officers are well aware that the administration of a compulsory registration system would impose formidable and socially valueless new burdens on the police service, and impose duties on non-offenders far out of proportion to any utility it might have in dealing with major crime.

Between 1939 and 1952 the British population was registered, and identity cards had to be carried. But the major reasons for the introduction of National Registration Cards in 1939 – wartime evacuation and mobilisation measures, the anticipated lack of census data for planning purposes (a census had been planned for 1941), and the introduction of a rationing system – provided a rationale for identity cards which does not exist in any form today. (Nevertheless, vestiges of the wartime National Registration scheme remain to this day, in the form of the National Health Service Register.) Some recent, limited proposals for ID cards have been turned down. When, for example, Prime Minister Margaret Thatcher attempted to bully the Football Association into using identity cards to control entry to football matches during 1985, her initiative was completely rejected by the police. As an authoritarian, high-profile political response to the problem of hooliganism, the idea appeared attractive until the police pointed out that it would make the situation worse. ACPO officials dismissed the value of identity cards, stressing that it might make crowd control even more difficult.

It is generally claimed that information given to government departments is not used without consent for purposes different from that for which it has been provided, and that safeguards against unauthorised access are strict. But this is quite simply not the case. Extensive and sometimes highly speculative details about private lives are garnered by DHSS investigators, and traded with police, social workers and housing departments. VAT inspectors from the Customs and Excise department have provoked anger in business quarters by using confidential data given to other departments in their enquiries about small traders or company finances. The Inland Revenue, police and security services all consider that they should have *carte blanche* to see any personal information, confidential or not, held anywhere in government. The information privacy of those who are not white Europeans is extensively breached by social security officials, who may demand that claimants prove their qualifications for British residence, or who secretly pass personal details of claimants to the immigration department for checking. Some health service administrators have behaved similarly.

These are some more examples of systematic breaches of rules of confidentiality by government departments:

The Defence Ministry has stated (in evidence to the Lindop committee) that the security services 'have access' to all confidential data.[9]

The Inland Revenue has sought a general dispensation to obtain any confidential information from government departments which they think relevant for tax purposes; other ministries endorse this claim.[10]

A secret L Code issued to DHSS officials urges them systematically to use information about legal-aid applicants, contrary to confidentiality provisions of the 1984 Legal Aid Act.[11]

The Ministry of Defence wanted to extend the vetting of its staff and members of the armed forces, so as to determine if they disagreed with government policy.[12]

Many of the more disturbing examples of improper record linkage or information handling concern the police. Unauthorised access to police information, certainly at the level of criminal records, has repeatedly been demonstrated to be almost trivially easy. Provision is also made for criminal record information to be communicated officially to a wide range of statutory and other bodies.

Much unnecessary information has been circulated and stored in the police service – particularly in local 'intelligence' indexes, which are often gathered and recorded with insufficient heed for accuracy, propriety or the dangers of leakage. The principle that information should be obtained and used only 'fairly and lawfully' is not respected by the police. The Data Protection Act (in Section 28(4)) specifically permits the police to continue to flout this principle – on the basis of the somewhat tendentious argument that not using illegally acquired data would prejudice law enforcement.

Information is certainly improperly input. The NCCL magazine *Rights* reported that police officers invited to attend social work case conferences had been found to be transferring information gained to central police records.[13] The practice was detected when police enquiries were made following a training conference which included (unknown to the police officers taking part) a wholly fictional case. Soon afterwards, social workers were surprised to be telephoned by Scotland Yard officers who sought further details on the fictional family.

Few cases of official record leakage, however, could be more chilling than that which involved TV researcher Jan Martin in October 1978. Ms Martin worked for an independent film company which had been asked to make public relations films by builders Taylor Woodrow. She had to be 'security vetted', and her employer was then told that she had 'terrorist connections'. Ms Martin was the victim of an erroneous dossier in Special Branch and MI5 computers. Were it not for a stroke of good fortune, her entire future life and career would have been damned (see page 286).

There are many other case histories of actual damage which have reached the public record. They include the following:

Cornish musician Demeiza Val-Baker was arrested outside

Plymouth in 1983 on suspicion of carrying drugs. She was told that a police computer check on the car she was driving had revealed that she lived at an address which had previously been searched by the Drugs Squad. Although eight months pregnant, she was held in custody, stripped naked and searched. No drugs were found.

The car belonged to her father, a novelist. His house *had* been searched in 1981 by the Drugs Squad – in error. After the search was complete, and no drugs found, the police discovered that they had gone to the wrong address. They paid £250 damages to Mr Val-Baker. But the record of the raid, and the suspicion attached to that fact alone, had not been extirpated from police records. His pregnant daughter suffered for it.

London company director Leopold Rubner was arrested in Stoke Newington in 1975, whilst driving his pregnant wife to hospital. A PNC check 'revealed' that the car – his car – was stolen. It had been stolen two months previously, but had been recovered, and had been reported recovered. However, Mr Rubner was not given the benefit of the doubt, and was detained.

Torquay businessman David Morrell was arrested in 1975 for a £2 parking fine, unpaid by a company of which he was secretary. When being arrested, he was told only that the 'computer' had listed him as 'wanted'. The PNC, or other records consulted, had not however revealed the triviality of the offence for which he was sought.

When John Moore appeared before Birmingham magistrates accused of drunkenness, he was falsely said to have 'previous' – a conviction for gross indecency in Coventry two years before. A West Midlands police superintendent admitted four days later that the record was false, having been confused with another man by the PNC's checking system 'due to the closeness of their dates of birth' (in fact a year apart).

Anthony Brumwell was sent to jail at Bradford for six months; he was freed when he established that he had two, not eight, previous convictions, as claimed on the record produced in court.

Ronald Powell, a black youth, spent a month in jail as a result of yet another mix-up. He was jailed after being arrested for affray, when magistrates were told of a long string of previous convictions including a six-month jail sentence. But the offences had been committed by a man called Newell; police had mixed up two similar criminal records numbers, and put Newell's offences into Powell's file at the Criminal Records Office.

Even when errors on the PNC have been detected by the victim, correcting the mistake can prove an ordeal. A Kent driver appealed to the National Council for Civil Liberties in 1980 after local police told him that they were unable to correct an erroneous PNC record accusing him of a dishonesty offence – stealing a car. The driver was told by a member of the Kent Police, 'I have had an up-to-date enquiry made of the computer ... unfortunately there is nothing I can do to assist in the correcting of the computer record.' It took two years before the Home Office could confirm that the PNC computer record had been corrected.

Another motoring offender, one Robert Scott, never got rid of a false criminal record, first put against him in 1965. The record was lengthy, and included sex offences. Scott blames subsequent difficulties in obtaining employment and being refused permission to foster children on the continuing circulation of unchecked and evidently unchangeable untruths about his character.

Worse fates have befallen other victims of police computers abroad. A 20-year-old French hospital worker was shot dead by French police when his vehicle was checked on their national police computer, and erroneously reported as stolen because of an Interpol error.[14]

Computer system designers are familiar with a difficulty they call GIGO. It stands for: garbage in – garbage out. Any storage and retrieval system has the problem that its information output can only be as good – or as bad – as the information input. The computer is rightly regarded as the dumb servant; the danger of a computer system such as the PNC being fed with errors is that it may distribute those errors widely and multiply their possible consequences. The PNC thus has the potential to turn a limited local problem into a countrywide disaster, and has done so. Since the Home Office apparently intends that most PNC data of the type concerned in the above examples will be accessible to the subject, the danger from erroneous information should be reduced by the new Data Protection Act. All but the first and last cases in the list above might well have been avoided.

These dangers were carefully noted by an ACPO committee in 1979 when they put off any plan to install a national computerised criminal intelligence system. Not every Chief Constable was impressed with the Thames Valley Police 'Collator Project' computer, which held local intelligence records, nor with its widely reported difficulties and low acceptance rate amongst police officers. Merseyside Chief Constable Kenneth Oxford remarked in 1979 that the project had 'inherent dangers'. Confining such sensitive, unconfirmed and speculative material to a local force would minimise the risk of leakage, and the damage from any error, he argued.

Regularly explored by the news media, the threats and benefits of computer technology are often presented in accordance with a number of preordained stereotypes. There are benign stereotypes, in which computers are presented as beneficial aids to efficiency; and there is the Big Brother story of computer databank abuse and similar shocks. Another kind of report – a hardy perennial of British journalism – is to demonstrate what 'snoopers' can do. Alarming revelations make good copy. Such an exercise, as noted previously, was mounted by the *Sun* newspaper against Labour MP Michael Meacher in early 1982, a month after Meacher had un-successfully attempted to introduce his Private Member's Bill on data protection.

As in most such exercises, the private detectives concerned claimed no difficulty in checking police records. They also inveigled information about Meacher's health, family life, mortgage and other circumstances from doctors, building societies and similar sources. They reported that they had made:[15]

> a complete background search ... as to criminal record. Results of these enquiries came back that he is of impeccable character.
> He has only been married once and there are no signs of extra-marital activities ...

For a fee of £517.50, the private detectives had been able to amass a considerable quantity of both publicly accessible and private material. The snoopers used by the *Sun*, Ian Withers and Nationwide Investigations, have long been in the business, and had been sentenced to imprisonment in the past for 'public mischief' offences, but the convictions were eventually overturned on appeal to the House of Lords. After Meacher protested in Parliament, Mrs Thatcher promised to introduce the Data Protection Act. Not that the new Act would avail any other MP being similarly treated in future; most of the information the Withers had obtained came from manual records (exempted from the Act).

Criminal intelligence data, and even Special Branch information, has often and easily been improperly obtained from police records, manual or computerised – sometimes by unscrupulous actors employing nothing more than a plausible telephone manner and a good knowledge of police jargon. These are some of the known cases:

> A former Nottinghamshire police inspector and a director of the former Ladbrokes casino empire tapped massively into the PNC for nine months in 1977 and 1978. Their purpose was to obtain the names and addresses of the customers of rival London casinos, whom they hoped to poach. Spies for Ladbrokes wrote down car numbers seen outside the other casinos. In 1981, the two men received suspended jail sentences after admitting corruption in agreeing to bribe a Nottinghamshire police sergeant to get the information from the PNC.

> Nottinghamshire police subsequently suppressed, for political reasons, details of the confession and suspension of another police officer in 1980 for selling information from the police computer. To keep the affair secret, the officer was merely transferred instead of being punished. A petty

criminal from Nottingham, who admitted receiving computer information from the officer, boasted that he still had other contacts feeding him computer information 'for my own purpose'.

In January 1981, a Sheffield policeman who had used the PNC to harass women members of a health club in Sheffield was fined £75 for making offensive telephone calls. The policeman, a member of South Yorkshire police, had spied on the women dressing and undressing at the gym, and had then noted their car registrations, which he traced on the PNC. After being caught, the policeman resigned before being convicted by magistrates.

Two Thames Valley Police Authority members, including Oxfordshire County Councillor Julian Jacottet, reported serious leakages of sensitive police computer information in August 1981. One man had failed to get a job after police records, noting that he had previously been stopped by police during sex with a woman in a car, had been passed on to a prospective employer. In another case an Oxford publican had regularly obtained details of customers he did not like through police computer checks on their vehicle numbers.

Senior police officers subsequently attacked the Police Authority members and a local newspaper which had first carried the story, threatening the newspaper with a ban on local crime news from the police. The officers claimed that the 'shoddy' report lacked evidence.

In 1981, the *Observer* ran a series of articles demonstrating how easily sensitive police information was handed out on the telephone. First, they rang Scotland Yard, whose computer bureau carried out a PNC check. To do this, a specialist telephoned the ex-directory number of Scotland Yard's Computer Bureau and identified himself as a detective sergeant at an outer London Metropolitan Police station. He said, 'Our [local PNC] terminal's out. Can you do a run for me?' The answering officer obliged immediately. Then the journalists rang Brighton police station where a collator checked on two names, and read out details filed at the station, including names, dates of birth, addresses, and details of an arrest (no conviction) under the Prevention of Terrorism Act.

A Northumbria police collator did a check on local records and used the PNC to get further information on personal addresses, at the bogus caller's request.

All the police forces concerned said that it should not have happened; Sussex Police claimed at the time that 'Things aren't done on the phone like that now.'

Two weeks later, and despite 'new safeguards', the *Observer* repeated their experiment, getting information over the phone from police computer operators in Nottinghamshire, Durham, Merseyside and Kent, including the claim from a Liverpool police file that a local man was a homosexual.

Two days after that, one of the authors exposed a Windsor private detective who had bought and sold police computer information. The detective was a former Thames Valley police officer, Mr Malcolm James, who had access to PNC and the local police intelligence computer information, crime reports, criminal records and intelligence through his former colleagues. James charged £4 for each computer check. After the allegations were made, two policemen were suspended. One left and the other was sacked after disciplinary hearings. However, the Director of Public Prosecutions opted not to prosecute the private detective under the Official Secrets Act for obtaining unauthorised information.

Two former Metropolitan Police detectives then revealed that private security staff working for the Sultan of Oman at his private estate in Britain were able to carry out 'dozens' of checks on prospective staff to be employed at the estate. An estate security team, run by two former Royal Military Policemen, was able to procure the checks through a liaison with Thames Valley Police HQ officers, one of whom was on occasion driven around in the Sultan's Rolls-Royce Silver Wraith, and lunched. According to a former Metropolitan Police detective who worked as a guard at the site, batches of 30–40 prospective staff names were submitted for PNC 'traces', with occasional positives being found. The former detective asserted that, even with his London policing experience, he 'didn't know of anyone who could get half the things done that were done in Thames Valley'.

Another example of the easy access to police records enjoyed by security operatives came from a London magazine which printed memoranda circulated in the London Hilton hotels, referring to their security managers' 'scrutiny on new hired employees with regard to police records'.

Special Branch files were penetrated in 1982 and details published of a file on a former anti-apartheid campaigner. Questioned about the leak, the Special Branch immediately changed the number of its computer enquiry bureau and suspended all telephone enquiries.

In 1985, it was reported that over 100 officers in 39 police forces in England and Wales had been put under investigation by the Police Complaints Authority. The PNC had allegedly been used by these officers to discover the names and addresses of vehicle owners who were being offered prizes in a petrol-station lottery game.[16] The offending officers contacted drivers of vehicles selected for prizes and offered them the information about where to claim their prize in return for a share of the winnings.

In none of these cases were police officers actually convicted of offences concerning leakage, abuse or failure to safeguard police information. Only one officer was prosecuted – unsuccessfully. This is despite official claims, made in early 1982 by the then Home Office minister Timothy Raison, that 'severe penalties' faced all abuses of the PNC.

A widely publicised threat to information privacy stems from technical breaches of computer security systems, whereby unauthorised third parties are able to 'tap' databanks, or where authorised users obtain data to which they are not entitled. Generally, technical security threats to personal privacy are of a minor character compared to the dangers discussed elsewhere in this chapter. Personal data will seldom have a high enough financial value (as opposed to, for example, electronic funds transfer information) to attract determined attempts to penetrate an installation or subvert its staff. A different category of threat is posed by mischievous computer system users and enthusiasts – now called 'hackers' – but their numbers and abilities are wildly exaggerated in popular newspapers and magazines.

Specialists argue that a secure computer system affords better protection against accidental or unauthorised leakage of information than manual records. They point out that stealing information from within a computer requires expertise and, usually, familiarity with the system being penetrated. Anyone can in principle raid a manual file and read ordinary papers. Against this, however, is the increased possibility of unauthorised access because of the large number of terminals (which are often physically and geographically widespread), and the fact that, once inside, an information raider can extract and copy vast tracts of information. Moreover, it is comparatively easy electronically to conceal a covert entry – by posing as an authorised user or by disguising the entry to the system altogether.

Most breaches of computer network security and privacy seldom reach public attention. It is believed that many – perhaps most – are never detected. And when fraud or abuse is detected – as the examples of police computer leakages demonstrate – there is strong internal pressure merely to rectify the breach quietly, rather than announce it by having an offender punished. There have been no formal studies or analyses of the extent of data tapping or computer record theft in Britain, except for a few reports mentioned above. In contrast, computer fraud, where money or resources have been stolen, has received a certain amount of systematic attention. The results of these studies provide at least an indication of the potential threat to personal privacy from lapses of computer security.

A first-ever survey of British computer fraud was conducted by the Department of the Environment's Local Government Audit Inspectorate in 1981. All the computer users who responded, including central and local government, had been promised total anonymity, and the report's authors had no way of telling how many frauds went undetected or how many significant detected frauds had not been reported. Twenty per cent of the 328 respondents reported a fraud or breach of computer security in the previous five years – some 67 incidents in all. These were said to have cost the computer users a total of £900,000 as a result of theft or the loss of resources. Only one of the cases had resulted in a criminal prosecution.

How many of these frauds might be relevant to tapping information out of an official computer databank?

Roughly one third of the breaches of security reported were committed by people who could as easily have extracted and sold the personal data as they could have committed commercial frauds. Government installations are as vulnerable as any other – but the identity of the computers in the survey which fell victim to each fraud or abuse was kept secret.

One instance of unauthorised access to personal data was reported, even though details of breaches of privacy had not been requested. It concerned an unidentified computer department employee who had extracted details of others' wages. Another case involved the removal of lists of a company's customers by a departing salesman. On many occasions, computer staff – managers and operators alike – had availed themselves freely of computer resources. Twelve managers had been able to set up their own private businesses – or even computer bureaux – on employers' computers. One enterprising manager and his wife set up their own company to sell processing time to the husband's employer – on his own computer. In another case employees dialled into a system to play chess. Two enterprising operators set up a mail-order business selling computer-generated biorhythm charts. Some programmers copied and sold programs and software; one fraud was based on a secret alteration to the computer's programs. Three programmers altered programs or input data or instructions to sabotage the computer; one of them was successful in 'crashing' the computer (bringing it to a halt).

These incidents, and the evidence they provide of the rate and extent of potential databank abuse, do not encourage confidence in the likelihood that personal data will remain secure inside a large computer. Successful technical assaults on official computer systems have often been mounted by

students and others with specialist knowledge. Even the PNC –
through special connections to the ordinary telephone
system for emergency police use – has not been immune to
this type of leakage. Non-police users have reportedly been
able to 'log on' to the system and extract information.

The managers of any large computer installation, particularly those offering bureau services, are extremely familiar
with attempts by hackers to make unauthorised use of
terminals and computer connections, other people's files and
programs – the more determined will not stop short of tapping
into complete international networks. At worst, these attacks
may be motivated by fraud; more often than not, they are
simply done for the sake of the challenge.

On major ICL 1900 series computers in the 1970s, students
were able to take over the entire computer installation as and
when they wanted, by means of a very simple password-
defeating device. A major computer network run by the United
States Advanced Research Projects Agency (ARPA) – part of the
US Department of Defense – also received devoted attention
from international hackers.[17] ARPANET, as the system is called,
was set up in Britain in 1973. Connected to powerful university
and research-centre computers in Britain and elsewhere, the
network is financed by the US navy.

ARPA established a free, permanent link to the United States,
where over 50 major computer centres could provide enter-
tainment and a wide variety of programs and data. Enthusiasts
made connections with ARPA through public telephone
networks, using codes and identities given to legitimate users
to 'log on'. Others, including programmers and operators at
the Rutherford science laboratory near Oxford, had direct
computer-to-computer connection to ARPA in the United
States. They soon established communications links with like-
minded individuals on the other side of the Atlantic.

By granting data subjects the right to obtain damages if they
are injured or inconvenienced by data which has leaked to
unauthorised third parties, the Data Protection Act imposes a
general duty on computer users to maintain adequate technical security. Security requirements are also specifically
imposed on computer bureaux by the data protection principles. If sued, users or bureaux would have to prove that they

had taken 'such care ... as was reasonably required to prevent ... [unauthorised] disclosure or access'. Although government departments cannot be prosecuted for criminal offences, they can face lawsuits for damages. However, the burden of the evidence in this chapter has been that the threat stems from administrative and bureaucratic practice and malpractice rather than from the nature of computer technology.

4 From the Cradle to the Grave

The most threatening development in government databanks, so far as privacy is concerned, would be the development of a central population register – probably accompanied by the introduction of a standard personal identification number, and the use of that number to link records now widely separated. The Lindop committee were particularly concerned that such a system should only come about, if at all, after considered debate and as a result of special legislation. It should never be allowed to happen haphazardly or by stealth.

But this is precisely what is now happening – not by sinister design as such, but in a series of steps intended to suit administrative convenience. The future is indeed threatening. Present trends suggest that the government will integrate the databanks and computer operations of the DHSS, Department of Employment and the Inland Revenue by the year 2000. At the same time as this happens, the Inland Revenue may be granted formal powers to tap other government records and confidential personal information (as well as already having general exemption from the Data Protection Act). Statutory controls on the dissemination of Inland Revenue information may be weakened. It appears from present practice that personal information in the centralised DHSS network will be widely accessible to other government agencies. Two major national databanks – the NHS Central Register at Southport and Edinburgh and the DHSS National Insurance General Index near Newcastle upon Tyne – are already used by MI5 and the police as central population registers through which individuals can be traced.

Whatever may be omitted from a national register, however, there will by the year 2000 be a government central computer network recording the name and number, current address, date of birth, sex, identity number, family relationships and many other particulars of virtually the entire population. Linked to the network will be at least 60,000 VDU terminals, to which 200,000 civil servants may have access. Most of these terminals will be installed by 1990. Through a proposed government data network and other systems, the central computer will be connected to all the local offices of the Inland Revenue, DHSS and Department of Employment. There are plans for the direct exchange of personal data with major employers' computer systems, banks' and Post Office financial networks, and perhaps also with local authority, health authority, hospital and Home Office computers. We cannot now foresee what attempts police lobbyists may make to have automatic access to this new network or to copy its central database. But unless new administrative practices are introduced soon, the basic information held on the central computer will be routinely available to police, Special Branch and security services, if these services wish to make 'non-trivial' enquiries.

Through this new network, much personal information which the individual has to provide, for example to claim a benefit, or to an employer – will be routed through successive computers to wind up on a 'central index'. Even if no new law is passed, the effect of the system will be to create a national population register which each individual is obliged to inform of changes of name and address (and often a great deal more). Moreover, by the same time, the majority of adults (on present plans) will have been issued with a National Insurance (NI) 'Numbercard', laying an easy basis for the future introduction of a national identity-card system.

The central computer, formally the Departmental Central Index (DCI) of the Department of Health and Social Security, will be located in Washington New Town. It will replace the current computerised DHSS general index, which holds, against every NI number, surname and first two forenames, address, sex and date of birth.[1] The central index is the focus and centrepiece of the DHSS Operational Strategy, a major computerisation plan whose development and implementation will span 25 years. Based on a three-tier nationwide network, the installations of the Operational Strategy are intended to administer the entire social security system. This includes the collection of NI contributions and the payment of unemployment benefits (presently administered by the Department of Employment), supplementary benefit, government pensions and many other allowances.

As the register of every individual with whom the DHSS or Inland Revenue has dealings, the central index will include anyone who has ever been employed; anyone who has claimed a benefit since the late 1970s; all pensioners; anyone attending school in or after 1975; and everyone born after 1964. Very few adults or children will not fall into one of these groups. In 1982, the DHSS described the central index as 'a powerful tool, holding or providing access to personal information about virtually every citizen'.[2] Plastic identity cards may be used as a standard means of accessing the information held on the index. In 1982, this possibility was said to be 'sufficiently attractive to merit further study'.

The Operational Strategy is, according to the DHSS, the 'biggest computerisation programme in Europe'; its scale is certainly far beyond anything yet seen in Britain. 'A fully integrated computer network is the government's policy,' said Secretary of State Norman Fowler in August 1985. The Operational Strategy will eventually create an enormous pool of centrally accessible personal data, officially known as the 'whole person concept'.

The 'whole person concept' has developed within the DHSS since 1977 (when plans were first devised for the new strategy), and now means a single computerised personal record within which the department would hold a very wide range of data pertinent to claimants' or employees' circumstances. This record will include 'all [the] relevant data about the person' on: family relationship(s); residence; housing; health; financial expenditure; income; employment and employer; contribution records; benefit office, claim and payments information.[3] Information held about children (on child benefit records) will be linked to that on their parents or other adults 'as appropriate'. Records of spouses, cohabitees or adult dependants would also be interlinked. The DHSS holds that 'a central index and the use of a single reference number (i.e., the NI number)... is considered essential'. It adds, 'The needs of the other government agencies are another important factor ... The development of the DHSS system [should take] account of the situation, problems and intentions [of other government departments and agencies].'[4]

All this information, moreover, 'should be available at the point of [any] enquiry or claim'. Within the DHSS alone, by the mid-1990s, this will mean that data is accessible from 25,000 terminals. No detailed proposals have yet been advanced as to how staff who are authorised to use VDU terminals will be prevented from unauthorised general access to personal records. On the contrary, the thrust of government plans so far has been to make the information as widely available as possible, including to the Department of Employment (another 10,500 terminals) and the Inland Revenue (25,000 terminals). A plan to transfer the new national computerised index of personal names and NI numbers to the Inland Revenue was quietly acknowledged by the government in April 1982 – provoking some alarm.[5] 'Where will it all end?' asked Conservative MP Charles Irvine. Since 1984, some Department of Employment offices and the Northern Ireland DHSS have also had access to the general index in order to trace claimants or their NI records. Such access will be generally available to these and other government departments when the central index itself starts to become available nationally. At the time of writing, this is planned to happen in 1987 or 1988.

The new links planned between the DHSS and Inland Revenue are steps towards the complete integration of the tax and social security systems. Because of interlocking arrangements to swap information about tax and national insurance contribution liabilities, or benefit payments, the two departments already exchange a great deal of information on claimants and employees – some 60 million items of personal data per year. Linked records have been established, covering 37 million people. The Inland Revenue collects NI contributions from employers for the DHSS; while the DHSS notifies the Inland Revenue of any taxable benefits that it pays. Many large employers already provide the government with information on employees and their PAYE and NI contributions in the form of computer tapes. These are sent to the DHSS Central Office in Newcastle (see below), where the information is processed and passed on to the Inland Revenue.

Meanwhile, the Department of Employment's 1100 local unemployment benefit offices (UBOs) act on behalf of the DHSS in supervising unemployment benefit payments. The employment department also administers checks on the unemployed (the process of 'signing on'), and investigates whether or not claimants are genuinely 'available for work' through regional benefit investigation teams (RBITs, known as 'Rabbits').

Some social security benefits are already payable through the taxation system, requiring employers in effect to act as a paying office for benefits. Statutory sick pay is currently put into the wage packet or salary cheque by employers on behalf of the government. In the future, formerly separate personal benefits, such as family income supplement (to be renamed family credit), will also be paid through employers. One effect of the changes will be that some recipients of family credit (and any other benefit that will in future be treated as a 'tax credit'), and who are or will come below the threshold for paying income tax, will have their normal pay 'topped up' by the benefits. In a further broadening of these information-swapping links, the government intends to call upon employers to provide basic details, such as names and addresses, on their employees from their computerised payrolls. In June 1984 Parliament was told that:[6]

> The employer is likely to have the most up-to-date information, for example, on the employee's address. In these circumstances, where the employer is willing to supply computer tapes containing the employee's address, together with the other basic information referred to, the Inland Revenue proposes to use that source rather than the Department of Health and Social Security exchange.

These developments will enormously increase the data traffic between the Inland Revenue and the DHSS. More alarmingly, the new tax credit plans mean that personal information will increasingly be passed to employers. Credits in the wage packet imply that an employer will automatically be given details of an employee's family and other circumstances (at least indirectly) which the employee may wish to keep secret. Similarly, PAYE information passed through the DHSS necessarily means that the DHSS is given information which they do not need. As we show below, government departments have sometimes not hesitated illegitimately to breach the widely proclaimed confidentiality of personal information.

In order for the social security, employment and revenue departments to share data and keep it up to date, they must agree to a common means of identifying individuals. A 1982 report on the DHSS Operational Strategy noted that:[7]

> The timescales for the computerisation of the PAYE project (expected to take most of the 1980s) and the social security Operational Strategy are similar. It is therefore highly desirable to ensure that data used across the two departments are in compatible formats from the start of both developments.

The report also foresaw a 'substantial increase in the volume of exchange of information between the DHSS and IR', which 'reinforces the need for a central index to enable records to be located'. Both the DHSS and the Inland Revenue therefore had to use the NI number as the 'main key' to records.[8]

Although the possibility of linking taxation and benefit records in this way has clearly been under official consideration since the mid-1970s, DHSS officials denied to the Lindop committee any intention to centralise and amalgamate their own records, let alone link with other departments.[9] But integration plans derived impetus from the efficiency scrutinies of the civil service conducted by Sir Derek Rayner during the early 1980s. Rayner recommended the issue of plastic NI Numbercards[10] and, in a 1982 study of the social security system, commended the linkage of the two computer operations on grounds that it would be 'more efficient to gather the data in one place and use it'. Although the wider considerations of information privacy were said to be 'outside [their] competence', Rayner's team nevertheless reported that their proposal 'will be regarded by some as too much like Big Brother'.[11]

'From the cradle to the grave' was the motto Beveridge adopted in his original 1942 design for the postwar social welfare system – a caring, planned and concerned system that both insured individuals against needs when they could not work (national insurance) and provided a safety net (national assistance) to keep everyone out of poverty. The Beveridge plan has led to today's huge, unwieldy bureaucracy. By 1980, the Operational Strategy review politely noted, DHSS operations had become 'heterogeneous and relatively unco-ordinated'. By 1985, the social security system was administered through almost 2000 different centres, annually handling 24 million claims for 34 different benefits, and paying out nearly £40 billion in claims.

The Newcastle Central Office was first established in 1948 as the central repository for records of NI contributions, and for assessing benefit payments which were based on contribution records. It continues to provide official enquirers with details of NI contributions and benefits paid. By 1980, Central Office held more than 50 million separate records, all on paper, and handled 85 million enquiries every year. Other, currently separate, central or local filing systems are used to administer major benefits (e.g., child benefit or supplementary benefit). Because each benefit is handled separately, the DHSS has an average of five manual or computer files on each claimant.

Central Office, spread around the Newcastle area, was first computerised in the early 1970s. Until then, Central Office was not so different from the hypothetical tennis-court filing system described in Chapter 2. Maintenance of most of the department's records depended entirely on almost Dickensian labour-intensive techniques, with armies of clerical staff laboriously entering data into NI ledger sheets. Each personal contributions 'record sheet' was updated annually as stamped NI cards were returned to Newcastle by employers or contributors. The NI number originally had mechanical significance as a means of finding a record sheet in a hundred voluminous rooms or 'ledger sections'. NI numbers are allocated at random. Random distribution was originally intended to ensure an even spread of NI cards returning from all parts of the country throughout the year. But, since 1981, every child has been identified automatically on the child benefit computers (in Washington) and information passed to Newcastle so that they may be allocated an NI number on or after their 16th birthday.

At the start of 1982, over 50 million names were computerised on the general index of NI numbers. Now an on-line enquiry system, the general index has 140 terminals. Full searches to trace a specific name or number take only a few seconds, as against many minutes (or even hours) to search manual ledgers. Pensions, too, are computerised, and the general index now automatically identifies people approaching pension age; a claim on their behalf is then initiated. At North Fylde near Blackpool a separate computer complex administers other benefits which do not depend on NI contributions, including war pensions, disablement benefits and the family income supplement. In 1980, a limited service to DHSS local offices, called Datalink, provided staff with an additional facility to exchange information about maternity benefit and sickness pay with Central Office computers. But the Datalink service is not on-line; enquiries are accumulated at each local office during the day and then sent overnight on the telephone network at cheap rates. No further developments of this kind are expected until the end of the 1980s.

Unemployment benefit, in contrast, has traditionally been administered by the Department of Employment. Unemployment benefit officers (UBOs) are operated for and serviced with information by the DHSS. But the growth in long-term unemployment during the 1980s has meant that well over 50 per cent of those who have to register at unemployment benefit offices in order to claim other benefits have exhausted their right to unemployment benefit.

Unemployment benefit is paid for by NI contributions and thus requires access to DHSS Central Office records. Supplementary benefit is means-tested and administered by DHSS local offices. The affairs of a claimant receiving both unemployment and supplementary benefits are dealt with jointly by UBOs and the DHSS, a further ill-co-ordinated complexity of the social security system. Both the Rayner scrutiny team and the House of Commons Public Accounts Committee have strongly recommended a 'single office' to handle all benefits for each claimant – be it a DHSS office or a UBO.[12]

During the 1970s, most of the UBO system was computerised. The new network is known as the National Unemployment

Benefit System (NUBS) and is operated from two DHSS computer centres, at Reading and Livingston. Since computerisation began, the scale of unemployment has grown to more than seven times the level that the NUBS computers were originally intended to handle. In consequence, the unemployment benefit system has been one of the economic growth areas of the decade. Originally envisaged to deal with about half a million unemployed (and an absolute maximum of 600,000), individual NUBS computers have proliferated with rising unemployment. The number of UBOs now linked to the Reading and Livingston centres has doubled since the system started. During the 1980s, as the two centres re-equipped with new-generation ICL 2966 computers, computer orders were continually being repeated to handle the rising claims workload. There are now 12 computers at the two NUBS centres; there may soon be 20.

Enquiries from UBOs about NI records are now sent directly to the NUBS computers and there collated onto magnetic tapes. The tapes are then taken to Newcastle Central Office to be 'run through', and returned to update computer personal files on new claimants. Unemployment benefit payments are then calculated and Giro cheques issued. NUBS data are also passed on tape by the DHSS to the Inland Revenue so that unemployment benefit payments may be taxed, if required.

The present NUBS system is not very advanced. Teleprinter terminals temporarily store information in the form of punched paper tape, which is then transmitted to Reading or Livingston via permanent, slow-speed telegraph lines. Payments to unemployed people are sent out from these two centres. It was acknowledged in 1985 that personal files on the NUBS computers hold 'complicated and technical' files on people claiming unemployment benefit – covering some 41 separate items of basic personal data, including marital status; whether the claimant is a student; his or her nearest post office; reasons for withholding any benefits; attendance day at the benefit office.[13] The data is accessed using the claimant's NI number.

Data tapes prepared by the NUBS computers are also now used to calculate unemployment statistics, at a Department of Employment computer centre in Runcorn, Cheshire. NUBS tapes are sent daily to the main computer, called JUVOS (Joint

Unemployment, Vacancies and Operating Statistics), which maintains the unemployment register. Information transferred from NUBS to JUVOS comprises name, NI number, date of claim, date of birth, sex, marital status, student status, post code; and, if appropriate, a marker to indicate that the claimant has found employment and can be deleted from the unemployment register. In January 1986, the government began a trial experiment at three unemployment benefit offices to test the feasibility of specially collecting ethnic data on claimants. Eventually such ethnic data may be put on the JUVOS computer.

Combining the local office files of the Department of Employment and DHSS with the Central Office files – as planned in the Operational Strategy – will result in the compilation of a substantial profile on most people who have ever had contact with UBOs or the DHSS. Child benefit files at Central Office, for example, will provide details of parents or relationships with other adults. The NI contributions files contain basic personal information plus, directly or indirectly, details of employers and of periods of service in the armed forces, records of imprisonment, maternity, sickness or unemployment. Files of benefits for invalidity or disability are linked to dossiers of medical records and assessments carried out by the department. Means-tested benefits administered by DHSS offices require claimants to disclose wide-ranging and sensitive personal information. For these benefits, interviews and enquiries will often be held to supplement the basic information provided by claimants themselves. Furthermore, both 'Rabbit' squads and DHSS fraud investigators are expected systematically to record and investigate third-party allegations about potential frauds and other unverified or speculative data about claimants' personal lives.

Unsurprisingly, therefore, the amount of sensitive information within and flowing between Newcastle and NUBs, UBOs and DHSS local offices provoked a special warning from the Lindop committee that 'vigilance' was required. The committee took note of the long-term plans of the DHSS, and warned that placing DHSS local office data on computer could 'pose a threat to the data subject's interest'. The report stressed the importance of having the (proposed) Data Protection Authority 'consider the DHSS information network carefully' in order to 'offer the DHSS an independent view'.[14] But in pressing ahead with the Operational Strategy, the government has made no concession whatsoever to this careful and considered view.

In theory, the wholesale computerisation of social security data could be of great value to claimants. It could help remove difficulties put in their way when they have to deal with multiple benefits offices and differing claims procedures. The DHSS claims that, for this reason, its Operational Strategy has been generally supported by welfare rights and advice organisations. The present scheme of differing benefits, each with its own rules, regulations, referral procedures, voluminous coloured forms and separate claims offices, are a bureaucratic jungle in which many claimants (and officials) lose their way, resulting in frequent wrong assessments and over- and underpayments of benefit. The complexity of claims procedures, and the often coercive and sometimes unpleasant way in which some benefits are administered, also discourages the take-up of benefits to which claimants are entitled.

An integrated computer system could make one officer, in one office, responsible for assessing all the benefits due to a single individual. Similarly, the DHSS 'whole person' database could be used systematically to identify claimants who had not applied for benefits they needed, and to which they were entitled. The integrated database could help eliminate the problem of overpayment or underpayment through clerical error. The obligation to repay innocent overpayments, when discovered, can create as much financial hardship for claimants as underpayment. The new computers may also help eliminate such embarrassing problems as the continuing dispatch of letters and benefits to dead people from one DHSS benefit office after their death has been notified to another office.

But will the computer systems of the DHSS Operational Strategy match the promises which are now being made for them? It seems unlikely. The government's main interest in the strategy is the apparent opportunity it affords of making large cuts in the civil service. It is hoped that, by 1995, DHSS staff will be reduced by some 25,000, with a net saving of over £100 million a year. Savings as high as £1.9 billion have even been predicted.[15] But staffing levels have already been pared to the bone, even as the number of claims have proliferated with rising unemployment – at a high cost to the quality of service provided. While official lip service continues to be paid to increasing the efficiency and attractiveness of DHSS offices, it is all too obvious that the government has much political capital invested in making claims for supplementary benefit, at least, as unpleasant as possible.

In any case, much of the critical detail of the Operational Strategy remains to be determined. The original plan involved a series of 14 individual projects costing, at 1981 prices, some £700 million.[16] As the strategy proceeds, the DHSS hopes eventually to integrate information held in local offices, on the central computers at Newcastle and North Fylde, and on the NUBS computers at Reading and Livingston, into a single national network. The amalgamated 'whole person' data will then be held in a network of 'area' computers each connected to the central index. The central index will be the apex of the three-tier system, with the area computer centres forming the second tier. The exact number of area centres to be established is not yet settled, but will probably be between five and ten. Computerised local offices form the third and lowest tier (see Figure 2, opposite). The area computers will serve both UBOs and DHSS local offices.

The central index computers will provide a reference index to all other computer records on each individual, no matter where they are held. At first, these records will be held at existing national computer centres. Then, as equipment at these centres requires replacement, the data will – on current plans – be decentralised to and amalgamated in the area centres. To the existing DHSS information will be added data 'reference groups' on non-DHSS aspects of an individual's life in which the department claims a 'legitimate business interest'. These include employer, hospital or custody establishment (e.g., prison).[17] Other plans for the central index include recording individuals' aliases or former names, and the facility to identify someone from information other than name or number. During 1985, the DHSS ordered nine ICL 39/80 computers, sufficient to equip the first three area computer centres at Livingston, Peterborough and Bristol. The

Figure 2

Central Index and DHSS Computers*

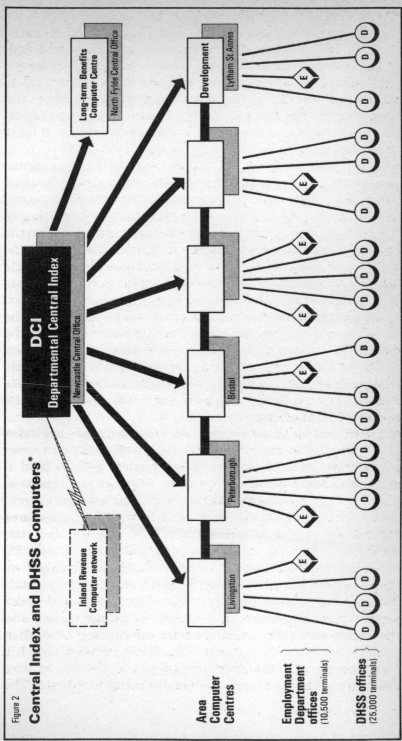

Long-term Benefits Computer Centre
North Fylde Central Office

DCI
Departmental Central Index
Newcastle Central Office

Inland Revenue Computer network

Development
Lytham St Annes

Livingston

Peterborough

Bristol

Area Computer Centres

Employment Department offices (10,500 terminals)

DHSS offices (25,000 terminals)

*Details of the Operational Strategy computers were still being finalised in 1986. This diagram shows the expected structure of the system, as planned in 1984.

new computers will be equipped with the powerful CAFS tracing system (see page 42).

The first installation, in 1987, will mark the start of the assembly of the largest computer database in the country. A minimum of 180 gigabytes of personal information will eventually go on-line. Roughly 4000 VDU terminals will be linked to each area computer.

This aspect of the Operational Strategy is known as the local office project (LOP). The first phase of LOP is intended to computerise the burdensome routine calculation and payment of supplementary benefit. The second phase will extend the system to cover incapacity benefits, including sick pay and other benefits, now handled by the North Fylde computers. Later in the 1990s, through the central index and area computers, local office terminals may be able to access information on pensions or child benefits. Eventually, as the present NUBS system is replaced, information on unemployment benefit, other benefits and NI contributions will be integrated as a single database.

The first major strategy project of this kind to go into operation was TRES (the Terminal Replacement and Enquiry Service). Between 1985 and 1987, all unemployment offices were being provided with fast, on-line access to the two NUBS computer centres. Ten thousand VDUs will eventually be installed in some 1100 UBOs, linked to NUBS via Honeywell minicomputers in the larger offices. The link to NUBS uses the British Telecom data network Switchstream – a cheaper alternative to permanent connections. 'Packets' of data are sent into the Switchstream system as required, and rapidly routed to the chosen destination. The £70 million TRES system will provide UBO staff with access to the computer records of over three million unemployed claimants. They will be able to make enquiries, send information and update computer records from remote keyboards.

By using Open Systems Interconnection – a standard type of computer to computer communication – the new DHSS computers will be able to undertake new tasks. For example, several types of long-term benefit are already sent direct to claimants' banks; in future this could be done entirely without paper, using automated credit transfer (ACT). DHSS and Employment department officials have already considered linking their computers directly to the BACS banking system (see page 61).

The recent history of government computer projects suggests that the Operational Strategy will not follow the smooth course charted for it in the early 1980s. The DHSS computerisation plan is littered with failures – the most striking of which was the sudden abandonment of the first and most important project in the strategy itself, called CAMELOT (computer-aided mechanisation of local office tasks). CAMELOT had similar initial objectives to the current LOP system – the computerisation of supplementary benefit assessments and payments. During 1980, prototype area computers were installed in Reading and Bath, linked to five local offices near Bath. Later, 26 large CAMELOT computers were to be installed at 12 regional centres. During 1979, the department anticipated that the CAMELOT system would be operational in Bath by 1981, and nationally by 1987. £6 million was spent on it, and a team of 50 worked on its development.

But, early in 1982, CAMELOT suddenly disappeared into a black hole inside the DHSS – since when, without explanation, neither its name nor attributes have been mentioned again. A veil of secrecy still cloaks the 'technical reasons' said to have caused its sudden failure.[18] On the day that CAMELOT was supposed to be complete, the first phase of LOP, its replacement, will not even have begun operating. As a stopgap measure, the DHSS in 1985 introduced a system called LOMP – the local office microcomputer project. British Telecom are supplying 2600 Merlin microcomputers to 450 DHSS local offices, where they will be used to calculate supplementary benefit claims, pay fuel bills and keep track of paper files within the office. But the LOMP micros neither store nor check data, nor communicate with the DHSS central computers.

The CAMELOT disaster, however, is only exceptional in the degree to which its very name now embarrasses the DHSS. When, in 1980, the first Datalink connections between Newcastle and local offices were turned on, they generated 'gibberish'.[19] During 1982, the DHSS decided to pass responsibility for the administration of housing benefit payments to local authorities. Some 23 months' notice was then given to ICL before the scheme came into operation in November 1983, to enable the company to develop standardised computers and software for the local authorities. But the housing benefit computers failed. Backlogs of claims built up everywhere, often of six months, sometimes of two years. A DHSS review admitted two years later that the transfer of housing benefit was a disaster for claimants and authorities alike, provoking 'acute confusion and long delays, creating distress and hardship'.[20]

Another change to the early phase of the Operational Strategy has been the abandonment of plans to introduce a benefit calculation system to be used by claimants themselves. This could have offered a further clear advantage to claimants from DHSS computerisation – by 'targeting' those who are entitled to claim, but have not done so.

The development of such programs for claimants began in the early 1970s. One such system, at Surrey University, was first tested in Brighton late in the decade. It attempted to calculate entitlement automatically, and – in its initial form – was to be used only by the claimant, who would respond to questions asked by the computer. In 1981, the Surrey development was enthusiastically backed and funded by the DHSS. It was field-tested during 1982 and 1983. But, by then, the idea of allowing claimants to use computers directly had been dropped, and the system was reconsidered for use by DHSS officials instead. Since then, projects specifically intended to help claimants have ceased to be separately identified in Operational Strategy plans.

Prospects for the effective computerisation of DHSS operations diminished further when, in 1985, the government announced a series of radical reforms for the welfare state. Many of the Operational Strategy projects had to be partly or completely replanned. For example, the first phase of the LOP project is to be rearranged to cope with the replacement of supplementary benefit by income support. Other means-tested benefits are to be reduced or changed, and the planned introduction of a partial tax credit system means a complete revision of some computerisation plans. Nor does the government propose to stop tinkering with the system.

But the final hurdle, at which the Operational Strategy may

yet fall, is the high walls of the Treasury. Even in 1982, it was acknowledged that to concentrate data on the scale suggested 'might in practice prove too expensive if carried to its limit'. By 1984, projected savings from the LOP project had fallen from £380 million to £66 million, as projected staff cuts fell dramatically. Very few people in government or Parliament were prepared to believe the revised figures. The government's intention to cut jobs by installing computers has also provoked determined civil service union opposition. Newcastle Central Office has been the scene of many lengthy and costly strikes. Caught in the crossfire between the unions and the Treasury, funds for and the ultimate success of the costly Operational Strategy projects look increasingly vulnerable.

Among government departments, the DHSS operates the largest personal information databanks and has on occasion provided striking examples of the coercive exploitation of the imbalance of power that the possession of such private information confers. Since 1980, growing battalions of DHSS fraud investigators and roving specialist claims control units have investigated the personal lives of well over a million claimants. These investigations, often highly publicised and frequently grotesque in nature, have not infrequently been portrayed as though conducted in the spirit of a vital crusade against alleged dole 'scroungers'.

As part of this economic warfare, information held in the personal files of the unemployed has repeatedly been trawled and traded with the police in order to target hundreds of thousands of claimants – on the basis of, at best, generalised suspicions. During 1983, the DHSS and ICL started developing an 'expert system' to automate and extend their secret targeting methods (described below).

In this context, it is worth noting, however, the evident intention, on the part of ministers and sections of the media, to portray claimants generally as at best feckless and at worst unwilling to work and out to milk the system. A notorious joint DHSS–police operation in 1982 – Operation Major – demonstrated this practice in action. 'Scroungers' were made a public issue when, on 2 September 1982, 286 people were arrested in Oxford after they entered a fake temporary social security office, set up by the Thames Valley Police and the DHSS. Banner headlines announced the melodramatic 'sting', and press reports inflated and wildly exaggerated DHSS claims about a 'fraud ring'.[21]

During the 1980s, the social security system has increasingly been driven towards means-testing, shifting the onus onto the individual to prove personal need. Means-testing requires the employment of thousands of additional officials to obtain information and check claims; and it requires the claimant to surrender dignity and privacy to reveal increasing amounts of sensitive personal information. Officials also derive considerable power from being allowed to make discretionary judgements about personal circumstances. Means-testing directs financial resources away from providing benefits into amassing information about the private lives of the poor. The handling of information in the DHSS is structured at least as much towards withholding benefits as towards providing them.

The sweeping changes in the social security system announced in 1985 imply further risks to the privacy and integrity of claimants' personal lives. For example, payments from a new 'social fund' may be supervised by local boards of worthy citizens. Local officials and other appointees might sit on a supervisory committee to take final decisions about social fund payments. These 'worthies' would have access to personal dossiers, and the information therein would, it appears, be exchanged with other public authorities:[22]

> There will be need to be clear links with the work of social service and health professionals who may also be involved in helping the same person. The views of outside professionals may have a part to play in helping officers reach judgements on individual cases.

'Local people,' the green paper claimed, 'are best placed to make that judgement.'

In searching for potential fraud, DHSS investigators are instructed further to extend official information-gathering activities to include 'checks of other [government] departmental records, discreet enquiries of employers, business associates or neighbours'. Investigators are encouraged, if time permits, to engage in 'approved special investigation methods' including 'observation, shadowing, liaison with police, and checking of vehicle numbers'.[23] Other departments' files, including information from the DVLC at Swansea, are made available.

DHSS regional fraud directorates have also evidently interpreted this instruction as licensing full-scale exchanges of information with police criminal records and criminal intelligence. Early in 1985, the NCCL received copies of what were effectively joint DHSS–police files, drawn up in one DHSS regional office. The files contained police photographs of claimants, details of criminal records if any, full personal descriptions, medical information, vehicle licence numbers and ownership details, as well as NI and criminal records numbers. The civil servant who leaked the information told NCCL that the regional office and the police were engaged in a two-way information trade. The police would 'trawl' through lists of claimants to help the DHSS select suitable targets for mass fraud investigation. In turn, it was said, social security staff would provide the police with confidential information on claimants, and even try and get details on 'people not even claiming' in whom the police had an interest.[24]

Officially, there are 1250 DHSS fraud investigators,[25] augmented by an elite of 175 officers in specialist claims control units (SCCUs). These officials operate in teams of six, tour DHSS local offices, and spend a few weeks in each. Between March and May 1984, for example, one such unit visited Scunthorpe seeking out people 'with a suspiciously high living standard', according to a leaked DHSS memorandum. (Such individuals, it should be noted, might be identified through a failure to appear obviously impoverished on a weekly benefit payment of £23.)

High on the SCCU investigators' hit list in Scunthorpe were single parents, the able-bodied unemployed, and other groups of claimants who were assumed a priori to be moonlighting, including:[26]

> [those with] a suspiciously high standard of living [or] who have the skills which allow them to take part-time work, such as typing, car repairs and building. Claimants who have relatives who are self-employed or in business will also be investigated. Single-parent families will be investigated where children are of school age and 'there are signs of unexpected affluence'.

Based on these criteria, no fewer than 7000 out of 12,000 claimant files were selected for special examination, in a town with a 30 per cent unemployment rate as a result of the rundown of the steel industry.

The SCCUs generally use a specified checklist of six factors elicited from case papers, including occupation (when employed). Skills such as plumbing and decorating attract special attention. Besides occupation, units also check other indicators considered relevant – such as single women with children. Such women are high on the SCCU hit list; they are always assumed to be cohabiting with a man until the contrary is proven. Investigators make overt or covert enquiries, perhaps using paid snoopers or informers, in an attempt to discover even a temporary sexual relationship which could be used to sustain an allegation of fraud.

Such gross intrusions on personal privacy are occasioned by the nature of means-testing. When entitlement depends on differentiating claimants' 'needs' based on factors which include their intimate personal relationships, then surveillance of such relationships becomes an inevitable part of the discrimination process.

The effectiveness of such investigations is highly questionable. Sweeping allegations about hundreds of millions of pounds of fraudulent benefit overpayments made in the early 1980s have been scaled down dramatically, and estimates are no longer quantified. Real frauds against the social security system do take place, but the scale of their occurrence and the official surveillance effort that is launched in response stands in striking contrast to the treatment of tax offences by the Inland Revenue. Tax evasion cases are virtually never prosecuted, despite huge sums involved.

In 1984 a clever system to help SCCUs target claimants was proposed to the DHSS by ICL and software consultants Logica. The new computers would first mimic, then improve on, the units' work. We have obtained a copy of the confidential proposal.[27] Financed under the government's Alvey advanced computing programme, ICL and Logica's ultimate goal was an 'intelligent knowledge-based system' (IKBS) which would select new target groups for investigation, refining its methods as time progressed, seeking maximum 'cost-effectiveness' in reducing claims.

A prototype expert system 'would assist fraud officers in selecting on a logical basis the most promising cases for investigation'. Fraud, the proposal notes, was 'currently *high profile* within the DHSS ... [a] more effective choice of investigations could be of importance both from a financial and a public relations viewpoint'. The system was described like this:

> Fraud officer puts into the computer details extracted from case notes of all candidates for investigation.
>
> Either the computer or the fraud officer selects cases for investigation, together with reason for choice and method of investigation.
>
> Fraud officer updates case details with time spent, methods used, outcome, at regular intervals.
>
> The computer recommends when asked: cases to close; new cases to investigate; priorities in case load; and prompts on actions.

The proposal added that:

> The major benefits of the [expert system] are that by slowly building and constantly analysing a database of cases selected for investigation, the way will be paved for a *computer scanning of an on-line database* of case records ... In the longer term, initial data entry will not be required as on-line case notes can be scanned by computer. [Our emphasis].

An expert system can formulate rules and hypotheses as it obtains more information, both raw data and through its own experience. It may, for instance, recognise trends and patterns that are not obvious from superficial inspection. An expert system would, as a database of cases builds up, seek out new 'exploratory variables', which might be used to target claimants on the next round of investigation: 'In the long term, the system will be best justified by an ability to scan case files in the database, selecting some for high priority investigation.' At slack moments, the computer 'supersnooper' might be asked to examine 'a sample of cases where there is no prior reason to suspect fraud' to see whether some then might not be 'more worthy of investigation'.

After the ICL/DHSS CAMELOT project collapsed, and prospects for the computerisation of local office files receded into the 1990s, plans for an SCCU system were put on ice. The reason given publicly for this was that not enough of the necessary data existed in electronic form. The DHSS also experienced enormous staff resentment at the effects of the SCCUs' investigative methods. During 1985, ministers decided that they should abandon targeting, computerised or otherwise, and investigate only anonymous tipoffs and staff suspicions.

Apart from established links between the Inland Revenue and the Department of Employment, the confidentiality of DHSS information is readily breached. Public statements by the department on this issue appear to be pious claptrap – for example, the assertion that 'the Department would not disclose an individual's address except for strictly limited purposes', or that 'personal information held in departmental records is regarded as confidential and is not normally disclosed to a third party or another government department without the consent of the person concerned'.[28] There are thousands of cases on the record in which the DHSS has transferred personal information without individual consent (millions, if one includes the bulk transfer of information from the NI general index to the Inland Revenue). We have discovered not a single instance in which officials first sought permission of the person(s) concerned. Nor can the department's internal regulations or conduct be held to justify the claim that such disclosures are 'strictly limited'. Some disclosures made systematically by sections of the DHSS are not even lawful.

In 1984, the Legal Action Group discovered that the department's legal aid instructions manual, or 'L Code', contravened the 1974 Legal Aid Act – which prohibits disclosure of information about a legal aid application without the subject's consent. The information provided by an applicant has to be used only for the purpose for which it is provided – assessing legal aid entitlement and contributions. The confidential L Code, however, instructs officials to pass on any information that they think may affect supplementary benefit or other claims – for example, revealing the whereabouts of a man owing maintenance to his wife to a DHSS local office where she may be claiming benefit.

To hide this illegal traffic, when passing on confidential information a legal aid official must ask for an 'understanding that ... the source of the information will not be disclosed'. In authorising such behaviour, the DHSS cannot even enter the white collar criminal's common plea that they didn't know they were breaking the law. Soon after the Legal Aid Act took effect, the DHSS asked the Lord Chancellor's Department to alter the law to permit other uses to be made of the information provided.[29] Permission was refused.

Similar official conduct is illustrated in a circular, obtained by the authors, which accompanied the issue of tables of National Income Statistics (NIS) prepared by the DHSS since 1975. The NIS tables give the annual distribution of PAYE earnings by regions in the UK. The information 'is derived from the linkage of Inland Revenue PAYE data and DHSS National Insurance information'. The tables are 'based on a sample of 1 per cent of persons with a National Insurance number'. There is nothing sinister about these statistics *per se*, but they may have been prepared in breach of the Taxes Management Act 1970, which requires an oath of confidentiality of Inland Revenue staff, who may *not* disclose information to other departments. The terms of the accompanying circular, dated March 1980, makes officials' nervousness about this activity all too clear:

> These data are supplied ... on the strict understanding that they are for use within this Department only and that *no reference to them, not even to the existence of them,* will be made to persons outside this department (including local authorities). [Our emphasis.]

The most disturbing aspect of both the L Code and NIS cases is that, in both instances, a more or less plausible argument could be put before public and Parliament by the DHSS for making the information disclosures concerned. Official willingness to enter furtive agreements to breach clear statute law for relatively trivial cause can give the public no comfort about how personal information will be protected in future – when regulations like those quoted at the beginning of this section are weak, heavily qualified and not enforced by statute.

For example, individual personal data from DHSS records are regularly and informally passed to public agencies such as the police, who are permitted to receive any information 'in cases of other than trivial crime'. In evidence to the Lindop committee, DHSS officials admitted that their regulations allowed wide discretion over confidentiality:

> Information may be disclosed without necessarily obtaining prior consent in connection with a person's need for further asistance, or in order to meet a welfare or statutory requirement, or where the Department considers that it is in the public interest to do so.

The DHSS view of the public interest was not further defined, but appears to allow considerable discretion. Information *would*, they said, be disclosed in specific circumstances to:[30]

Civil courts – for maintenance proceedings.

Police – where 'more than trivial crime' is involved.

Customs and Excise – for investigating serious offences.

Inland Revenue – when they are seeking tax arrears which include arrears of national insurance contributions.

Ministry of Defence – in cases of desertion from the armed forces.

Official guidance to the police from the Home Office stresses the general utility to police investigations of DHSS information. The advice is contained in the *Consolidated Circular to the Police on Crime and Kindred Matters,* which promises that the DHSS will consider assisting the police, *'normally orally and in confidence,* in investigations of offences other than those of a trivial nature'. (Authors' emphasis.) The circular explains for police benefit the utility of the Newcastle general index as an almost complete population register of names and addresses, adding that local supplementary benefit offices may 'have information about some persons for whom there is no central [DHSS] record and may occasionally have an address not yet shown in the central records'. It suggests that the DHSS can usually be relied on to provide police with 'the last recorded address', as well as date of birth and some earlier addresses. Generally, police are told to keep secret these breaches of personal confidentiality by the DHSS:

The fact that assistance has been given, or information has been passed, by the Department of Health and Social Security under the procedures described ... should, as far as practicable, remain confidential.

Even with such ready co-operation to hand, however, it is evident that police needs, in a significant number of cases, have given rise to exchange of information well beyond even the lax letter of official policy.

Perhaps the most striking example of DHSS–police co-operation to come to light recently was the wholesale police trawl of Newcastle NI contribution files during the hunt for the 'Yorkshire Ripper'. Some 17,000 men and their DHSS records were investigated in the search for a Sunderland man who had later moved to West Yorkshire. (A Sunderland accent had been detected on tapes that the police believed – wrongly – they were receiving from the Ripper.) Consent for the Ripper operation seemed justified in admittedly exceptional circumstances; the consent, moreover, was given in a public and considered way. But, because of erroneous police judgements, access to DHSS personal files was to no avail in catching the mass murderer.

Private detectives seeking personal information appear to face little more difficulty than the police in getting information from the DHSS/NUBS system. An enquiry file compiled in 1984 by an Isle of Wight investigation agency, and obtained by the authors, reports of a Mr F—: 'I had hoped that unemployment records may have revealed something but my source has been unable to locate a claim in his name – presumably because he's doing very nicely knocking financial institutions.'

The Home Office circular advises police officers to quote the NI number when contacting Central Office or DHSS local offices. 'When a National Insurance number is known,' it says, 'it should always be quoted ... As much information as is known should ... be given when making an enquiry.' Requests for other, more sensitive types of information may also be made to the managers of DHSS local offices. No special safeguards or restrictions are specified. The circular also advises police to seek DHSS information when 'tracing addresses of Commonwealth immigrants and aliens'. Information may also be offered to the police by NHS and DHSS administrators:

> Officers of the Department of Health and Social Security may themselves report to the police on a confidential basis any evidence of obvious malpractice by aliens or Commonwealth immigrants revealed during the course of departmental work; as, for example, when an application by one person on behalf of another for an insurance card suggests that either person is illegally in the United Kingdom.

As a matter of course, the DHSS passes on information about claimants who are thought to be subject to immigration control. Many instances have been recorded of DHSS officials' excessive zeal in passing information about black people to the police or immigration authorities. Personal information from means-tested benefit applications has been found in police files on immigrants, and with the illegal immigration intelligence unit computer at Harmondsworth (see page 171). Government immigration regulations and official attitudes to their enforcement have granted DHSS staff a dangerous discretion to require non-white, non-European applicants to prove that they are British citizens or otherwise authorised to settle in the UK.

These procedures have attracted unfavourable comparisons with South African 'pass laws' which control the movements of blacks. Requests to black citizens making fresh claims to produce their passports continue to be widespread. The practice of demanding passports has resulted in at least one judgement against the DHSS under the Race Relations Act. In 1984, an Indian-born resident, asked to produce family passports when seeking for an allowance for his wife, successfully won 'technical' damages in a case against the DHSS.[31] In the same year, a black social security officer and one-time DHSS fraud investigator accused officials of the department of racial discrimination, citing in evidence an astonishing official handbook on immigrants, which was still being distributed. The handbook described West Indians in Britain as being frequently promiscuous because of a history of 'studbreeding' by their ancestors whilst plantation slaves.[32]

The Inland Revenue will complete its national computer

databank during 1989. The new tax network not only mirrors the DHSS system in many respects, but is also to draw upon basic data from the general index, using the NI number as the key identifier for individual taxpayers. Under the direction of the Central Computing and Telecommunications Agency (CCTA) of the Treasury, the development of the DHSS and Inland Revenue systems is being co-ordinated to provide 'future governments with options' for creating an integrated national databank. Such a move would undermine still further the principles of data protection, since all Inland Revenue data (and Customs and Excise VAT information) is, under Section 28 of the Data Protection Act, exempt from subject access if it is held for the purpose of 'the assessment or collection of any tax or duty' and its disclosure would prejudice that purpose or the detection of crime. The Inland Revenue thus shares with police and security organisations the right to tap information from other computer databanks, without such disclosures having to be notified to the public or data subjects in the Data Protection Register.

The Inland Revenue computer network will include eleven regional processing centres operating two main systems: COP (computerisation of PAYE, Paye As You Earn taxation); and CODA (computerisation of Schedule D assessment, for self-employed people). More than 25,000 terminals will eventually be installed in 600 tax offices across the country (about 17,000 for COP and 8000 for CODA). Between 1986 and 1988, on average, one new tax office is planned to go on-line every day. Eventually, about 28 million PAYE taxpayers will be recorded on COP, with some 3.5 million more self-employed taxpayers' records on CODA. The system will also computerise some 1.1 million records on employers. The complete network may use up to 50 large ICL computers.

Ministers agreed to the £228 million COP/CODA plan in October 1980. An initial seventeen ICL 2988 computers were ordered a month later. A National Development Centre for the COP system at Telford was set up in 1982. Uniquely for a large-scale government computer project, the COP plan has proceeded ahead of schedule and at less than the originally estimated cost. The first tax office, Wolverhampton, went 'live' in December 1983. It was connected to the Telford

development centre, which also houses the regional processing centre for the West Midlands. Other regional centres were
thereafter due to go 'live' at two to three-month intervals (see
Table 2, page 63, for their locations). COP records are to be completely computerised by 1988; the CODA scheme should be
completed by 1989. A national communictions network, using
high-speed British Telecom data links, will enable all the COP
computers to work together – forming, in effect, a single
databank.

As indicated earlier in the chapter, several significant steps
have already been taken towards the integration of DHSS and
Inland Revenue records. Compatible technical standards and
common record formats have been planned. The same type of
computers (ICL 39/80 or Estriel) have been ordered for future
regional computer centres in COP/CODA, as for the DHSS local
office project; and they will use the same data communication
method: Open Systems Interconnection. The Inland Revenue
has also been given the complete, computerised DHSS general
index. The information was passed on so that the Inland
Revenue might 'utilise basic information … from DHSS records in order to avoid the substantial and expensive task of
keying in that information from its own paper records'. The
data transferred included the name, number, date of birth
and title of anyone recorded on the general index. Other
information reaches the Inland Revenue from computer tapes
supplied by employers.[33]

A feasibility study for a full-scale joint Inland Revenue–
DHSS database was launched in 1985. The study followed a
pilot exercise in 1983–84, when the Inland Revenue inspected
3000 DHSS records in a search for self-employed taxpayers
who were not recorded as paying NI contributions. During
1985, ministers were also due to consider the 'confidentiality
issue' – specifically whether the oath of confidentiality, which
the law requires of Inland Revenue staff, could be relaxed so
that data could be passed to the DHSS.[34] However, the Inland
Revenue has been given unrestricted access to most DHSS
information since 1982.[35]

The Inland Revenue also plans to establish a rapid national
tracing service based on NI numbers. The first tracing computer, with records on over two million taxpayers in Scotland,

was installed at the East Kilbride PAYE centre in 1982. The tracing system is based on the hardware equivalent of free text retrieval, ICL's Contents Addressable File Store (CAFS). This will be used to track down taxpayers who may change address, and for other investigative purposes – such as cross-referencing bank account or payments information to a particular taxpayer's file. Given only partial information about name or address, CAFS can locate a person's name and NI number (and hence their tax records). In a letter to Paddy Ashdown MP in October 1984, Treasury minister Barney Heyhoe acknowledged that the tracing system would eventually be extended to include all Inland Revenue district offices. It would provide, he said, 'facilities to perform National Insurance number and name and address tracing for taxpayers both in and outside their regions'.

Previous Inland Revenue attempts to computerise its operations were almost complete failures. The first computerisation plan was formulated in the 1960s; nine computer and office centres were to be set up to cover the whole of the PAYE scheme across Britain. But only one of these – Centre 1 at East Kilbride in Scotland – ever started operations. The rest of the plan was quickly shelved.

Centre 2 was indeed built, at Bootle – but a six-year-long electricians' strike began just as the computers were about to be installed. They were moved to Liverpool. At the same time, however, the PAYE scheme was altered, and the government first suspended and then cancelled the computerisation plan. At East Kilbride, the technology of the 1960s did not permit fast on-line computer operation; extensive form-filling and card-punching was required to move data to or from the computer. A government proposal in 1972 to move to a tax credit system sounded the death knell for the scheme. Centres 3 to 9 were forgotten, while Liverpool became a general computer centre instead. The Liverpool computers now hold a small databank of 500,000 records on subcontractors in the building industry – workers colloquially known as 'the lump'. It also operates the MIRAS and LAPR databanks, holding data on anyone claiming personal tax deductions for mortgages or life assurance policies.

Two tax offices at Shipley and Cumbernauld supervise the

collection of some £60 billion in taxes every year. In January 1984, dual ICL 2982 computers at each centre started operating on-line databanks on nearly four million self-employed tax-payers. Although the collection network is not part of the COP/CODA scheme, links between the two were recommended in September 1985, and were expected to be approved by ministers for the early 1990s, as was a system called OCTA (for On Line Corporation Tax Assessment). Confidentiality arrangements for the new system will include normally restricting access to any individual taxpayer's file to the district office dealing with it. There will also be standard physical security precautions, including keycards or badges, and passwords, to control access. Nevertheless, the COP/CODA system must make inevitable much wider access to personal tax records than is now physically feasible.

Meanwhile, the Inland Revenue is seeking almost untrammelled powers to obtain confidential personal information from any source. The proposal follows a departmental committee report on enforcement powers, published in 1983. The Keith report recommended that tax inspectors should be given powers to obtain any information on demand, including personal information given to other government departments in confidence. The powers recommended were almost as wide-ranging as those proposed by the government during the passage of the Police and Criminal Evidence Act. Although it would be normal for the taxpayer to be told of any such 'information notices' served on government departments or other third parties, Keith recommended that this requirement should be waived in cases of suspected fraud. There was, said the committee:[36]

> no valid argument of principle against powers being given to the Inspector to make specific information demands of officials of other departments in respect of identified taxpayers. *We so recommend.*

At the time of writing, detailed proposals were expected to be contained in a government green paper on personal taxation for publication in 1986. Legislation, in the form of a Finance Act, would follow in 1987. In canvassing other government departments in 1985 for their attitude to Keith's proposals, officials of the Inland Revenue's policy department offered a very wide interpretation of the recommendation. According to a memorandum leaked to the *Guardian*, the department 'presently intended' to seek powers to:[37]

> serve notice on other government departments to release data ... overriding any requirement as to confidentiality contained in any legislation under which the information was originally given.

Criticising the *Guardian* report, the deputy chairman of the Inland Revenue claimed shortly afterwards that it was 'wholly untrue' to say that existing government rules on confidentiality were 'frequently breached'. It was not untrue. Not only have there been other occasions, as described above, where officials have knowingly broken laws of confidentiality; but the *Guardian* itself had, some years before, revealed in a series of articles how easy it was for an adept trickster to obtain personal tax information from inspectors' files. The *Guardian* cases led to a major Home Office and police enquiry.[38]

Since the start of 1984, a NI Numbercard – resembling a standard plastic credit card, complete with signature space and a magnetic strip encoding the bearer's name and number – has been issued to everyone reaching the age of 16, and to anyone else registering in the NI system for the first time or applying for a new card. By 1990, nine million youths and adults are expected to have received them, with the total issued rising to about 24 million in the year 2000. Eventually, the cards could be used in automatic readers, similar to the present automatic telling machines (ATMs, or cash dispensers) installed by most banks.

The DHSS has been unforthcoming or uncertain in public as to why a magnetic strip was included on the Numbercard saying that they had 'no immediate purpose' for it in mind. But in a background briefing note, the department explain that:[39]

> [it was] provided against the possibility that, as the Operational Strategy develops, it will become desirable for the cards to be machine readable. It is sensible to incorporate such a feature from the outset since the additional cost is very small – approximately £10 per thousand cards.

The Numbercard may become the basis of a national

identification system. This will certainly be a contingency that has occurred to senior government officials. In the present circumstances, there is no cause for legislation to give legal effect to such an initiative. Instead, as Lindop feared, it may happen step by stealthy step. A future government inclined to curtail liberty will find it easier to introduce a compulsory and wide-ranging national registration system if the skeleton of such a system is already in place.

Despite government claims to the contrary, the Lindop committee concluded that the British NI number was already close to being used as a personal identity system. Although no further government proposals have been made for the use of the NI Numbercard, it is fairly certain that – for benefit claimants at least – its carrying will become obligatory. It did not take long for suggestions about compulsory carrying of NI cards to creep into public discussion. In August 1984, in what NCCL called the 'thin end of a nasty wedge', the Public Accounts Committee of the House of Commons suggested that casual workers should be issued with the new Numbercards and required to produce their cards when being paid – so that information about payments made to them could be collated successfully by the Inland Revenue.[40]

Warning bells should ring particularly loudly if, following the introduction of new police powers under the 1984 Police and Criminal Evidence Act (see page 194), and the more widespread issue of the Numbercard, police officers generally start asking to see a Numbercard as a possible proof of identity during street stop-checks. An early move in this direction would be heralded by the wider inclusion of NI numbers in police record systems. By the time such a development comes to cause public alarm, it may be too late to turn back.

Increasing centralisation of government records in the manner described above seems to make the gradual evolution of a population register and a personal identification number system almost inevitable, if present plans are not arrested. Such 'collation and centralisation', the Lindop committe warned, 'for however beneficial a purpose, would, in our view, be thoroughly undesirable. It would give any government too great a potential power over its citizens and it would be dangerous if it fell into the wrong hands.' Such collation of information, said Lindop, 'would present a considerable threat to the privacy, and perhaps the freedom, of the private citizen.' That warning has gone unheeded.

5   In Sickness and In Health

Few personal records have the same potential to damage personal integrity or privacy as those concerning health. Medical records detail information about individuals which has customarily attracted the most stringent protection. In the 1980s' debates about data protection, no area of information privacy provided a fiercer battleground. Many medical matters – information about sexually transmitted diseases, sexual preference, family circumstances, pregnancy, contraception, or mental illness – attract such sensitivity that, if patients and sufferers do not feel that they have a guarantee of confidentiality, they may avoid seeking treatment. Any failure to assure privacy of medical information may thus threaten health or lives.

Medical ethics clearly state that clinical information about patients must normally be confidential to members of the medical profession directly concerned in treatment. This cornerstone of doctor–patient relations originates in the Hippocratic oath, and is reflected in the rules of the General Medical Council. The GMC has struck off those practitioners who have gratuitously breached individual privacy for 'infamous conduct in a professional respect'. But in hospitals and clinics many non-medical staff necessarily handle confidential records. Rules of confidentiality should uniformly cover administrators, who are 'expected to conform' with the ethics of the medical profession. They do not always do this – leaving loopholes in privacy protection that have in the past been accidentally or deliberately exploited.

The introduction of computerisation to the NHS has been uneven and irregular, reflecting the administrative diversity within the different districts and regions of the health service.

Each of the 14 regional health authorities in England, parallel NHS agencies in Scotland, Wales and Northern Ireland and 201 subordinate district health authorities (13 health boards in Scotland) have autonomy in the selection of computers and software. Some larger hospitals have their own 'patient administration systems' and computers, while others may use that of the district or regional health authority. But many hospitals have no general computer facilities at all, except in specialised testing laboratories. A separate tier of NHS administration is the 98 family practitioner committees (FPCs), supervising general practitioners, many of which do use a standard 'family practitioner system' to maintain and amend their medical registers. A range of computer systems for GPs is also now available, but facilities vary widely. The result has been a disparate collection of health service computer systems performing different tasks in widely differing ways.

New blueprints for NHS computing have been drawn up since the beginning of the eighties. The new systems envisage computerised support for both front-line 'primary health care' by GPs and hospitals and for administrators concerned with community health. Hospitals' computerised patient administration systems (PASs) are to be standardised and linked to similar data held by family practitioner committees and health authorities. A key feature of these new plans is the collection of a 'minimum data set' about *every* hospital patient or health service client.

There will be a national network of NHS computers, centred principally at regional health authority level, but it is unlikely to be in operation until the mid-1990s. There will be no central NHS computer system as such. Each district authority will remain responsible for people in its area. Indexes of patients held at regional level may not necessarily include names or national identifying numbers, but will be linked to identifiable district health records, including individual hospital patient administration systems. PASs will not necessarily hold all or any of a patient's medical data, but will become increasingly important for the structuring and indexing of a hospital's clinical records.

As well as a standard set of information to be held in and transmitted from NHS computers, communications technology will be standardised, using the Open Systems Interconnection (OSI) system. In June 1985 the government appointed the software firm CAP to oversee this standardisation. Information from hospital and district computers will be passed on the OSI network to regional health authorities, there to be stored and processed for statistics and analysis by the Office of Population Censuses and Surveys and the DHSS. Planning for an NHS computer network began in February 1980, when a health services information steering group was appointed. The group is usually known as the Körner committee, after chair Edith Körner of the South Western Regional Health Authority. It studied wide-ranging information-handling problems within the health service – for example, ambulance maintenance – as well as personal, administrative and clinical records.

A second NHS computer committee – the Computer Policy Committee – was established in 1977, and has since reviewed technical systems and standards. The Computer Policy Committee has also stressed the importance of establishing a homogeneous, integrated NHS databank. Such a system would resemble the 'whole person' concept in the DHSS plan for social security computerisation, described in the previous chapter. (In March 1985, these two main committees merged into a single Information Advisory Group.) If all current plans are successful, the government will establish a national computer network which will hold and transfer personal health information in a way that a combination of technical incompatibility of records systems and administrative disorder has hitherto prevented.

The first step towards standardising and linking diverse medical records is the adoption of a personal identifier – in this case, the National Health Service number. NHS numbers are allocated shortly after parents register a newborn baby with the Registrar of Births, Deaths and Marriages. Local register offices then pass details of new registrations to the NHS central register. What we now know as NHS numbers were first issued in September 1939, just before the beginning of the Second World War, as National Registration numbers. Under the National Registration Act, identity cards and numbers were

issued to facilitate the control of rationing and to
census data for call-up into the forces. The Nationa
tration Office for England and Wales was set up in
port, and for Scotland at the General Register Office.

In 1952 National Registration and the carrying of ID cards
was discontinued. But the central register remained, and
became the pivot of NHS records. The Southport and Edinburgh offices continue to record the names, FPC codes, NHS
numbers and dates of birth of over 50 million people. The
register is at present kept on paper in England, but is fully
computerised in Scotland. At the time of writing there were no
plans to computerise the English register although this
would have obvious administrative attractions. But if proposals to computerise local register offices go ahead, it would
make sense to computerise at least the new entries to the NHS
central register at the same time, despite the substantial cost.

There is no statutory requirement for patients or doctors to
inform the NHS central register of a change of address. But a
patient who moves between areas, changing their GP and FPC,
will have that change of FPC recorded at the register. The
patient's new address will be recorded against their NHS
number in the new FPC's medical register.

Every GP is registered with a family practitioner committee,
and the committee is responsible for monitoring the number
of patients on each practitioner's register. Information is
regularly transferred between GP and FPC, and between FPC
and the DHSS, the National Health Service paymaster. The size
of each GP's register determines how much the doctor is paid.
The FPC also maintains records on the number and type of
drugs prescribed by GPs.

The Office of Population Censuses and Surveys, which runs
the NHS central register for the DHSS, acknowledges that the
register is not simply for use by FPCs:[1]

> The Central Register ... provides a means of tracing the where-
> abouts of missing persons but considerable restrictions are placed
> on its use for this purpose. *In the main* [our emphasis] this use is
> limited to such projects as medical research.

The central register is arranged alphabetically by name and
can be cross-referenced with a numerical index. Addresses are

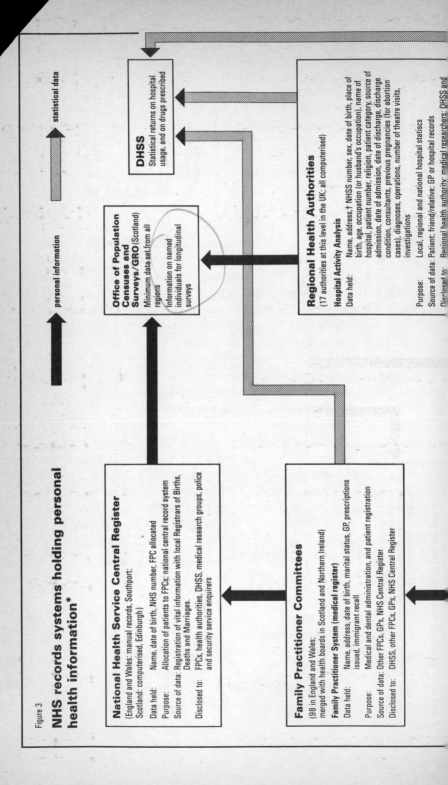

Figure 3

NHS records systems holding personal health information*

→ personal information

→ statistical data

National Health Service Central Register

(England and Wales; manual records, Southport;
Scotland: computerised, Edinburgh)

Data held: Name, date of birth, NHS number, FPC allocated

Purpose: Allocation of patients to FPCs; national central record system

Source of data: Registration of vital information with local Registrars of Births, Deaths and Marriages.

Disclosed to: FPCs, health authorities, DHSS, medical research groups, police and security service enquirers

Family Practitioner Committees

(98 in England and Wales;
merged with health boards in Scotland and Northern Ireland)

Family Practitioner System (medical register)

Data held: Name, address, date of birth, marital status, GP, prescriptions issued, immigrant recall

Purpose: Medical and dental administration, and patient registration

Source of data: Other FPCs, GPs, NHS Central Register

Disclosed to: DHSS, other FPCs, GPs, NHS Central Register

Office of Population Censuses and Surveys/GRO (Scotland)

Minimum data set from all regions

Information on named individuals for longitudinal surveys

DHSS

Statistical returns on hospital usage, and on drugs prescribed

Regional Health Authorities

(17 authorities at this level in the UK; all computerised)

Hospital Activity Analysis

Data held: Name, address,† NHSS number, sex, date of birth, place of birth, age, occupation (or husband's occupation), name of hospital, patient number, religion, patient category, source of admission, date of admission, date of discharge, discharge condition, consultants, previous pregnancies (for abortion cases), diagnoses, operations, number of theatre visits, investigations

Purpose: Local, regional and national hospital statiscs

Source of data: Patient; friend/relative; GP or hospital records

Disclosed to: Regional health authority; medical researchers: DHSS and

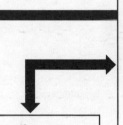

PATIENT

(Wide range of systems in use, some ad hoc. The description given is illustrative only)

Data held: Name, address, age, date of birth, occupation, ethnic group, register, examination notes, referral reports, prescriptions, NHS number, marital status, social class or occupation, ethnic group, telephone number, number of people in the patient's household

Purpose: Maintenance of personal medical records

Source of data: Patient, other authorities concerned (e.g., child in care)

Disclosed to: FPC, other GPs

Hospitals

(Wide range of systems in use)

Patient Administration System

Data held: Name, address, date of birth, marital status, sex, religion. Beds occupied, laboratory references (pathology, radiology, etc.)

Purpose: Identification of patient throughout treatment; sending mail

Source of data: Patient, friend/relative, GP, other doctors

Disclosed to: Available on request to any department in hospital

Hospital laboratory computers

Data held: Name, ward and consultant code and number, laboratory results. (Name not usually held for sensitive results such as VD tests)

Purpose: Production of reports, management statistics

Source of data: Laboratory and medical staff

Disclosed to: Laboratory, medical and nursing staff

Data held: Name, address, NHS number, sex, marital status, next of kin, GP, consultant, religion, occupation, last previous psychiatric care, age, date of birth, legal status (e.g., detained under the Mental Health Act), mental category, subnormal status, previous psychiatric in-patient care, diagnosis, outcome

Purpose: Local, regional and national hospital statistics

Source of data: Patient, friend/relative: GP or hospital records

Disclosed to: Regional Health Authority; medical researchers; others in statistical form only

---

District Health Authorities

(201 authorities in England and Wales: 13 health boards in Scotland: 4 health and social services boards in Northern Ireland. Most computerised)

National Child Health Systems

Data held: 1 Child register – name, address, date of birth, sex, NHS number, ethnic group, treatment centre

2 Birth information – number of births this confinemen:, live births/stillbirths/died, previous live births, stillbirths, and miscarriages, gestation period

3 Immunisation register – vaccinations (etc.), date given and treatment, centre at which immunisation given

4 Pre-school health – developmental examinations, results and date given, examination centre

5 School health – results of clinical examinations at school

Purposes: 1 To schedule immunisation appointments and pre-school health developmental examinations

2 For management purposes

3 For epidemiological purposes

4 For DHSS statistical returns

Source of data: Notification of birth and other reports from midwives, health visitors, administrators, GPs, reports from clinical medical officers

Disclosed to: Officials and medical practitioners within the District Health Authority

---

*Main source: NHS Centre for Information Technology.
Data Protection Guidelines on the Use of Computers.
DHSS. December 1984

†Names are not normally entered into the computer in 'most regions'; thus an individual can only be identified by recourse to the manual record (a hospital form) used to input the data.

not kept on the register, but are known to the FPC with whom
the person is shown to be registered. The FPC can thus supply
an address, if asked and willing. According to former MI5 staff,
the central register is also used by that agency to help trace
persons in whom they have an interest.[2]

NHS numbers are formed from codes indicating the registration district where a person was born, the year and quarter
of birth, and the birth register number within that area. In
England and Wales, this normally consists of five letters and
three or four digits (Scottish NHS numbers are allocated in a
slightly different way). The origin and form of the NHS number
is therefore quite different from the NI number system
described in Chapter 4.

Throughout the NHS, personal medical information in this
form may be found in over 300 administrative centres, as well
as in over 10,000 doctors' surgeries. Figure 3 (pages 124-5) shows
in detail the type of computerised or manual records that may
be held in each centre. It indicates what information is usually
held, to whom it is accessible, and with whom it may be
exchanged. These records may broadly be divided into three
categories.

The most basic raw data concern the personal health or
clinical medical records used in hospitals and in primary
health care by GPs. Clinical records handled by doctors and
other medical staff and specialists are familiar to ordinary NHS
clients; few people will have seen their clinical records other
than in a doctor's hands. Detailed personal medical data will
often be exchanged between surgery and hospital, but, save for
one advanced computer system installed in Exeter, such
clinical data is always sent in written form.

Second, there are registers maintained for community
health purposes, such as cancer surveillance or the monitoring and control of infectious or other transmissible diseases.
Registers and recall systems are used to support preventive
medical measures such as periodically summoning children
or others at risk for screening tests and immunisation. These
projects include both continuous national monitoring, such
as the Cancer Registration Scheme, and limited and local
research projects. Many of the larger schemes are organised by
the Office of Population Censuses and Surveys. Important

medical research activities also depend on the extensive use of detailed clinical statistics.

District health authorities are required to exercise surveillance of child health from birth onwards. Under the 1936 Public Health Act, all births – live or stillborn – must be notified to the health authority within 36 hours. So whether the birth is in hospital or at home, records are quickly established on both mother and child at a district health authority's computer — centre. A series of child-health computer systems now support long-term surveillance of children through infancy, immunisations, pre-school years and on through school days up to the age of 16.

The third category of health service information is straightforward administrative data on, for example, the occupancy of hospital beds, the management of waiting lists, or the workload in operating theatres.

FPC administrative records include medical registers, payments made to GPs, dentists, ophthalmists and pharmacists, and records of hospital inpatient and outpatient activity. Regional health authorities, all of which are computerised, are charged with the general administration of hospital facilities. The largest RHA computer network is the hospital activity analysis system, which holds over five million records on patients at area, regional and national level.

Administrative and statistical information such as that gathered by hospital activity analysis helps inform decisions about the allocation of scarce medical resources. Often, but not always, such information is held in such a way that the subject is unidentifiable or only partially identifiable. Under the new law, if data subjects are genuinely unidentifiable, the system concerned usually need not be notified to the Data Protection Registrar. But much statistical health information is necessarily related to specific individuals, so that records can be cross-linked – especially that held for such epidemiological purposes as ascertaining an apparent cause for cancers or tumours of a particular type, in a particular area or among an identifiable population group.

In the past, the distinctions between information collected for these different purposes have been relatively clear cut. They will soon become less so, and common data for many health service purposes could be held in a single computer database. Unsurprisingly, DHSS administrators anticipate labour savings when data can be collected once rather than several times. The second chair of the DHSS's steering group on health service information, Michael Fairey, stressed in 1985 that the distinctions between different types of information were becoming increasingly blurred: 'Information systems about patients have an administrative and clinical component; modern information technology allows both to be collected using the same mechanism.'[3] By April 1988, mandatory recommendations made by the Körner committee for the 'minimum data set' should be implemented throughout the health service. Every hospital and health authority in the country will be asked to collect the same items of information when dealing with a particular medical event (see Table 3).

Table 3
DHSS recommended 'minimum data set' for health computers*

---

1 Number or identifier of patient
2 Sex
3 Postcode of patient's address
4 Date of birth
5 Marital status
6 Category of patient
7 Code of GP
8 Method of admission
9 Source of admission
10 Wards occupied and period occupied
11 Codes of consultants/GPs responsible for care and period for which care took place
12 Method of discharge
13 Destination on discharge
14 Operative procedure
15 Diagnostic codes

---

* Items of information collected on all patients entering hospital.

The front line of the NHS continues to be the primary health care facilities offered in doctors' surgeries or in health centres.

1 and 2 A small computer of the late 1980s (*above*, an ICL 30/30) has three times as much power, and ten times as much storage capacity, as computers of the early 1970s which would have filled the hall shown below

3 (*Opposite top*) Computer-controlled scanner uses three television cameras to observe the registration numbers of vehicles travelling towards London on the M1 motorway. The registrations are then checked against lists of stolen/suspect vehicles held on the Police National Computer

4 (*Below left*) The Police National Computer building and communications centre, in Hendon, north London, is protected by high-security equipment and crash barriers

5 (*Above*) Experimental mobile computer data link and map terminal installed in police patrol car

6 (*Below*) Typical computerised local police command and control centre at Lewes, Sussex, headquarters of Sussex Constabulary

THIS DOCUMENT IS GOVERNMENT PROPERTY

NOTES FOR THE COMPLETION OF PARTS 2, 3 AND 4

General

1. BEFORE MAKING ENTRIES IN THIS DOCUMENT STUDY THE FOLLOWING NOTES AND PARTS 2, 3 AND 4.

2. Your prospective employment will put you in touch with information of outstanding security importance. The Government have decided that special inquiries must be made about the reliabi those in such employment.

3. So that these inquiries may be made you are asked to complete this Document FULLY AND ACCURATELY in black ink, or typescript, using BLOCK CAPITALS. It will be seen that parts 2 are similar in content; this is necessary to enable two forms of enquiry to be made simultaneously. Do not leave blank spaces; if an entry is inapplicable insert "No" or "Not Applicable" (N/A), as priate. Continue in Part 4 if insufficient space is available in Parts 2 and 3, noting against your entry the number of the relevant Section. If you are positively unable to enter any required parti precisely, enter as much information as you can and state briefly why you are unable to enter all the information.

Character Referees (see Part 2, Section 15, and Part 3, Section 17)

4. Character referees are required.

   (a) YOU SHOULD:—

   (i) Nominate two or more persons, Service and/or civilian, who are British subjects and, together, have been well acquainted with you in private life during the past five years. If this cannot be covered by only two referees, more are to be nominated.
   (ii) First ask their permission. If there is insufficient time to do so, submit their names and explain to them, as soon as possible, that you have taken the liberty of so doing.
   (iii) Ensure, wherever possible, that they are located in the U.K.
   (iv) Always give the addresses at which they can be most easily contacted.

   (b) YOU SHOULD NOT:—

   (i) Nominate anyone who is related to you by either blood or marriage.
   (ii) Nominate anyone you know in an official or professional capacity, e.g., a police officer   icial, etc., etc., unless he has some knowledge of your privat

5. THE INQUIRIES THAT WILL BE MADE WILL NOT NECESSARILY V   FEREES.

Political Associations (see Part 2, Section 21, and Part 3, Section 23)

6. In answering the questions on political associations yo   n which is generally held of the organization or pers question, even if you do not endorse that opinion. T   ffirmative answer will not necessarily disqualify yo appointment, but since it is Government polic   consideration.

Action following Completion of

7. When you have   3, and Part 3, Section 25.

8. Unl   personal reasons, you wish to send it direct
M

Correspondence to this address must be under double cover. The outer envelope should be addressed to
The Secretary PO Box 500 London SW1P 1XH and not to any individual

PO Box 500
London SW1P 1XH

Telephone 01-491 4488 ext.

Your reference   ----

Our reference   S4/F7/14/2

7 *(Opposite)* A Positive Vetting (PV) form is the first stage in getting top-security clearance for government work. All information from PV enquiries is fed to MI5, the Security Service, for checking against their records

8 and 9 *(Below left)* The Security Service headquarters at Curzon Street House in London's fashionable Mayfair district. The service prefers to be known to, and communicate with, the outside world as 'Box 500' – sometimes, just 'Box'

10 *(Below right)* MI5's first major computer, an ICL 1907, was installed in this top-secret centre, codenamed 'MoD-X' in Mount Row, Mayfair (now closed)

11 (*Above left*) Jim Hogg, a trade union activist in Dumfries, discovered he was the subject of a secret MI5 computerised 'permanent file' when a letter about him from his local Special Branch to MI5 was leaked to the press (see page 286)

12 (*Above*) Because of shortages, MI5 placed its first-ever public advertisement for staff in the late 1970s. Applicants were offered a grade higher pay than in any comparable civil service computer post. The advertisements were placed through an employment agency

13 (*Left*) MI5 executive Albert Crassweller, head of MI5's 'FX' division. His responsibilities include planting long-term infiltration agents in trade unions, professional and radical organisations and political parties, and environmental and peace groups. Their job is to gather inside information for MI5 files

14 *(Top)* Experimental machine-readable passport (MRP) terminal installed for trials at Heathrow Airport

15 *(Above left)* The 'machine-readable' page in a sample passport. A computer scanner can read the two lines of text and symbols at the bottom of the page

16 *(Above right)* A National Insurance Numbercard, first introduced in 1984. The Numbercard is at present the most likely basis for the introduction of a full-scale identity card and population registration system in Britain, were such a system ever to be desired

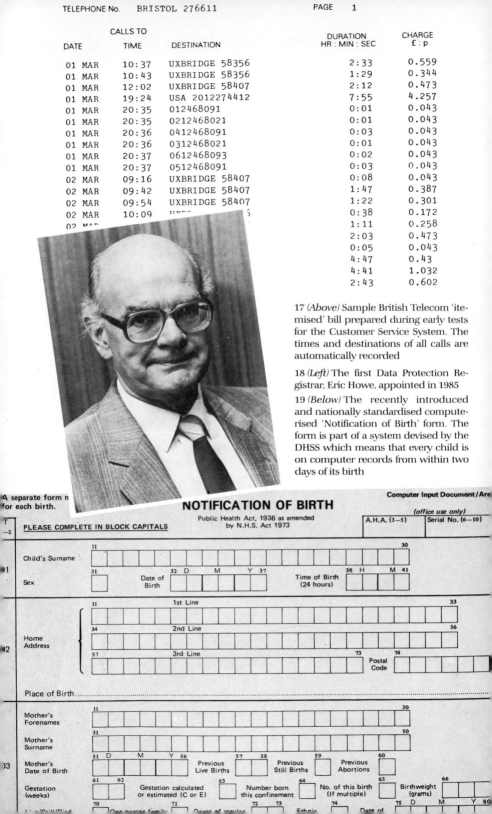

TELEPHONE No.   BRISTOL 276611   PAGE   1

CALLS TO

DATE	TIME	DESTINATION	DURATION HR : MIN : SEC	CHARGE £ : p
01 MAR	10:37	UXBRIDGE 58356	2:33	0.559
01 MAR	10:43	UXBRIDGE 58356	1:29	0.344
01 MAR	12:02	UXBRIDGE 58407	2:12	0.473
01 MAR	19:24	USA 2012274412	7:55	4.257
01 MAR	20:35	012468091	0:01	0.043
01 MAR	20:35	0212468021	0:01	0.043
01 MAR	20:36	0412468091	0:03	0.043
01 MAR	20:36	0312468021	0:01	0.043
01 MAR	20:37	0612468093	0:02	0.043
01 MAR	20:37	0512468091	0:03	0.043
02 MAR	09:16	UXBRIDGE 58407	0:08	0.043
02 MAR	09:42	UXBRIDGE 58407	1:47	0.387
02 MAR	09:54	UXBRIDGE 58407	1:22	0.301
02 MAR	10:09		0:38	0.172
02 MAR			1:11	0.258
			2:03	0.473
			0:05	0.043
			4:47	0.43
			4:41	1.032
			2:43	0.602

17 (*Above*) Sample British Telecom 'itemised' bill prepared during early tests for the Customer Service System. The times and destinations of all calls are automatically recorded

18 (*Left*) The first Data Protection Registrar, Eric Howe, appointed in 1985

19 (*Below*) The recently introduced and nationally standardised computerised 'Notification of Birth' form. The form is part of a system devised by the DHSS which means that every child is on computer records from within two days of its birth

A separate form n
for each birth.

NOTIFICATION OF BIRTH

Public Health Act, 1936 as amended
by N.H.S. Act 1973

Computer Input Document/Are

(office use only)

| A.H.A. (3—5) | Serial No. (6—10) |

PLEASE COMPLETE IN BLOCK CAPITALS

Child's Surname

Sex   Date of Birth D M Y   Time of Birth (24 hours) H M

Home Address
1st Line
2nd Line
3rd Line   Postal Code

Place of Birth

Mother's Forenames

Mother's Surname

Mother's Date of Birth D M Y   Previous Live Births   Previous Still Births   Previous Abortions

Gestation (weeks)   Gestation calculated or estimated (C or E)   Number born this confinement   No. of this birth (If multiple)   Birthweight (grams)

Here, personal medical histories are still almost entirely recorded on paper, although more and more doctors are trying out small microcomputers to store clinical as well as administrative information. Knowledge of the extent to which general practitioners are computerising their records is fragmentary, as no NHS organisation keeps a check of these systems. However, a 1985 survey by a major educational institute estimated that fewer than a thousand – barely 10 per cent – of general practices in the UK had a computer. Many of these systems consist of no more than a small microcomputer holding names and addresses of a doctor's patients. But some practices, probably around 500, have more sophisticated microcomputer systems and software, holding personal health information on patients. All such systems will have to be registered with the Data Protection Registrar. Access to clinical records held on such systems usually requires a password security check. Personal medical histories are called onto the screen by entering a patient's name, NHS number or practice file number. The data – a sequential historical record – are similar in structure to the standard paper records. There are lists of attendances at surgery, clinical notes, symptoms presented, diagnoses, and drugs or other treatment prescribed.

The simpler microcomputers hold routine data including the name of the doctor who usually sees the patient in question, and the patient's name, address, sex and date of birth. Further details may consist of a list number or other identifier, the NHS number, marital status, social class or occupation, ethnic group, telephone number and number of people in the household where the patient lives.[4] Additional medical data may cover problem warnings, such as allergies, drug sensitivities or drug abuse, epilepsy or diabetes. Information concerning the prescribing of drugs may also be held either with patient records or on a separate index for reporting to family practitioner committees. The basic register may be used as a mailing list as well as for clinical work. More advanced computer systems could automatically generate requests for screening or immunisation measures – by, for example, selecting girls approaching puberty for immunisation against rubella, or instigating recalls for cervical smear tests.

Much of the early work on the computerisation of GPs' records was carried out by the Exeter Community Health Services Computer Project, first set up in 1969. The project now provides on-line facilities to hospitals and health centres in its area. Project staff investigated how a single patient record could be utilised by GPs, hospitals and community health services. They told the Lindop committee that:[5]

> The objective of the single computerised record is that data collected during all episodes, whether dealt with by GPs, outpatient department or inpatient departments of hospitals, together with results of tests such as X-rays, blood samples, etc., shall be available from a single source by those who require the data for a specific purpose.

The DHSS funded the Devon Area Health Authority to set up an experimental on-line system linking two health centres (one urban and one rural) and two hospitals (one specialised and one general) within the South Western Regional Health Authority. Three other urban health centres could access and amend the databank from terminals located in the area's general hospital. The complete medical records of the patients attending each health centre were put onto the computer. The system allows authorised members of the primary care team to read and amend the medical record of each patient, as well as updating records of prescription details. These facilities are widely used to produce repeat prescriptions automatically on request.

The first 'live' records were put on the Devon system in 1974. With both hospitals fully registered, there were some 300,000 names on the databank. Personal health data on each patient includes NHS number, blood group, details of past and present illnesses, details of attendances at hospitals, results of treatment, hereditary tendencies or illnesses, allergic tendencies and results of psychological tests. Complete microfiches of patient records are produced for doctors making house calls.

The Exeter primary care system has inspired further projects aimed at computerising clinical health records, both in GPs' surgeries and in hospital wards. Experience gained at Exeter has been used to develop smaller computerised medical systems for individual GPs. Because of financial constraints, there has been no comparable community-based health project anywhere else in Britain. But the DHSS decided in 1979 to have the Exeter system software adapted for smaller, stand-alone machines of use to GPs. Private companies have also based commercial computer packages for GPs on the Exeter project. During 1982, Information Technology Year, the Department of Trade and Industry funded the installation in GPs' surgeries of 140 microcomputers supplied by two companies, British Medical Data Systems and CAP. After two years, GPs were said to approve of the systems installed, but were critical of poor instruction manuals and training, as well as of the performance of other private companies who had been employed to transfer onto computer data from paper records.

A key aspect of the Exeter system is its arrangements for allowing each user to see only authorised items of data. Nurses, for instance, might not see full clinical records but could check ward and bed occupancy. Administrative and statistical data, such as the number of beds occupied in any given period, can also be generated for the health authority from the integrated database of patient records.

Besides confining personal health care information to authorised users, the Exeter system has fields of 'suppressed data' on personal medical records. Such data is of special sensitivity and is not displayed on the screen without entry of a particular password. As a fictional example, a woman's initial record might show that she had given birth twice, once to a stillborn child, and that her mother was diabetic. An indication that further information was suppressed would be given. On going to the confidential file, the doctor might see that her father was described as alcoholic, and her housing conditions as 'poor'.

The designers of the Exeter system evidently found a need to give special status to what might be described as hearsay or subjective opinion. A system like this, with multiple levels of security, may cause concern in some quarters; it could be used to hide doctors' opinions from critical review rather than to protect the privacy of the patient.

Other sensitive information may be generated by the conjunction of individual records – perhaps those organised into family or household groups. The organisation of GPs' records on a household basis permits the construction of a demographic breakdown, allowing greater surveillance of personal relationships than has existed hitherto. Not only is each composite record sensitive in itself, but a collection of medical files may be in effect a local population register. Such indexes resemble the electoral roll, except that they include people under 18 – and will necessarily reveal more about family and other relationships. One general practice reported in 1985 that they had indeed generated much new and sensitive information through a computerised household analysis:[6]

> Using the household index we produced a list of every household in which there were two or more different surnames, which numbered 369 out of the total of 3719 households. This shows extended families, other family relationships, cohabiting, and that new patients have moved into the residences of former patients who may have left the district some time earlier. This list was of interest to the partners, showing domestic situations that they had not previously recognised.

The ready availability of information of this kind may be of special interest to non-medical officials – for example, to police wanting to know the personal relationships between members of a household in order to determine associates, or to DHSS 'snoopers' trying to prove cohabitation in order to reduce benefit entitlements. Since personal information within both the NHS and the social security system is ultimately the property of the Secretary of State, its easier availability on computer could tempt DHSS investigators into systematic misbehaviour – as has happened, for example, with legal aid assessments (see page 108). As we detail later, police officers have not always been willing to regard personal medical information as inviolable.

Standard computer codes relating to diagnoses are already frequently used in the health service. The commonest code, called OXMIS, consists of up to six digits for all diagnoses or problems likely to be encountered in general practice. There are well over a thousand classifications. For example, OXMIS classifies abdominal pain as 7855D, and zoster (herpes) as 053. OXMIS coding economises on computer space and systemises classification of ailments so that information in each file may be retrieved more easily. The standard ailment codes enable

doctors to identify patients in particular categories of illness so
that common features can be identified.

The widespread use of on-line computer facilities during
consultations in GPs' surgeries is years away, although key
data and indexes for paper records will increasingly be held on
computer. Complete personal medical histories will remain
on paper for the immediate future. It will also be some time
before medical expert systems are offered to assist in diagnosis
(as opposed to simply retrieving information during consultation). But such expert systems have long been the subject of
extensive research and development under the rubric of
'computer-aided diagnosis'.

Family practitioner committees are the first administrative tier
in the health service. They administer the provision of general
medical, dental, ophthalmic and pharmaceutical services in
their area, answering to the DHSS. Their records include the
registration of over 50 million patients, 22,000 doctors and
12,000 dentists. FPC medical registers were first automated in
1972; a standard computer system was later developed by the
Trent Regional Health Authority, and endorsed by the DHSS in
1981.

FPC computer systems maintain comprehensive lists of NHS
numbers, patients' current and any former names, previous
and present addresses, and previous and present GP and
FPCs. Typically, each FPC will hold several hundred thousand
patient records, although some hold as many as a million.
Although under present administrative arrangements the
medical records of patients changing doctors are transmitted
via FPCs (on paper), the committees do not hold clinical
medical details on paper or computer.

By 1985, 40 of the 98 FPCs in England and Wales had
computerised their registers. A particularly sensitive aspect of
the new systems is the monitoring of immigration status or
'immigrant recall' (see Figure 3, pages 124–5), covering anyone
granted NHS facilities while subject to immigration control.
After a year of such a person registering, this status is
automatically reviewed to see if the visitor has left.

FPC computerised record systems alone can operate specialised recall or screening facilities for the adult population,

since FPCs alone operate full population registers for their area (in contrast, districts only have information on children, and regions only on hospital patients). A key example is the recall of women of a vulnerable age for cervical cancer (smear) tests. The computer can automatically remind those who have not had a smear test within a recommended period to attend for tests if they wish. Such 'pro-active' health measures are extremely effective if properly applied. But a 1985 survey by Frank Dobson MP found that one third of the 201 district health authorities in England and Wales had not arranged for their FPCs to operate a scheme for the screening of cervical cancer. Ninety per cent of these said that they lacked the resources to fund such a scheme. Only 10 per cent of authorities had a computerised recall system; the remainder operated either a manual system or none at all.[7]

Such community health surveillance measures have led to a proliferation of standardised national computing systems over the last ten years. The first in a chain of four health monitoring schemes, most now computerised, is Notification of Birth, through which all births have to be registered to the district authority. This is separate from registration with the Register of Births, Deaths and Marriages.

Most health authorities have computerised their child registers, known collectively as the National Standard Register and Recall System, whose purpose is to notify those responsible for continuing care of the mother and child.

Birth forms for submission to the register may include highly sensitive questions relating to parental status, legitimacy of the child (i.e., parents' marital status), ethnic group, parents' country of origin, 'home conditions' and parental occupations (from which standard social class may be determined). Although the law does not require every question to be answered, in practice doctors, midwives or others attending birth will normally provide all the information asked for. Parents are not necessarily told that this information is being gathered, do not get copies of the birth form, and are not informed that some or all of its contents will rapidly enter a national computerised register. The process alarmed at least one professional body giving evidence to the Lindop committee, the Health Visitors' Association, which feared that 'there was no guarantee that the government could not use the information for other purposes'.[8]

During 1977, the Lindop committee surveyed the information gathered by 33 health authorities on Notification of Birth forms. Seven authorities, they found, wanted to know the ethnic group of the mother; three wanted to know her country of origin; and 32 recorded previous miscarriages or abortions. There was a wide range of additional items, many sensitive, gathered only by a minority of authorities. Because of the diversity of information collected in this way, the DHSS's Körner committee recommended future standardisation of the system.

Notification of Birth forms are the responsibility of district health authorities in England and Wales, and Scottish regional health boards. A repeat survey of Notification of Birth forms in 1982 by *Computing* magazine showed that there had been a shift to adopt a new standard form promoted by the DHSS.[9] But the standard DHSS form still seeks sensitive information about previous abortions, parents' ethnic group, one-parent families and parents' occupation. The form asks for data in such a way that, when provided, it may be rapidly entered in a computer.

The information asked for but not immediately required for the planned child health system is used for analyses of vital statistics by the Office of Population Censuses and Surveys. Such analyses have been used, for example, to isolate risk factors causing stillbirths. Medical research units remain strongly in favour of gathering extra information of this kind, despite the risks to privacy posed by a growing pool of computerised data. According to one such research group:[10]

> If suitable statistics are available, they can be used to see if the prognosis for disadvantaged groups is improving or deteriorating. Statistics can also be used to assess the extent of the need for specialised services. For example, if a district has a sizeable population of women of black African origin, it should consider the possibility of setting up a scheme of screening for sickle cell trait ...

The Lindop committee, however, concurred with the fears expressed to them about the Notification of Birth form. They felt strongly that the nature and use of information gathered for such statistics should be carefully checked; it was 'a good example of applications which should come under the independent scrutiny of the [proposed] Data Protection Authority'.

Since 1978, the National Standard Register computer system has been extended to include immunisation, pre-school and school health 'modules'. The second stage of the scheme, pre-school health information, was finally introduced in June 1982 after lengthy argument and professional concern (particularly from the BMA) about the adequacy of privacy safeguards. The pre-school health module recalls children as required to hospitals or clinics for medical examinations. As with the Notification of Birth scheme, the information may also be used in compiling health statistics.

The BMA argued that the organisation in charge of the project, the DHSS's Child Health Computing Committee, had not established clearly defined safeguards to protect confidentiality between doctor and patient. The association complained that the government committee was:[11]

> trying to pull the project off on the cheap; its supposed ethical principles which guarantee inviolability of records in no way lessen our fears ... We are not happy that the information won't be used by the government for its own purposes.

Ironically, the Conservative opposition of the day vociferously supported the BMA, and demanded that the computerised child health system be halted until adequate data protection laws were passed.[12] Five years later, in office, the same party attempted to render such medical records naked of protection in the face of immigration, police or other enquiries.

After the BMA's objections to the system, the DHSS agreed the following safeguards:[13]

> Identifiable information should be regarded as held for the specific purpose of the continuing care of the patient and should not be used without appropriate authorisation or the consent of the patient, or guardian in the case of a child, for any other purposes.

> Access to identifiable information should be confined to those persons clinically responsible for the patient during the episode

from which the data has been collected (or their succes
the purpose for which it was supplied. The author
discretion to release the information in the best interests
patient.

An individual should not be identified from data supplied for
statistical or research purposes except when follow-up of the
individual is a necessary part of the research.

The third stage of the national child health system, the school
health module, covering children aged from 5 to 16, began
trials in 1983. Screening tests and immunisations are organised on a slightly different basis; children at a particular school
requiring immunisations or examinations are periodically
identified, and medical visits arranged. At each examination,
the doctor is provided with a computer printout for each child,
showing immunisations received to date and the results of the
two most recent computer-recorded medical examinations.
The system can also indicate by a 'flag' that more detailed
medical information is available on manual files. The school
health module also permits the doctor to have printed out a
record card for cases where the child requires special supervision or care. From 1985 on, children's records in this stage of
the child health system could be examined and amended via
on-line terminals in some district health authority offices.

The success of these community health systems depends
entirely on maintaining an up-to-date child register. The
register keeps basic personal data on each child, the name of
their GP, and subsequently school particulars and other
identifiers. There is no national register as such in the child
health system; data is held by each of the 201 district health
authorities. By 1985, over 50 per cent of districts had computerised their child registers. The DHSS was encouraging the
remaining authorities to follow suit.

The highest tier of health service administration, regional
health authorities, also operate computerised registers, the
largest of which are the hospital activity analysis (HAA) and the
mental health enquiry (MHE). HAA is primarily concerned with
the use of hospital beds and other resources; the MHE is a
similar system for in-patients in psychiatric hospitals and
units or in special hospitals. The two systems will eventually be

superseded by a standardised approach to monitoring patients on admission to and discharge from hospital. Each of the 14 regional health authorities (RHAs) in England, and their Scottish and Welsh equivalents, have their own computers to store this information.

Information required by regional health authorities for the HAA and MHE is supplied by hospital administrative staff. The information requested – which includes the religion, age and occupation of the patient – is listed in Figure 3 (page 124). In the MHE, there are further questions about alcoholism or drug abuse. Answers are usually recorded manually, although an increasing number of hospitals either have their computers linked to those of the RHA or use the RHA computer directly.

Hospital computer schemes are split broadly between patient administration systems (PASs), concerned with managing the whereabouts of patients and the use of hospital resources, and those technical systems concerned primarily with scientific data, such as laboratory computation. Limited steps have been taken towards putting clinical examination and investigation information onto on-line systems. PASs may sometimes go under different names – for example patient movement record, or master index system – but all serve essentially the same purposes. Somewhat similar to a system for reserving seats on an airline, a PAS's primary function is to book patients in and out of beds, wards and operating theatres. It maintains waiting lists for admission, outpatient clinics, examinations or clinical tests. Other facilities may include recording the movement of patients' medical records to and from the hospital register. Staff availability and consultants' bookings at outpatient clinics are also recorded on some PASs.

Individual PASs may be used within a single hospital or may form part of a network shared by hospitals in a health district or larger area. Small and specialised hospitals may have terminals to a PAS computer in a large general hospital. But at present, PASs differ not only from one RHA to another, but between hospitals in the same region. In future, information on hospital activity will be transferred direct from a hospital to the RHA computers.

Both the DHSS and commercial computer companies have experimented with expanding PAS facilities to include patients' complete medical records. ICL, which has already supplied such systems to more than a quarter of the district health authorities in the UK, offers progressive expansion of patients' files, and prospects for computers to operate as a single network. ICL's latest PAS uses the Contents Addressable File Store (CAFS) to locate medical records by reference to content rather than personal identifying numbers. CAFS makes it possible to ask very wide-ranging questions about the hospital's data and, according to ICL, 'substantially increases the speed with which random enquiries to large files of data can be answered'.

In 1984, four RHAs (West Midlands, Northern, South East Thames and North West Thames) formed an inter-regional consortium with ICL to promote the extension of PASs. The first step will be to record and link a hospital's main patient indexes to information from pathology and radiology laboratories, and obstetrics departments.[14]

During 1985, the North West Regional Health Authority became the first RHA to attempt to computerise patient (and staff) records across an entire health region. The system would include computer records on all hospital patients, details of diagnostics and therapeutic services, as well as a range of other administrative schemes. The plan would cost over £30 million by 1995, involve 36 minicomputers in 19 health districts, and hold the records of about four million patients attending 130 hospitals in the region. A full-scale hospital patient system, with clinical data included, would be developed later. The minicomputers, although geographically separate, would form a single co-ordinated network. But like so many other ambitious computer projects, the North West RHA scheme was, at the time of writing, plagued by contractual difficulties and software problems.[15]

Many physicians have refused to co-operate with hospital activity analysis and similar schemes because of fears about confidentiality. The issue arose dramatically in 1973, when medical staff at four Buckinghamshire hospitals withheld their co-operation from the Oxfordshire RHA in the construction of a unique centralised databank in which information derived from HAA and MHE reports would deliberately be linked. The aim of the Oxford Record Linkage Study was to 'create records of events affecting named individuals in order to study the development of people's health over a period of time', the Lindop committee was later told. In order to do this, the study could not use unidentified patients; the computer had to hold their names. For over two years, some 50 consultants in the Aylesbury area privately refused to supply names and addresses of their patients. They finally made the dispute public when they realised that they were getting nowhere with the DHSS by keeping the matter out of the public eye. The head of the consultants' committee, Richard Pryer, explained that the group feared the increasing trend in the early 1970s for subpoenas to be issued against health officials, rather than doctors, in order to obtain medical records.[16] Psychiatrists generally were also leaving names and addresses off the MHE forms. This practice continued, as the first report of the Körner committee acknowledged in 1982:[17]

> A significant and increasing proportion of psychiatrists are not submitting named data to the DHSS for reasons of data confidentiality; at least 16 per cent of all records are submitted without the patient's name.

The medical profession was split over whether or not to accept the precautions offered by the DHSS regarding data protection. Many doctors refused to supply names and addresses on HAA forms, despite assurances from the DHSS that these computer records are only *partially* identifiable – because a person can only be fully identified by cross-reference to manual records.

The MHE proved to be particularly controversial because information is not only more easily identified with individuals under this scheme but – according to the National Association for Mental Health (MIND) and other organisations concerned with the mentally ill – the forms are very often completed by non-medical staff. As a result the data they contain, particularly concerning diagnosis, is unreliable. There were particular worries that unreliable and inaccurate information could be linked to an identified individual. One such case was disclosed in 1983, when a man was released from the Rampton special hospital after it was found that a medical record stating that he bit the heads off chickens and assaulted small girls was untrue.

In 1977, the DHSS assured the Lindop committee that personal information gathered in the MHE would be held separately from individual identifying details. But, four years later, this assurance had failed to convince those psychiatrists who were still not supplying names and addresses of patients on one in every six MHE forms submitted.

New health information systems have been proposed by the DHSS's Körner committee. Körner recommended replacing such operations as the MHE, HAA and Notification of Birth requirement (in hospital) with a 'minimum data set'.[18] This information (listed in Table 3, page 128) would be gathered on all hospital in-patients. It is of course a *minimum* data set, the purpose of which is to enable data about patients to be transferred between FPCs and health districts and regions – primarily for administrative purposes. After 1988, district health authorities are obliged to ensure that the 'minimum data set' is collected, so that this information may be passed to RHAs.

The committee also recommended that certain information *not* be included in the minimum data set, namely:

patient name; national [i.e., NHS] number; social class derived from occupation; ethnic origin; place of birth; religion; follow-up arrangements on discharge; vaccination(s) given; adverse reaction to drugs.

The committee did not reject this information because it would be unwise to collect such data, but because these items did not fulfil three criteria it had laid down for the minimum data set: they are not required by district officers; they are not easy to collect; or their collection might be disproportionately expensive. Under the Körner proposals, district identification numbers are used in place of the NHS number for locating hospital records. Körner noted that, because the NHS number was not widely used by hospitals (as opposed to FPC registers), it could not be an effective part of the new system:

We see advantage in using a national number to identify patients. Although all health service users have a unique number, the NHS number, which would allow the national linking of district records, it has been little used and consequently has proved difficult to collect. We reluctantly accept that in the foreseeable future there is no prospect of a national number being used universally but would like to encourage local experiments with the use of the NHS number.

On social class, the committee looked at the possibility of collecting information by means other than by asking patients about their occupation. Properly to code social classification from occupation requires a clerical officer with specialised knowledge. Körner commented:

> In addition, precise rules need to be adopted for classifying retired people, women and minors, which are groups that always pose particular problems in an occupation-based classification.

One proposal was to assess social class from patients' post-codes – presumably using a similar classification system to the ACORN codings used by direct-mail companies. (Postcodes are part of the minimum data set.) But this would be an insidious method, particularly as patients would not be aware that, by giving a postcode, they were also being allocated a presumed social class. Such a method would be doubly dangerous since the probability of error in obtaining the postcode is high, and the validity of applying ACORN-type socioeconomic codings to one individual is questionable. Yet information derived from such codes might be used to make significant decisions about the use of NHS resources.

The Körner committee had wanted to assess social class differences in the use of hospital beds, in order to identify class inequalities. But in the absence of necessary safeguards and a sophisticated approach, there were evident dangers. In the event, Körner recommended that social class be established from other, more accurate, sources, notably the Registrar of Births and Deaths: 'He is responsible for generating the NHS number and specially trained to obtain data about occupation,' the committee noted.[19]

Family planning clinics presented special problems regarding the proposed minimum set. The Körner committee recommended that a computer file should be opened on each person (almost all women) attending a clinic each year. The file would record the method of contraception prescribed and other personal data, including age. This latter information would be grouped in seven categories, or five-year age-bands, including an 'under-16' category. The possibility of automatic identification of girls under 16 receiving contraceptive supplies has particular significance in the light of the controversial Gillick case, in which the complainant unsuccessfully sought a judicial ruling that, if an under-16-year-old was being prescribed contraceptives, doctors should in all circumstances override confidentiality and tell parents. Although the claim was rejected by the House of Lords, the case was extremely controversial and a clear reminder of the special sensitivity of medical data.

Remarkably, Körner also proposed computerising probably the most sensitive data handled in the health service: the sexual-contact tracing services operated by STD (sexually transmitted disease) clinics. The purpose of the computerised tracing service would be to report to health authority administrators the effectiveness of contact tracing, when an STD patient had been found to be suffering from a transmissible disease. Counsellors at STD clinics normally try and persuade such patients to identify, so far as they can and are willing, their recent sexual contacts who might have become infected. The information passed on, the Körner committee said, would not 'have to include name or identifying number'. But the STD clinic would, of course, retain full identifying particulars of both patients and their contacts.

At a time when an epidemic of a novel, grotesque and fatal infectious disease is rapidly spreading in the population, it is difficult to imagine a more foolish or irresponsible suggestion than the creation of computerised STD contacts registers. The start of 1985 saw widespread hysteria amongst media commentators and legislators as a result of publicity given to AIDS. Much of the publicity was informed by a scarcely disguised and ill-tempered prejudice against gay men. Then, with remarkable speed, the government tabled new infectious disease regulations to permit the compulsory hospitalisation of AIDS sufferers, though they stopped short of making the disease formally notifiable under the 1936 Public Health Act. To do so, they were strenuously warned, could undermine public health, since many people who feared that they were at risk from AIDS might avoid treatment if this meant their name going onto an official register, with an attendant high risk of future coercive measures being employed against them. The population most at risk from AIDS rightly perceived that the government might be readier to try and use coercive means to isolate possible sufferers than to pay for the necessary research into preventive measures and possible cures. This threat remains potent as the disease spreads and public fears increase. It would be foolish for anyone in the health service to introduce the possibility of creating records that might later become a register of AIDS carriers and their contacts – against whose interests or liberty special authoritarian legislation could one day be devised.

Two computer systems that hold information on people attending STD clinics are to be found at the Westminster Hospital and St Thomas's Hospital, both in London. Rather than holding patients' names, both systems store identifiers which relate to manual records. The Westminster Hospital system is used primarily to identify trends in the spread of particular infections. Each record contains information on the number of sexual contacts, the age and sex of each person, and any complications that have arisen in the course of treatment. By October 1985, the system had accumulated some 2000 records.

Outside access to personal medical information should always be a decision for the clinician caring for the individual patient. However, there are a few legal circumstances in which doctors must disclose information – generally, these are in cases concerning infectious diseases, dangerous drugs, births (including abortions and stillbirths) and deaths. But the matter of the ultimate legal ownership of clinical records is a contentious issue. The BMA argues that doctors own the files; the DHSS maintains that legal ownership of a physician's files, and consequently the information therein, resides with the Secretary of State.[20] In protecting information privacy, there is also the practical problem that, while GPs may easily control records held in their own surgeries, this is more difficult for a hospital physician who is part of a large organisation. Records held in hospitals are, for this reason, more vulnerable to disclosure to non-medical third parties.

So far as compulsory disclosure is concerned, some 25 infectious diseases, including polio and typhoid, are notifiable, and doctors must always report cases found to health authorities. Doctors are also obliged to report to the Home Office's Chief Medical Officer anyone who they 'consider or [have] reasonable grounds to suspect' is an addict of heroin, morphine, cocaine or other dangerous drugs. They may do this without the patient's consent or knowledge.

That is all a doctor is obliged to report – but it does not satisfy police and other authorities. In 1979, the BMA was outraged to discover that police officers were making systematic attempts to get information from doctors and other NHS staff. In one case, an inspector in a regional crime squad had written to family practitioner committees urging them to assist in the tracing of a person wanted for questioning. The inspector wished each committee to:[21]

Make a search of existing records to establish if X had registered with a doctor as a temporary patient.

Check on future records to establish if X, using one of a number of aliases, registers as a temporary patient.

Consider circulating an alert to local doctors in the area.

Make other enquiries that the committee considered worthwhile in an effort to trace this person.

On another occasion, police asked for, and received, help from an administrator in one RHA. The case came to light because the administrator concerned wrote to other regions, and to their district health authorities, asking for their help in apprehending a woman wanted by the police. The police knew that the woman they sought was in need of medical treatment and must go to a doctor. The BMA protested that:

The incidents ... show that the police are attempting to persuade doctors, and other NHS staff, to act as some form of information collectors ... Doctors are also being asked to play a part in the apprehension of patients wanted by the police.

The BMA warned that the disclosure of information without the consent and in the absence of a court order would be 'to the detriment of patients' generally, and would 'destroy a fundamental principle in medicine'.

The BMA was strongly critical of the Data Protection Bill's provision for confidentiality of medical records. It was particularly concerned that third parties such as the police, security services or Inland Revenue were to be licensed to have what would otherwise be unauthorised and unlawful access to health data in the possession of doctors. Complementary arrangements had also been made in Clause 10 of the Police and Criminal Evidence Bill. This clause, as originally designed by the government, gave the courts the power to force doctors to disclose confidential medical information to the police. In 1982 the BMA said:[22]

> There are no safeguards in the Bill to ensure that the information about innocent people will be held in confidence by the police and will be destroyed at the end of the inquiry. There is nothing in the Bill to prevent the police acquiring information thereafter in connection with trivial or less serious offences. [Clause 10] would allow a judge to issue an order *ex parte* without giving the doctor an opportunity to present a case as to why the application should be refused.

The government eventually conceded that both proposed pieces of legislation were unacceptable. After a series of meetings in 1984 between BMA President Sir Douglas Black and the Home Secretary, it was agreed that medical records should be safeguarded from third-party interference. Black particularly feared the tapping of health authority or hospital files without doctors' consent. In a last-minute amendment to the Data Protection Act, the Home Secretary took powers to curtail third-party access, including that by police and security services, to health data.

It was decided that the form of these safeguards would be agreed by a special interprofessional working group on access to personal health data, which was then convened by Black. The regulations had not been issued by late 1985, but their terms were anticipated by a DHSS circular, written in October 1985, on a code of confidentiality on personal health data. The code prescribes that:[23]

> Health authorities hold information only for the benefit of a patient's health. This information is confidential and should not be given to third parties. Professionally qualified people have a duty to protect this confidentiality.

Doctors (etc.) will entrust personal information on patients to health authorities on the understanding that the information will remain confidential.

Information on people other than the patient, which is held for the benefit of the patient's health, will be treated in a similar, confidential manner.

These rules, however, may be broken on occasion:

[The code] states that disclosure of personal health information without the patient's consent can only be permitted in certain strictly defined circumstances where the law or the public interest may prevail over the individual's right to confidentiality.

The 'strictly defined circumstances' cover the prevention, detection or prosecution of a serious crime and cases involving national security. Personal confidentiality may also be breached 'to safeguard public health' and for 'health research'. The medical research exemption requires that this may be done without the patient's consent only if an appropriate ethical committee (which should include lay members) has satisfied itself that 'a sufficient case for dispensing with the subject's consent has been made out' and has approved the proposals.

In cases of crime, any disclosure must concern a crime 'sufficiently serious for the public interest to prevail', and it must be likely that, without disclosure, the task of preventing or detecting the crime will be 'seriously prejudiced or delayed'. The police must also undertake that personal health data will not be used for any other purpose, and will be destroyed once the patient is prosecuted, discharged or acquitted. Following the intervention of the medical lobby, the codes of practice likely to be provided for under the Data Protection Act may provide reasonable protection for confidential health data from access by third parties such as the police. Any request will have to be accompanied by a certificate from a senior officer explaining the purposes for which access to information is sought.

The special provision for disclosing information on grounds of 'national security' should be exceptional, and the medical professional responsible must be satisfied that disclosure is necessary by seeing, if required, 'a certificate signed personally

by a cabinet minister or by the Attorney General or the Lord
Advocate under section 27 of the Data Protection Act'. This, the
code says, 'may be treated as conclusive'. But, even if such a
certificate is issued, there will be no compulsion on the doctor
to disclose. Equally, the wording of the code does not *require*
such a personally signed certificate. It is just that such a
certificate can be deemed 'conclusive'. A health professional
could still secretly disclose personal health records on
grounds of national security if he or she 'is satisfied that
national security is involved and that disclosure is necessary to
safeguard security interests'.

The Data Protection Act also allows the Home Secretary to
make special regulations concerning subject access to personal medical records. One of the data protection principles
states that subjects should normally have access to their
records. But the Act modifies this principle in relation to
health data so that individuals are not necessarily given full
access to data on their 'physical or mental health or ... sexual
life' (Section 2.3). Both the Home Office and DHSS consulted
interested parties on the appropriate form for subject access;
Sir Douglas Black's working group on access to personal
health data had recommended that health professionals
could at their own discretion withhold patients' files if they
believed such an action to be in the best interests of the
patient.

Black's recommendation would cover all health service
medical data, whether held by GPs or hospitals. It could also
include medical reports held elsewhere, for example by
insurance companies or employers. But opinions on medical
matters by non medically-qualified persons would not be
exempt from subject access. The arguments advanced by
medical professional groups in favour of restricting subject
access include the vexing question of disclosing a diagnosis to
a terminally ill patient, and fears that a patient's knowledge of a
particular diagnosis might somehow impede treatment. Some
professionals have argued for complete exemption from
subject access, but this would be clearly incompatible with
the European Convention on Human Rights (see page 22).

In fact, some GPs already have a policy of letting their

patients see their entire medical records without qualification, insisting only that, if advisable, they first see the files in the presence of an adviser or counsellor – who would explain technical information and help the patient understand or adapt to unexpected revelations about their health that might previously have been withheld. Some hospitals have adopted not dissimilar practices with their computerised records. St Thomas's Hospital in London, for example, has a general policy:[24]

> to let patients see what information is held about them on the databank. [But] where the doctor feels that it is not in the patient's interests for the information to be disclosed, the matter is referred to the consultant in charge of the case in the first instance. The consultant would usually take into account the opinions of the other medical staff involved in the care of the patient, including the patient's GP. Under certain circumstances, the patient's family may also need to be taken into account. At present, ultimate responsibility for the disclosure of information to the patient rests with the patient's consultant.

The Black working group also recommended that, instead of the usual 40-day period within which a computer user must furnish to a data subject the details of his or her files, there should be a six-month delay in revealing health data. This would provide a 'cooling-off' period, the working group said, to allow for diagnoses to be confirmed and counselling to be offered to data subjects. But the report did not offer a unanimous view of whether or not, if data was to be withheld, this fact should be revealed to the patient concerned. In some circumstances, this would be tantamount to revealing the data itself.

In general, Black recommended, parents should have the right of access to their children's medical records – although some matters, such as the prescription of contraceptives to a girl, should remain confidential to the patient herself. Any code of practice should not be confined to computerised records. The working group pointed out, rightly, that 'public expectations may be raised for similar principles to operate in respect of manual records'.[25]

The right of a data subject to seek damages under the Data Protection Act, if they can show that they have suffered from inaccurate information in their records, means that subject access may pose a threat to some health professionals. If, for example, a GP or FPC official entered an erroneously late recall for a woman to have a cervical smear, they might be sued if she contracted cancer as a consequence of the failure to implement preventive measures in time.

If the proposed code of practice were adopted, without an effective right of appeal, then it is likely that the risks of civil action following disclosure of mistakes may tempt some physicians dishonestly to claim exemption on the grounds of 'the best interests of the patient'. If doctors are to be the ultimate arbiters of whether people may see their medical files, then there must be an effective and reasonable appeals procedure. However, an appeals procedure based on the patient taking the initiative will not work if patients are not told that information is being withheld from them.

The growing network of NHS computers, and the planned standardisation of communications methods and record formats, all make the resolution of such dilemmas increasingly urgent. Whereas the interests of the medical profession almost entirely align with the interests of data subjects so far as third-party access is concerned, they can diverge sharply sharply in the case of subject access. But the greater problem is the attitude of administrators. In the computerisation of the health service, as in the computerisation of the welfare state, administrative insensitivity to information privacy issues remains disturbing.

6 At Home and Abroad

Government central databanks to service the welfare state or levy taxes will, as we have seen, be in operation well before the turn of the century. No other collections of private data in public hands will rival the scale or the sensitivity of the data held in DHSS, Inland Revenue and National Health Service computers. But, by the year 2000, there will probably be other comprehensive computerised national population registers in existence. The basis of some of these new registers will be addresses or locations rather than names. (Government databanks described elsewhere in this book are, generally, indexed by name.)

This chapter describes those government databanks associated with lifestyle or location. The areas covered include the planned surveillance of international travel; the census, electoral and other population registers based on association with an address; and national records of ownership and usage of property and of cars, telephones or television sets. Other relevant databanks are concerned with the use of public services, such as secondary or higher education – and the involuntary use of other public services, such as prisons and borstals.

Travel and communications will come under increasing scrutiny towards the end of the century. Government plans for the automated surveillance of international travel will begin to be realised after computerised passports are first issued to British citizens in 1987. Hitherto, immigration control has affected mainly the foreigner, black and Asian, against whom the immigration system quite explicitly discriminates. Records of more than a million foreigners entering and leaving the country every year are already computerised. The new passports are intended to facilitate checks on the international movements of British citizens.

Some travellers are already under the surveillance of two sophisticated computer systems known as IVAN and CEDRIC. They are run respectively by the Immigration Service and Customs and Excise, and maintain records not only on people suspected of drugs smuggling or illegal immigration, but also on the friends and associates of such suspects.

Plans for the computerised surveillance of international travel have already attracted considerable public attention. In February 1983, at an international air terminal at London's Heathrow airport, the Immigration Service began tests on new computers which could automatically scan 'machine-readable' passports (MRPs). Almost eighteen months later, the government announced that, from 1987 on, all British passports would be machine-readable. A statement by the Home Secretary claimed that the first objective of the new scheme was 'to provide a speedier service to the travelling public'. But the Home Office's actual purposes were rather different. They wanted to:

Automatically identify those on a special warning list – the 'suspect index' – so that their movements might be tracked, or other action taken.

Make automatic records of all passengers entering and leaving the UK – a 'traffic index'.

Maintain a check on all visitors subject to immigration control, identifying those who have not left within an allowed time so as to pass their names on to the police or to special immigration tracing units.

These proposals are described at length in confidential 1980 and 1981 Home Office and Immigration Service reports obtained by the authors. The new computerised passport-reading system formed part of a series of projects called INDECS (the Immigration and Nationality Department Electronic Computer System). The more sensitive aspects of INDECS remained under wraps until revealed by one of the authors early in 1983.

Planning for INDECS began with studies by the Home Office/Metropolitan Police Joint Automatic Data Processing Unit (JADPU) between 1974 and 1978. The first JADPU report, in 1975, recommended the computerisation of the traffic index on Home Office computers in Croydon. A second report in 1978 looked at the problems immigration officers faced in effectively checking incoming passengers against the voluminous suspect index, and studied the feasibility of computerising it. The report proposed that immigration officers enter personal details (often abbreviated) via a keyboard; a VDU would return a message saying either NO TRACE or that ACTION should be taken, according to a list of code letters. The message on the VDU might refer the immigration officer to a 'suspect circular' giving further details about the passenger.

Table 4
Passport checks – major Home Office 'suspect index'
action categories

Code	Meaning
A	Notify Box 500 [i.e., MI5] of the passenger's arrival; if possible ascertain destination.
J	Ditto – but without arousing passenger's suspicion.
S	Point out to Special Branch officer in attendance.
Q	Refer to Suspect Circular for further information.
C	Refer to Immigration Service headquarters before landing.
B	Passenger is mentally ill or unbalanced.
O	Point out to customs officers.
R	Refuse leave to enter.
D	Passenger subject to deportation order.

The original INDECS plan was written in 1979. It had five phases. Phase 1 was to be the computerisation of the increasingly congested traffic index – which, by the late 1970s, had to deal with over 12 million visitors a year. Phase 2 of INDECS combined a suspect index 'feasibility study' with a test of the new passports. Subsequent stages of INDECS would fully automate the suspect index; automate the department's own offices; and provide statistical information. Eventually INDECS would embrace a full-scale national network of 500 terminals at ports of entry, coupled to electronic filing systems holding and processing details of visitors, 'suspects' and applicants to settle or for British nationality. It was hoped that all immigration and nationality department activities would eventually be automated.

British immigration control only affects those who do not have either full British citizenship or residence rights in the UK. Everyone else, including EEC nationals and British passport holders without residence rights, are subject to control by immigration officers at authorised ports of entry to the United Kingdom. According to the Immigration Service's general instructions:

> The purpose of immigration control is to ensure that people coming to the United Kingdom from abroad are admitted only in such numbers and for such purposes as are consistent with the national interest.

Detailed objectives, it is stated, include the desire 'to protect the resident labour force' and 'to keep the rate of immigration within limits at which it will not give rise to serious social problems'.

Some travellers coming to Britain are subject to an initial 'pre-entry' control, and may require visas, letters of consent or entry clearances in order to be able to enter. The second phase of immigration control, at the actual port of entry, is conducted by immigration officers. They work closely with Special Branch ports units. Post-entry control is concerned with the detection and (usually) expulsion of overstayers – who have remained in the UK after a permitted period – and with the apprehension of illegal entrants who have bypassed control checks.

As a result of the first Aliens Act, passed in 1905, police officers as well as immigration officials have power of surveillance over foreign visitors after their entry into the UK. After the Second World War, this was codified to require any alien over the age of 16 who was in the country for three months to register at a police station. Each police force maintains a register of aliens, while a central register is kept by the Home Office. Many registers are now held on local police computers. Except in London, the supervision of alien registration is normally a Special Branch task. Registered aliens, including students and migrant workers, have to notify the police within a week of any change of address or employment, or if they get married. They can be deported if they are convicted of a criminal offence; or if the Home Secretary thinks that their presence is not 'conducive to the public good' – a provision allowing wide scope for political judgement which was used to deport German student leader Rudi Deutschke in 1970, and American journalists Mark Hosenball and Philip Agee in 1977.

From 1945, the Home Office has also maintained a record of visitors entering and leaving the UK. This procedure became standardised with the requirement for all visitors to complete landing and embarkation cards, some of which then form the traffic index. (The remainder are used for compiling statistics.) The landing cards record the traveller's name, nationality, passport number, place and date of birth, occupation, sex, and address to be visited in the UK.

The rules which govern both immigrants and visitors to Britain are often unreasonable both in principle and in application. For this reason, the increasing effectiveness which Immigration Service computerisation may bring is *ipso facto* a threat to civil rights, particularly to those Britons whose families originally came from the Indian subcontinent. Many people with legitimate reasons to visit or settle in Britain, including close family ties, can be caught and punished as 'overstayers' because they – and often the officials with whom they deal – do not understand the arcane complexities of British immigration rules.

Even when the law is correctly applied, it violates international human rights standards and, in particular, principles about not separating family members enshrined in the European Convention on Human Rights. The Home Office may deliberately keep husbands and wives separate for many years, or refuse residence rights to a husband or wife whose spouse and children have the right to residence in Britain. The Home Office deliberately and illegally discriminates against Asians whose families are settled in Britain. To do this, they have devised a system of entry clearances; all family members who wish to settle in Britain are required first to obtain such clearances.

The entry clearance procedure is merely a disguise for a

covert immigration control system intended severely to limit the number of Asians joining their families settled in Britain. For Americans, Europeans, Canadians or Australians, obtaining entry clearance is not subject to unusual delay. In the Indian subcontinent, however, the Home Office deliberately employs far too few entry clearance officers for the known case load, in order to build up long queues and thus 'regulate' the number of Asians coming to Britain to settle. This system, which the Home Office itself believes is contrary to British law, and a breach of the European Convention, was set out at length in a leaked confidential briefing that civil servants prepared for Home Office minister David Waddington in 1985.[1]

Indeed, when the Commission for Racial Equality proposed to hold a formal investigation of the immigration control system in 1980, the Home Office went to the High Court to try to ban the inquiry, on the grounds that 'by its very nature the immigration control system was based on racial discrimination'.[2] But, after 18 months' delay, the investigation went ahead. It found that the Immigration Service's determination to find and exclude the minority of applicants who are ineligible to settle in the UK had often resulted in unfair and racially discriminatory treatment of the majority who *were* entitled to settle. It was the 'poor and black [who] had the biggest obstacles to face', the commission said. 'New Commonwealth' blacks were 40 times more likely to be refused entry as 'Old Commonwealth' whites. So far as the post-entry control of immigrants was concerned, the Commission for Racial Equality noted, Home Office computers, police operations and intelligence networks, and information exchanges between government departments had on occasion contributed to the serious disruption of good race and community relations in the UK.[3] Looking behind this, the commission found that the baseless racist fear of a potential 'tide' of Asian immigrants 'continues to inform official thinking'.

The first steps to implement the INDECS immigration control computers were the computerisation of the traffic index, the testing of the automated suspect index, and the computerising of the central intelligence index – a databank used by the Immigration Service's illegal immigration intelligence unit.

After 18 months' development and a three-month trial run, the computerised traffic index became operational in August 1980. Numbers on landing and embarkation cards completed by visitors were 'paired', so that INDECS could more effectively match the cards and detect overstayers using numbers rather than names.

At first, about 50,000 visitors a month were recorded on INDECS. But INDECS phase 1 was not a technical success, and was still officially regarded as 'under development' three years later. By February 1984, INDECS held about 1.5 million records on visitors, about whom information could normally be obtained using the passengers' landing-card numbers. The databank may also be searched using a person's date of birth, name, nationality, or by reference to the date when the subject is due to leave the country.[4] Although the INDECS computer is located in Bootle, Merseyside, landing cards are sent to the Home Office Immigration and Nationality Department offices at Lunar House, Croydon, for entry to the computer. By April 1985, there were 14 INDECS terminals located in IND offices.[5]

At the time of writing, INDECS was still not able to process details of all passengers arriving in or leaving the UK. 'Technical constraints,' the Home Affairs select committee was told in 1985, had prevented the 'recording on the computer of all of the large numbers involved'.[6] Whether a card goes into INDECS or the manual section of the traffic index or is not indexed at all depends on the nationality of the passenger, the intended duration of stay and the purpose of the visit. The criterion for entry into INDECS is that the passenger is admitted by an immigration officer in the so-called 'Code 3' category, usually meaning that the officer is doubtful about the passenger's intention to leave at the end of the permitted stay.

INDECS automatically prepares lists of persons who are still in the UK after the expiry of their permitted duration of stay. Until 1984, this information was first sent to a special Home Office section called OTIS (the Overstayer Tracing and Intelligence Section) whose teams would, within two months, make inquiries at the overstayer's last given address. But overstayers were seldom found. The OTIS teams were outstandingly unsuccessful in tracing overstayers, with a failure rate exceeding 90 per cent. After 1981, when the Metropolitan Police decided that they were best equipped to carry out overstayer enquiries alone, the failure rate climbed to more than 97 per cent. The Home Office then dropped this method of attempting to find overstayers, relying instead on tipoffs from informants ('denunciation') or on information supplied by other agencies such as the Inland Revenue or DHSS.

A visitor can avoid the dangerous stigma of being categorised as an overstayer by applying to the Home Office for an extension of stay. If this is granted, details are passed to INDECS. If a visitor has to register with the police, this information is also noted on the computer. Police forces will inform the Home Office of any person who has failed to register, and this too is recorded on INDECS.

Information about apparent overstayers or those failing to register is sent to the Metropolitan Police Aliens Registration Office in London. Eventually (since overstaying or failing to register, like illegal entry, is a criminal offence) details of alleged immigration offenders may be entered on the wanted/missing persons index of the Police National Computer.[7] At the time of writing, this information was transferred by manual means from a standard PNC terminal. A direct computer-to-computer link (or a tape transfer) may be considered for use in the future, but would inevitably result in up to 1000 false 'wanted' entries each year on the PNC, since at least 2 to 3 per cent of identifications of overstayers on INDECS are officially acknowledged to be erroneous.[8]

Substantial amounts of data are therefore routinely exchanged between police forces, the PNC and INDECS. In February 1984, the Home Office estimated that such transfers occurred about 60,000 times a year. Personal information about immigrants is additionally passed to the police 'in connection with the investigation of possible immigration offences', while 'occasionally ... information may be disclosed to other government departments'.[9]

The second phase of INDECS began with the machine-readable passport experiment at Heathrow. The House of Commons Foreign Affairs Committee had been told in June 1982 that 'trials of an experimental computerised suspect index are shortly to commence at Heathrow airport and elsewhere'.[10] The 'world-wide adoption of machine-readable passports' would, the Home Office said later, enable the INDECS computers to feed back information to immigration officers while they were checking travellers.

But the main advantage of the MRP experiment, if successful, would be to make automated checks of arrivals or departures against the suspect index, thus greatly enhancing the scope and effectiveness of travel surveillance. The suspect index is a 'list of the names of persons in respect of whom Immigration Officers are required to take certain action', according to Immigration Service general instructions. The criteria for inclusion on the list are that 'the persons concerned represent a serious threat to the public good, public order or national security, and might otherwise not be identified'. The criteria, it has been claimed, 'do not otherwise take account of political views'.[11] The index includes names supplied by police forces and Interpol, by the Security Service (which prefers to be known to immigrant officers by the mystificatory title of 'Box 500'), and from police and Immigration Service intelligence units.

The confidential INDECS study, written in 1980, noted that 'One of the major benefits of an automated machine readable passport system is the potential for performing automatic SI [suspect index] checks.' The main value of MRPs, according to these Home Office papers, would be in 'obtaining very fast and effective checks against a much larger Suspect Index'. The report adds, 'If demand were met, the size of the Suspect Index could almost double within two years [and provide] an increase of 161 per cent on weekly updating volumes ... an effective SI system can only be achieved through some form of automation.' The criteria for categorising 'suspects' would become less stringent than hitherto. The new system would also facilitate exchange of data with police and security service computers. The terms of reference for INDECS phase 2 included greater surveillance on British travellers, and included the need to study 'to what extent the preferred solutions could be applied to the British arrivals control desks'.[12]

At present, the suspect index is a black or blue book which immigration officers carry and have on their desk as travellers come through immigration control. The book, slightly smaller than A4 size, contains about 450 pages, with roughly 40 names on each – a total of about 18,000 names. It is officially classified 'confidential'.

The first section of the SI is a 'rapid clearance index', which is used at periods of peak pressure on immigration control points. It contains the names of a small number of people thought to be particularly dangerous. The next section, the largest, lists the names of foreign nationals. The last section is reserved for British and Irish nationals. Many of those listed in the British/Irish section are dual nationals of the two countries. But 20 of these pages contain the names of some 800 British citizens who are not linked to Ireland. Half of these, some 400 names, are of 'security interest' (the remainder are children who are wards of court).

In 1984, among the 400 names in this section were those of Vanessa Redgrave, the actress and one-time leading member of the Workers Revolutionary Party; writer and former student leader Tariq Ali; Kim Philby, the Soviet spy who left the secret service for Moscow a quarter of a century ago; and Peter Wright, a retired MI5 branch director living in Australia who had told the British press of his fears about spies inside MI5 itself, and thus himself became an official Security Service surveillance target. Like Wright, anyone publicly criticising British intelligence services is made an MI5 counter-espionage target, and becomes subject to surveillance. In 1984, suspect index entry number 49940 contained roughly the following information:

> Campbell, Duncan. Investigative journalist involved in exposure of government intelligence.

Actions A, S and Q (see Table 4, page 153) were prescribed in the case of this individual, requiring immigration officials to alert MI5, Special Branch officers and others to his arrival or departure. In practice, this surveillance measure is fatuous, since British citizens are not subject to immigration control, and cannot be stopped and questioned. The suspect index is in practice almost never checked as they pass through. Even when the passenger mentioned above drew immigration officers' attention to the existence of the 'confidential' SI 'warning', they refused even to look at the index, taking such remarks to be the tiresome jest often made by passengers about being 'in the book'.

The problem of exercising surveillance over British travellers has long been recognised. As early as 1978, the JADPU report warned the Home Office that 'declining rate of checking carried out especially in the British control indicated the need for a fundamental reappraisal of procedures'.[13]

The Immigration Service general instructions also tell officers to report to 'Box 500' details of British passengers who come on a long list of categories of British citizens in whom Box 500 has expressed an interest. They include those 'attending a communist sponsored or other event of apparent security interest'; 'passengers travelling to a communist country for a stay of three months or more'; and 'passengers who appear to be of security interest including those with extreme Right-wing affiliations'. For non-British citizens, Box 500 also gives a long list of categories of traveller in whom they are interested, including most Armenians, Japanese who visit the Middle East a lot, Irish people visiting eastern Europe, and those associated with 14 named alleged communist-front organisations, such as the World Peace Council.

In addition to the main suspect index, which is relatively long term and updated every six months, ports of entry are given a 'short list' of people who may be expected to travel to or through Britain in the near future. This is more ephemeral in nature, consisting of:

> [the] subjects of special messages from Box 500, the police or other sources. Such persons should remain on the short list for fourteen days unless the message is repeated . . . Officers will be expected to keep a special watch for them during that period.

The short list is necessary because of the severe difficulties faced by immigration officers in checking the book against every passenger entering the UK.

The first trial of MRP scanners started at Heathrow airport on schedule in February 1983. Other terminals were due to be installed later at the port of Dover and at Gatwick airport, but neither of these got properly off the ground – and the Heathrow experiment stopped after less than two years. For the duration of the trial, the only passengers carrying MRPs were Americans. Details of all Americans appearing in the SI were therefore recorded on microcomputers, to which passport-reading terminals were connected. Plate 14 shows a passport-reading terminal ready for use at Heathrow. When the experiment ended, the equipment was moved back to Lunar House in Croydon, the headquarters of the Home Office's immigration department, for further development.

At the commencement of the Heathrow trial, the Home Secretary repeated an earlier statement that 'the equipment will be entirely self-contained ... and will not be connected to any other computer system'.[14] It was true that the experimental system was 'entirely self-contained', but the plan in Whitehall was to move forward to 'a national network of MRP terminals'. The 1980 Home Office report had foreseen that:

> The computer systems might be linked to form a distributed network encompassing the whole country with the centre of the network located at the Home Office ADP [automatic data processing] unit in Merseyside.

MRP computer terminals, it was suggested, would be linked to minicomputers – one each for Heathrow and other large ports, with smaller ports sharing single systems. These would in turn be linked to the Bootle computer. Once such a network was in place, and after most nations had moved to MRP procedures, all travellers coming to Britain would be automatically checked on the suspect index, and cleared only after the computer had responded with a NO TRACE signal. Foreign travel by Britons who were put onto the expanded and automated SI would also be recorded.

The important part of the MRP is a single laminated plastic page, which registers the traveller's name, nationality, date of birth, sex and passport number. The basic specification for the MRP was drawn up by the International Civil Aviation Authority (ICAO) in 1980, some 12 years after the proposal was first mooted. ICAO anticipated that the MRP would be used by many member countries to investigate wide-ranging checks on their citizens and visitors. They noted that:[15]

Some countries may wish to record the inward and outward

movements of all categories of travellers; some countries may wish to record the inward and outward movements of some categories only; and others may be concerned only with partial controls for specific groups.

The personal data page of an MRP is not unlike that of an ordinary passport. But the same details also appear in a standard machine-readable form at the bottom of the page. At a control point, the machine-readable page is inserted into a slot in the MRP reader. The reader is linked to a computer and the traveller's details are read by the computer. The technical process involved is similar to the reading at cash tills of bar-coded pricetags on retail goods. However, rather than bar codes, MRPs use ordinary letters and numbers and are read by optical character recognition (OCR) computer scanners.

The use of OCR permits passport holders themselves to read the information stored on the passport. Several 'check digits' are included in the reading area, but these contain no extra information about the bearer. It will not be possible for immigration authorities covertly to add extra data to the MRP. Such practices *have* been detected in the past; for example, coded pen marks on visitors' passports have been used to record officials' suspicions, or to denote someone refused entry to the UK.[16] In fact, during early ICAO discussions, the Foreign Office proposed that MRP personal details could be held on a magnetic strip – as on banking and credit cards; such a strip could have contained invisible, secretly coded information about the bearer.

The Home Office originally hoped that immigration officers at each air- or seaport would soon be able to use these readers, but many countries whose nationals visit Britain in large numbers are not committed to issuing MRPs. Most European countries plan to do so, together with the United States, Canada, Australia and some South American countries. In Europe, Belgium and West Germany have already begun issuing MRPs.

The German MRP doubles as a national identity card, which every citizen has to carry in public. The British authorities are well aware of this potential use of the MRP, but presently disavow its use as an identity card. A July 1984 Home Office briefing stated that 'some countries may issue identity cards in this [MRP] format. There are, however, no plans to introduce an identity card in this country.'

The British government decided to issue MRPs in 1981. Prime Minister Margaret Thatcher was said to be particularly keen on adopting the standard ICAO design. For some years, Britain and other member states of the EEC had bickered about the colour and style of the proposed common format 'burgundy red' passport, which had been agreed in principle in 1974. UK ministries took a prominent role in this bickering. The Foreign Office did not want a red passport at all; royal blue was their preference. But burgundy red and machine-readable they will be, ready for issue in 1987.

After the Heathrow trials, the British prototype MRP readers went into technological limbo, in order to be redeveloped to handle heavier levels of traffic and check passengers against a much larger suspect index. Official hopes that the redeveloped readers would be available in time for the introduction of British MRPs in 1987 had, at the time of writing, begun to look uncertain. Nevertheless, the Home Office's 'Forward Strategy', described in evidence to the House of Commons Home Affairs Committee in 1985, gave priority to the development of 'a centrally maintained computer index to all IND [Immigration and Nationality Department] warnings information', including listings of 'deportees, illegal entrants, those with serious criminal convictions, etc.'. This would produce the advantages of 'faster decision making in individual cases through the ready availability of warnings information, case histories or the rapid and reliable identification of the whereabouts of paper files' – for example, when dealing with applications for British nationality. But the department admitted to the House of Commons late in 1985 that the 'timescale for the [computerisation] programme is lengthy'.[17]

The dangers of travel surveillance in Britain to civil liberty (other than to racial equality) have so far been avoided because of the simple fact that the system doesn't work. The present manual suspect index is too overloaded to pose a serious political threat. But the operation of similar systems in West Germany presents both a striking contrast and a severe warning to the UK. As already mentioned, in West Germany, everyone must possess and carry national identity cards, which may be used as a passport when travelling between EEC countries. Although machine-readable identity cards are a recent introduction, German frontier controls have, for over 10 years, been computerised to some degree.

In one system, used for example at Berlin's Tegel airport, travellers' passports are placed face-down on a glass screen above a TV camera by the immigration officer. A second official sits in front of a VDU and types the data from the passport into a terminal to the local police computer. A warning list, similar to the British suspect index, is provided to the local police computer by the West German central police computer, INPOL. INPOL is operated by the *Bundeskriminalampt*, the German version of the FBI.[18]

INPOL clearly serves a surveillance role. Horror stories abound about its use, and in particular about its 'wanted persons' list (like that held on the PNC in Britain), within which there is a special category for persons under surveillance (also as on the PNC) called BEFA, short for *beobachtende fahndung* or 'observation [and] search'. Persons on the BEFA list are described as being suspected of breaking the law, but in cases where there is little or no evidence available to launch a successful conviction. Some on the list may merely be suspected of having the potential to break the law.

There are nine sub-categories of the BEFA list, and many who are neither lawbreakers, terrorists nor illegal entrants are included. BEFA 7 persons are those suspected of terrorist offences; BEFA 9s are participants in demonstrations. One group in the BEFA 7 section includes people found associating with suspected terrorists. They are coded BEFA 7K. 'Associating' means literally that, and does not exclude absolutely innocent association. People found by police in the same bus or train compartment, for instance, as a suspected terrorist have been registered in the BEFA 7K category. Such people would never know that their names have been placed on computer, yet may be subject to aggressive searching or worse each time they cross Germany's borders.[19]

The INPOL horror stories include the tale of businessman Romwald Neidermayer, who discovered after repeated rough searches that he had been given a personal BEFA 7 code as a 'terrorist contract' after his passport had been stolen.[20] Between 1976 and 1979, details from the passports of 100,000 West Germans who travelled to east European countries were secretly transferred to NADIS, the computer of the federal security service, known as the Office for the Protection of the Constitution, or *Verfassungsschutz*.[21] Using NADIS, the *Verfassungsschutz* administers the notorious German *Berufsverbot*, or 'forbidden beliefs' system, used to ban members of legal left-wing organisations from public-agency jobs, even in the state railway service. In 1977, the names of thousands of Germans aged between 20 and 35 who had crossed the country's *western* borders were recorded on the INPOL computer, as part of the search for the kidnappers of Hans-Martin Schleyer.[22] At the same time, instructions to border guards included the names of 789 left-wing political activists, 278 publications 'suspicious' persons might carry, and 239 organisations, on all of which they were expected to report.[23] Details of this extraordinary system emerged in the late 1970s during investigations by the director of the German data protection office, Hans-Peter Bull.

With facilities like these, machine-readable identity cards or passports become highly threatening to privacy, because of the way they can be used for internal control. An identity-card system makes it easy to set up roadblocks and monitor every person entering a particular area. This already happens to some extent in West Germany. After a serious crime, or before a demonstration, West German police have stopped people and taken down the names and numbers on their identity cards – a process that may soon be automated.

British immigration officers are asked by MI5 to take an interest in people carrying 'subversive' literature. West German border guards are given lists of published magazines divided into 'subversive' and 'non-subversive' categories. The West German lead in the technology of political and social control has been recognised in Europe, and has been endorsed by some as a model for other countries. Nearly a decade ago, the Council of Europe recommended the West German model as that on which other European countries should base their plans for computerising immigration control. A 1978 report on terrorism in Europe singled out the INPOL computer, located at Wiesbaden, as having made a significant breakthrough in tracing terrorists at home and abroad:[24]

> All Council of Europe member states would gain if the Wiesbaden computer were to become the basis of a databank on international terrorism, to be used not only after a major terrorist incident has occurred, but also on a regular basis through periodical exchanges of information.

To this effect, it was recommended that immigration and passport checks should be tightened – 'however repugnant this may sound to those for whom European co-operation means making frontiers less and less relevant'. Stressing that the security of VIPs as possible targets of terrorist attacks had had to be intensified in several European countries, the report advocated a new Europe-wide computer network as 'an essential requirement for controlling terrorism in a sophisticated intelligence gathering system'. The network would not necessarily involve computer-to-computer links (which would be politically unacceptable) but information could be transferred by 'secure telex lines between national police centres' in Europe to and from Wiesbaden and the INPOL computer.

In a series of reports on the 'easing of frontier formalities', both the Council of Europe and the Commission of the European Communities have recommended that member nations should 'consider the desirability of introducing … a national identity card system where there is none at present'.[25] The EEC has asked member states to minimise frontier formalities for EEC nationals travelling within the community, in effect replacing frontier immigration controls with internal identity cards and police checks. Such identity cards and the new machine-readable passports may not in themselves hold personal data that threatens the bearer's fundamental freedoms. But as the key to increased internal surveillance, with all the hazards that discriminatory suspect indexes and wide-ranging BEFA databanks bring, their widespread issue would unlock new dangers in the future. For Asians and others of New Commonwealth descent in Britain now, these dangers have been real for more than a decade.

Until black immigration was defined by some as a social

problem, regulated by law, and made a crime when unauthorised, there was no such thing as 'illegal immigration'. The Immigration Act of 1971 marked the end of a long process whereby British Commonwealth citizens lost their rights to visit and settle freely in Britain. Those who were settled in Britain at that time became subject to novel and discriminatory controls, including passport raids and requests from public authorities to prove their British citizenship. All these controls chiefly affected only Commonwealth blacks and Asians, and intentionally so, since both the Immigration Act and the subsequent 1981 Nationality Act explicitly discriminate against non-whites.

The 1971 Act created many new immigration offences; the police in turn created intelligence units in order to investigate the new offences. Special Metropolitan Police and Immigration Service intelligence units both date from this period. The Immigration Service Intelligence and Investigation Unit (ISIIU) was set up in 1970 at Harmondsworth, Middlesex, close to Heathrow airport. The Immigration Service also operates a privatised detention centre at Harmondsworth, where people refused entry may be held, often for lengthy periods. The Metropolitan Police Illegal Immigration Intelligence Unit was set up in 1972, and soon merged with the Central Drugs Intelligence Unit, sharing common offices, files and eventually an extensive computer databank.

The Immigration Service intelligence unit has a staff of 40. Its terms of reference are:[26]

> to collate, evaluate and disseminate information for the purpose of increasing the efficiency of the immigration control before, on and after entry; to liaise with the police and other Government Departments in connection with evasion of the immigration control, including clandestine entry.

Files are maintained on people overseas who are refused entry clearance or leave to enter when they come, or who have been deported from the UK. Files are also opened on anyone who has applied to stay in the UK, then decides to leave before the Home Office has finished considering their case.[27]

But the unit's main task is to assemble data on people who 'are considered to be involved in the abuse or attempted abuse of the immigration laws'. It collects both 'hard and factual' and 'intelligence' information. Information is supplied by individual immigration officers, by the central office of the Immigration and Nationality Department, by police forces, entry clearance officers (overseas), and, according to the general instructions, 'individual informers'. Unsolicited informers' reports on alleged illegal entrants are, it is claimed, 'carefully checked with a view to ensuring that they are accurate and ... that [the report] has not been furnished maliciously'.[28] This claim is nonsensical, as much of the information cannot be checked. Former Immigration Service officers dismiss it as 'quite untrue'.

Throughout its first decade of existence the intelligence unit used a manual card index – the central intelligence index. According to the Immigration Service general instructions, the objective of the index was to help investigators 'discover, frustrate and assist in bringing to justice clandestine immigrants and persons assisting them'. The index was split into eight sub-sections, of which the main three were:

Names index, with names and 'other particulars' of anyone including sponsors, businessmen, education establishments and other organisations who have come to notice 'in any way' in connection with suspected or attempted evasion or with clandestine entry.

Address index for the UK and abroad, cross-referenced to the names index.

Telephone index of the names and numbers 'found in the papers and diaries of would-be evaders'.

There were also indexes of planes, boats, ships and passports.

The Metropolitan Police Central Drugs and Illegal Immigration Intelligence Unit (CDIIIU) built up similar indexes. By January 1974, the unit had 76,000 names on file, and expected this to grow to 287,000 by January 1985 (see page 265). The CDIIIU files were computerised on the police C Department computer during 1978 and 1979. In August 1981, the immigration service got its own computer, colloquially known inside the service as IVAN.[29] Like the C Department computer, IVAN uses the free text retrieval software Status.

By April 1983, some 300,000 names and addresses were

recorded on IVAN files. The personal information held includes name, address, date of birth, nationality and the category in which the person is recorded. A year later, the Metropolitan Police – who had begun to find the invigilation of immigration offences irksome – disbanded their CDIIIU and withdrew the police liaison officers to the Immigration Service who had been stationed at Harmondsworth. The C Department computer was wiped clean of immigration intelligence information, which was transferred to the IVAN system during January 1984.

Personal information on the IVAN computer is retained for seven years, unless further information has come to light since its entry, or if 'suspicions about the subject's involvement in abuse of the immigration laws have been dispelled'. But the test of what sort of information from informers and other sources justifies an entry on the computer is extremely weak; the government has said that:

> It is not possible to state precisely what evidence is required of abuse or attempted abuse of the immigration laws before a person suspected of those actions has his particulars entered on the computer. Much depends upon the source and apparent reliability of the information.

IVAN also records 'certain addresses which have come to notice in respect of abuse or attempted abuse of the immigration laws'.

The Home Office advises immigration officers to consult the intelligence unit 'when there is some positive reason for thinking' that it might be helpful. Immigration officers can ring the Harmondsworth unit and ask for details, if they exist, on a person who is seeking entry to the UK. At least three terminals are available on-line, 17 hours a day.[30]

The ease of unauthorised access to information on IVAN and the remarkable extent of data transferred to IVAN from other government departments were demonstrated in February 1985 when callers posing as immigration officers telephoned the Harmondsworth unit and asked for details on six named individuals. In only one case did the intelligence unit ask for the caller to quote a warrant number. When enquiring about a Pakistani woman, the fake caller was cross-referred to one of her relatives, a British citizen settled in the UK, and then given extensive data about him which had clearly been extracted from a DHSS supplementary benefit claim:[31]

> He was made redundant five months ago from his job as a machine operator. He invested his £1,200 redundancy pay in property, purchasing a £16,000 house with a £7,000 mortgage and £9,000 savings. He also owns another house which is at present unoccupied and up for sale. His present income amounts to £90 supplementary benefit, which includes benefits due to his two daughters. He has £1,004 savings in a building society and a mortgage of £90 a month.

Besides working closely with Special Branch, the Immigration Service may exchange information with Customs and Excise, Inland Revenue or DHSS. Information from the intelligence unit can be obtained by police officers when making stop-checks or conducting other investigations. Information about National Insurance contributions can be obtained from the DHSS when required.

Since April 1984, the Home Office has also had responsibility for the Passport Office, previously a part of the Foreign Office. Some of the Passport Office's files have been computerised under a £165,000 scheme first revealed in 1982; the computer-isation plan includes providing 'facilities for the maintenance and search of Special Files and the Passport Warning List'.[32] The 'special files' list people who are not allowed passports. They are divided into four categories: children who are wards of court; people who are wanted for arrest or are suspected of a serious crime; people who have been repatriated to the UK at public expense and who have not yet repaid the return fare home; and those 'whose past or proposed activities are so demonstrably undesirable that the grant or continued enjoy-ment of passport facilities would be contrary to the public interest'. The Home Office says that this fourth category covers 'security cases', but that people who fall into it are 'extremely rare'. Questioned about the meaning of the term 'demons-trably undesirable activities', a Home Office spokesman said it was 'self-evident'.

The number of people in these categories was, in 1985, around 8000. Their names are listed on a small micro-computer, and applicants for passports are checked against the list. A sub-category of special files is the 'passport warning list', covering people thought to be resident abroad and who may apply for a passport at a British embassy. This list is sent out to all British embassies and is periodically updated. The Passport Office intends eventually to store on computer the names and personal details of all British passport holders – some 15 million people. The special files will also be held on computer for checking against applicants for new passports. The plan is to have the computer system operational by 1987, in time for the issuing of the new machine-readable British passports.

Questioned in 1982 about privacy safeguards in the Passport Office, the government claimed that passport information stored on computer would be given 'the same protection and privacy as the existing passport records'. This was a deliberately meaningless reassurance, as Passport Office information was even then acknowledged to be 'available on request' to the Home Office and Inland Revenue.[33] Rather more secret and more sinister is the Passport Office's practice of checking all passports returned for renewal for the presence of east European, Cuban or Chinese visas or entry stamps. If these are found, the passport is copied to MI5 (who are looking out for spies recruited by these countries) and to MI6 (who are looking out for travelling Britons as potential spies against these countries).

Non-whites who come to notice of the police in any way, particularly Asians, can often expect to face quite improper questions about immigration status. Dozens of cases have been recorded where British citizens and others settled in the UK, sometimes for decades, have been asked to produce their passports. The police have absolutely no authority to ask for passports, and even less right to regard the colour of someone's skin as *prima facie* reasonable grounds for suspecting an immigration offence.

But they do. A Southampton bus driver, fined £25 for speeding in 1980, was asked by Hampshire police to complete a detailed immigration-check form and produce his passport. He had lived in Britain for 20 years.[34] In 1983, three Nigerian students who caught a burglar and called the police were arrested and held in custody for 14 hours until they could prove that their presence in the UK was legal. The burglar, who was white, was released. In seeking to uncover immigration offences for which there is no reasonable suspicion, instead of dealing with actual and serious offences brought to their attention, individual police officers have gravely damaged race relations and the credibility of their service among the immigrant community. As discussed in Chapter 4, similar unpleasant and unlawful racial discrimination has also been exercised by some DHSS officials.[35]

The most controversial activity of the immigration intelligence unit has been its provision of targets for 'passport raids' run jointly with the police. Until 1981, police and immigration service teams periodically launched major raids (often in the early hours) against Asians' houses or places of employment. Everyone lacking a white skin was expected to produce proof of British citizenship or residence rights, or face arrest. After a particularly notorious series of raids in 1980, this policy was reviewed. The most grotesque of these 'fishing expeditions' was a raid on the Bestways cash and carry supermarket in London. Some 28 police and immigration officers removed 20 Asians to Kensington police station on suspicion of immigration offences. Of the 20 arrested, all but three were lawfully living and working in the UK.

After two further and equally controversial raids, fishing expeditions against Asians were ended, possibly temporarily. Raids have continued, but are usually conducted only in search of named individuals about whom there is prior evidence. Those arrested on such raids are questioned to obtain further information for the Harmondsworth intelligence unit. Diaries and lists of friends' names and addresses are entered into the computer, to create the largest possible database for future enquiries. Anyone associated in this way with someone 'coming to notice' of the intelligence unit may expect to be on the IVAN computer.

After the size of the IVAN databank (300,000 names) was revealed in February 1983, Liberal peer and immigration campaigner Lord Avebury warned that:[36]

> This is a very large number of persons. Only a tiny fraction can be those suspected of contravening the law ... it seems to me that we have very little safeguard against people being included in the file

for reasons which the public, if they could know of them, would consider to be grossly unsatisfactory.

When drafting the Data Protection Act, the Home Office did its best to ensure that no safeguards, neither registration nor subject access, would apply to IVAN or any other immigration computer. They also proposed that transfers of computerised information to the Immigration Service should not be registered. Immigration data would, they proposed, attract the same wholesale exemption as police, Inland Revenue and national security information. The intention and effect of the proposal was to stop anyone challenging an Immigration Service decision from seeing the computerised information about them which had informed the decision.

Eventually, the government had to back down at a late stage. The immigration exemption was dropped. Although the Home Office can still claim some exemption for its Immigration Service files (where actual crime is involved or suspected), most people will now get at least some access. The Home Office said in 1985 that:[37]

> The personal data held in the several computer systems used by the Immigration and Nationality Department are subject to the provisions of the Data Protection Act and will, in the majority of cases, be accessible by data subjects.

IVAN the intelligence computer has a brother called CEDRIC – the Customs and Excise Department Reference and Information Computer. Like IVAN and the Metropolitan Police C Department computer (with both of which it is closely connected), CEDRIC uses the Status free text retrieval software system and stores personal data on over 100,000 people. Although CEDRIC became operational in March 1983, its existence was not revealed to MPs for more than 15 months, and even then only by accident. At first, the special software system for CEDRIC performed badly and the customs service refused officially to accept delivery for more than two years.

CEDRIC's targets are people suspected of involvement in smuggling – mostly, drug smuggling. But the 100,000 names held include those whose connections with actual or suspected smugglers may be accidental, innocuous or erroneously recorded. The Treasury (which is responsible to Parliament for the Customs and Excise) has claimed that it would be 'a disproportionate use of resources' to attempt to calculate how many of those recorded on CEDRIC actually had criminal convictions. However, the computer was said to hold information on:

> Name, present address, any aliases, maiden name where appropriate, sex, date of birth, place of birth, nationality ... personal description, occupation, country of normal residence, passport details [and] telephone number.

Also stored are details of vehicles used by the subject, 'the role played by the subject', the 'type of case in which the subject is involved' and a 'description of the goods or services concerned'.[38] The Treasury statement to Parliament did not reveal the extent to which records may have been cross-linked by the investigators, or the existence of any indexes to vehicles or other property.

Much of the data on CEDRIC has been transferred from police intelligence indexes, and from such material as address books seized during raids or port checks. Details of passports and vehicles are easily obtained from the Passport Office and the DVLC. Telephone numbers obtained from personal documents, diaries and address books are widely regarded as useful intelligence data for cross-referencing and studying 'association networks' among those recorded on the computer. A Status enquiry will locate all references to a particular name or number held anywhere in the system.

CEDRIC superseded a manual card index, which in 1983 had held details of 70,000 people. In the first year of operation, the CEDRIC names index expanded to cover 106,700 – an increase of over 50 per cent. Between June 1984 and April 1985, some 3000 records were added to the file. But only 30 were deleted – which happens in circumstances when 'it appears that the department no longer has an interest in that particular subject'. Some 400 Customs and Excise staff had direct access to terminals; but any one of some 20,000 customs staff, from clerical officer upwards, could instigate a new record on any individual, British or foreign, whom they wished to investigate.[39]

During its first year, CEDRIC information was accessed about 50 times daily – 17,500 times in all. Some 25 CEDRIC terminals are situated in three London customs headquarters buildings; the computer itself, a Honeywell minicomputer with 1.2 gigabytes of disc store, is installed at the customs' computer centre in Shoeburyness, near Southend-on-Sea. One CEDRIC terminal is located within the Metropolitan Police National (formerly Central) Drugs Intelligence Unit (NDIU), where several customs officials work on secondment.[40] By this means, information can evidently be interchanged with police drugs unit officers – despite an early official denial that information from CEDRIC would be allowed to pass outside the Customs and Excise Department.[41]

In fact, CEDRIC and police computers will soon be integrated. The National Drugs Intelligence Unit has been made the 'central hub' of a new government campaign against drugs trafficking, and the focus for drugs-related intelligence for police forces and enforcement agencies.[42] In July 1985, Home Secretary Leon Brittan reformed the unit into a common police service. The NDIU, he said would be:[43]

> staffed by both police and the Customs services and have an enhanced intelligence-gathering and analytical capability sharing common data in place of the present divided system ... The new NDIU will give us the intelligence capacity needed to counter today's sophisticated drug trafficking groups.

A former Special Branch chief, Deputy Assistant Commissioner Colin Hewett, was appointed as the National Drugs Co-ordinator, a new post.

Although no further announcement was made, it was clear from the Home Secretary's statement that the police and customs services had been given clear political authority to embark on a considerable expansion and amalgamation of their separate but similar intelligence databanks. By January 1985, the former police Central Drugs Intelligence Unit had expected to hold some 60,000 records on the C Department computer (independent of the 110,000 on IVAN). The breadth and depth of surveillance may now be expected to increase dramatically.

Customs and Excise also operate a number of major

computers monitoring legal trade and supervising the collection of VAT. The VAT computer centre at Southend holds the names and addresses and financial details of all persons registered for VAT, about one million people in all. Most VAT paperwork other than payments and repayments is still processed manually. VAT investigation teams have provoked considerable ire amongst traders by unusual and intensive investigative methods, which have been reported to include spying on customers at a restaurant, taking vehicle registrations to trace them on the DVLC computer, and then contacting the customers to enquire about the value of meals purchased.[44] The objective was to see if the restaurant was falsifying its VAT returns; the customers' privacy was not an issue that concerned the customs service. Another newspaper revealed that small traders were being given an honesty rating from zero to 15 according to how co-operative they were thought to be; these scores were allegedly recorded on the VAT computer.[45]

There is one complete official population register with which everyone is familiar: the census. Once a decade since 1801 (save for the war year of 1941), every person in the country has been required to return personal particulars. In the latest census, 1981, questions about householders, their families, visitors, children and housing conditions had to be supplied to 100,000 official census 'enumerators'.[46] The next Census of Population will be held in 1991, on a date to be co-ordinated with other EEC countries. A mid-term compulsory census of 10 per cent of the population, as occurred in 1976, had been proposed for 1986 – but the £67 million plan was abandoned in 1983.

In charge of the census in England and Wales is the Office of Population Censuses and Surveys (OPCS), which answers to the Secretary of State for Social Services – but the 'strict confidentiality' of census information from scrutiny or access by others in government is said to be assured by the 1920 Census Act. (In Scotland, the General Register Office has the same functions.) For a period of 100 years, the information in the census forms is not available for any but a few very restricted purposes; it then becomes public.

The 1920 Census Act allows a census to be ordered by executive decree, but parliamentary approval is required for the contents of the order. Once the Queen has signed a census order, it is illegal to refuse to answer census questions, or to give false answers. The punishment is a fine. The questions proposed in each census are generally widely debated in advance. Since the most recent census (5 April 1981), information from the completed forms has been processed onto computer tape at a temporary data processing centre at Bootle; and then stored and processed on OPCS's two ICL 2966 computers at Titchfield, Hampshire. Names and addresses from completed census forms are not normally entered onto the computer.

In describing the 1981 survey, OPCS claimed that the census was 'not concerned with people as individuals'. It was taken 'solely to compile statistics about groups and categories . . . not to reveal, still less to make practical or administrative use of, information about any individual person'. This is misleading. OPCS does not advertise its conduct of a 'longitudinal survey', whereby since 1971 the movements and other 'events' in the lives of just over 1 per cent of the population are tracked through the entire lifetimes of the individuals concerned. Linking together the data from successive censuses, information is collated about named individuals who are selected on the basis of having one of four specific birthdates. The files of these people are then traced on the National Health Service central register in Southport – with remarkable effectiveness. In 1971, 96.8 per cent of people chosen for the longitudinal survey were traced in the register; in 1981, 98.5 per cent.

Because of migration (changes of address) during the period between censuses, OPCS uses the NHS central register (which is also in its care, for a separate purpose) to follow the survey targets as they move about within, or in and out of, the country. Information is also drawn from the registration of births and deaths, and from the cancer register. The birthdates chosen are secret, and OPCS has refused to reveal them on the grounds that individuals with those birthdates might then try to avoid taking part and thus 'distort' their statistics. They have not, of course, asked the 600,000 or so individuals concerned in the longitudinal survey for their consent that the census data they have provided, or the information they have given to NHS family practitioners, may be used in this way.

The census includes questions on usual address, past address, travel to work, place of work, occupation, country of birth, and relationships between persons at the same address. A separate series of questions is concerned with housing tenure and amenities. The form requires that everyone state their name, usual address and date of birth. OPCS says that this is necessary 'so that the householder (who is responsible for the form) can distinguish accurately between persons entered on the form'; in order to 'enable OPCS staff to identify the right person when information on the form is missing'; and 'to establish whether householders and others have discharged their legal obligations and provided all the necessary information'.[47]

Because of the compulsory and intimidatory nature of the census, OPCS goes to great lengths to convince the public that census information is kept confidential, and that every effort is made to ensure that information does not stray to unauthorised people. In evidence to the Lindop committee, OPCS therefore welcomed proposals for an independent Data Protection Authority, which would, it felt, help it to rebut attacks from a 'small but vocal fringe of the public which asserts that personal information is or could be used improperly'. Indeed, OPCS has a better record for respecting confidentiality than any other government department. The worst criticism it has suffered was for using names extracted from the 1971 census for follow-up specialised surveys of particular professions (such as of the number of people leaving nursing).

A year before the 1981 census, DHSS minister Sir George Young again assured MPs that 'The census forms and information on them ... will not be seen by anyone at all outside the census organisation.'[48] But despite such insistences, a survey carried out by OPCS after the 1971 census showed that a majority believed the census to be a 'means of providing a list of names and addresses for the government'.[49] It isn't – yet. But the determination of OPCS officials to maintain their reputation, on which public co-operation depends, is all that may stand between private census information and attempts by police, Inland Revenue or national security authorities to gain access to data they may think likely to be useful. Nothing in the

Data Protection Act provides extra safeguards for census data; indeed, the Act licenses OPCS to lie, if it wishes, about whether its data may be available to others 'in the interests of national security'.

The OPCS conducts many other surveys, based on data supplied by official organisations, or by using standard survey methods such as polling. It is also responsible for the registration of births, deaths and marriages. Information from local registrars on births, deaths and marriages has been collated centrally on computer since 1963. A report recommending a £4 million plan to install nearly 700 computers at local register offices was published in 1985. There were two options: a local microprocessor system which would rely on local storage; or an OPCS 'national databank'. The latter option was said to be 'more efficient'; it would link the NHS central register with registry offices and district health authorities in order to create a computerised population index,[50] and ultimately make possible the transfer of machine-readable data between the three agencies. The report noted that:

> If computers are introduced into the service, the system should be designed to make it as simple as possible for the necessary data to be transmitted automatically to the [district health authorities], and central notification may be the best approach.

This would involve some 23,000 items a week.

OPCS has also studied computerising the electoral register, nationally, for the same purposes. A working party on the electoral register was convened in 1974, and reported in 1978, strongly recommending the establishment of a national register. There were 'obvious political difficulties' and 'the serious threat to privacy presented by large scale collation of information about individuals would have to be faced'.[51] OPCS was then asked to study the utility of such a population register for preparing survey information more cheaply than by means of a full-scale census.

The main problem identified by the working party was the need to keep registers up to date and have them available for voting as and when required. At present, the registers are updated annually – and manually. The working party recommended that, as an interim step towards a national electoral databank, local authorities should computerise their registers in the same, standard way. No standard has been agreed, but new Representation of the People regulations came into force in February 1986, requiring local authorities to make electoral rolls available as computer-readable tapes or discs, as well as on paper.

So far, this has happened only in an *ad hoc* way. Council computerisation of local registers has also been proposed in the context of plans for comprehensive local authority data-bases which would include details on ratepayers, children and education, housing, the use of social services, and building and planning controls. Such proposals are periodic-ally revived and publicised, most recently as part of proposed changes to the rating system. But government-imposed cuts in local authority investment mean that comprehensive local authority databases are unlikely to be developed for a long time to come. Computerised electoral registers are of sig-nificant value – including financial value – to political parties and private organisations. As well as greatly reducing the labour of sending out election addresses, computers can store local canvassing lists, in which are compiled personal voting records together with information about voting intentions. Both the SDP and the Conservative Party have made extensive use of computers nationally to mail information and appeals to their supporters (see also page 59).

As described in Chapter 3, data from three public sources – the electoral register, the postcode system and the census – has been combined by two commercial agencies, CCN and the United Association for the Protection of Trade, to form huge private databanks (see pages 56–8). These organisations (and many others) use census 'small area statistics' in a way which comes very close to breaching individual privacy. Small area information is used to calculate general socioeconomic infor-mation about residents in each census 'enumeration district'. Residents' names are taken from the electoral register. The small area statistics, census critics allege, are compiled largely because of their potential commercial use – not to meet the real planning needs of public authorities.

Soon after the Post Office introduced the postcode system, it openly advertised its privacy-threatening facility to link previously unconnected computer records. Some 22 million addresses and 170,000 individual 'large users' of postal services are held on the postcode database. A full postcode database on computer tape, complete with ordnance survey grid references for each code, can be purchased from the PO for £20,000, and kept updated at a cost of £6500 a year. Postcodes are advertised as 'the most sensible national reference system' and 'ideal for computers'. Since then, many other databases have been constructed on the framework of postcodes. A personal address postcode is now routinely demanded on each occasion a citizen has to provide personal information, whether or not it is actually needed for the purpose of communicating with the person concerned.

Postcodes can often be used instead of names to transfer data between computers. For example, the details of anyone applying to the Post Office for personal mail to be redirected are now automatically sent to the TV licensing office, which is run by the Post Office. Separately, as part of plans to computerise counter services in main post offices, the PO has also proposed direct links to DHSS computers and the Swansea Driver and Vehicle Licensing Centre (DVLC), on whose behalf they receive and make payments of over a billion pounds a year. They might also link to airline or travel agents' booking facilities. A pilot scheme in the Thames Valley area will start in 1987, with the computerisation of 250 post offices. A national PO network with about 6000 terminals is planned for 1990.

Another computerisation scheme, announced in September 1985, will put on-line the records of the Land Registry. The registry holds details of land ownership (in areas where ownership has been registered). By 1987, it was expected that compulsory land registration would cover 85 per cent of the population of England and Wales. At the same time, the Law Commission has recommended that the Land Registry be opened to public inspection – instead of, as at present, requiring anyone wishing to investigate the ownership of private land first to have the relevant landowner's permission.

In contrast, virtually no attempt whatever is made to protect information about driving licences and vehicle ownership. Investigators and enquirers from the police and many other

public agencies are given free access to details of vehicles and
their keepers, for purposes which have nothing to do with the
'collection of vehicle excise duty and ... the enforcement of
vehicle excise and road traffic legislation' – the purpose for
which vehicle information is officially gathered.[52] The ease of
obtaining a vehicle registration in the course of enquiries, and
of subsequently tracing the keeper and driver through vehicle
registration files, has provided many with an attractive aid to
investigation. The handling of vehicle licensing data, both
before and since computerisation, offers as clear an example
as could be found of information collected for one purpose
being used, wholesale, for a multitude of other unconnected
purposes.

In 1984, the DVLC held 33 million vehicle records and 37
million driving licence records.[53] These files occupied 320 reels
of computer tape. In the same year, over five *million* items of
information were released from the vehicle licensing files – 2.8
million disclosures to the Central (parking) Ticket Office, 1.1
million to local authorities, 400,000 to the police, 30,000 to
other government departments, 25,000 to the general public,
and 636,000 to others (mostly manufacturers recalling vehicles
for safety purposes).[54] Information from *driving* licences was
released on over one million occasions – in response to 950,000
requests from the police, and 300,000 from other quarters,
notably the Inland Revenue. These figures exclude the number
of vehicle enquiries made directly to the Police National
Computer, now running at more than 20 million a year, making
a grand annual total of 25 million vehicle owners' checks,
almost none of them relating to the purpose for which the
information was originally given. The scale of these disclosures
has quadrupled in less than a decade.

Information from drivers' licences may be 'released only to
the police (for use by the courts), other licensing authorities ...
and to the Inland Revenue, to whom addresses are supplied in
certain cases to enable them to contact evasive taxpayers'.[55]
Anyone showing 'reasonable cause' may be supplied with the
name and address of a registered vehicle keeper.[56]

The police and local authorities are entitled to obtain
information from the vehicle register 'in connection with the
investigation of offences'. This does not provide the police with

a lawful right to obtain *all* information about *all* vehicles and
their keepers at *all* times in advance of and without reference
to any specific offence requiring investigation. Challenged by
the authors to provide evidence that they had been properly
asked to provide this information, the DVLC could not cite any
such request.

The wholesale and automatic transfer of vehicle data to the
Police National Computer was never sanctioned by Parliament
and is arguably far beyond the authority allowed in the 1971
regulations. Yet there can be little doubt that this transfer had
been anticipated from 1965 on, when planning for the vehicle
computer centre began, with the police represented in discussions. Had the government of the day chosen to be honest
about these intentions, they could have sought parliamentary
authority. They did not. The link to the PNC was one of two
remarkable pieces of administrative high-handedness which
have marked out the DVLC for much well-deserved criticism.
(The other action was the issue of a new-style driving licence
which misled holders about their opportunity to remove date
of birth details from the document (see page 71).)

The DVLC also achieved notoriety as the most spectacular
government computer flop of the 1970s. When it began
operating in 1974, it was the largest computer project of its
era. Reviewing its performance in 1975, the Commons Public
Accounts Committee found that the cost of the centre had
grown from £146 million in 1968 to £350 million six years later;
that it would need a total of about 8000 staff, as against original
estimates of 4000; and that its annual running costs were
almost treble the figures anticipated.[57] It started work late, and
immediately hit the headlines as enormous delays built up in
the issue of driving licences. Instead of local vehicle licensing
offices becoming redundant, 81 new offices had to be opened.
Plans to issue vehicle tax discs direct from Swansea were abandoned altogether. The project had been due for completion in
1974, but was not finished even in 1978. Until 1984, it was quicker for the the Swansea staff to use the PNC to check vehicle data
than it was for them to check on their own computer.

The DVLC, now working more smoothly with the aid of two
IBM 3083 computers installed in 1983, remains a vast data-
processing operation. One in eight letters delivered in Wales go

to the DVLC – some 250,000 forms a day. Processing these, 400 operators daily prepare about 30 megabytes of information (35 times the length of this book) for input to the system. Computer tapes containing all new vehicle amendments are sent daily to the PNC at Hendon. Discs may be used in future instead of tapes, but a direct computer–computer link has so far been ruled out on grounds of cost. A police liaison officer is permanently seconded to the DVLC, and has custody of the PNC terminal available there for cross-checking records on the PNC.

In addition to this, the DVLC receives computer tapes from an increasing number of police forces throughout the UK. On these tapes, local forces ask for information on vehicles and drivers, such as who was the registered keeper of a vehicle at a particular time, or the addresses of named drivers. The DVLC answers these questions and sends the tapes back to the appropriate force. In 1985, 22 police forces were using this facility, and another 12 had registered an intent to do so. A similar mechanism exists between DVLC and 14 local authorities who want to know the names of registered keepers of vehicles issued with parking tickets. Customs and Excise officers are given information from the DVLC on drivers and vehicles, as are Inland Revenue and DHSS investigators. The Inland Revenue acknowledges that, as far as it is concerned, this practice goes back to 1931. Anyone else with a 'reasonable cause' – for example, insurance companies claiming damages, or someone writing in to say that a car has run over their cat – gets the information too. A £2 fee must be paid for each vehicle enquiry.

Information about vehicle keepers goes on tape to the computers of the Metropolitan Police Central Ticket Office (CTO), which processes parking tickets issued in London and obtains the address for each ticket from the DVLC tapes. B9 division, which operates the CTO computer, also maintains a computerised evaders' 'blacklist', entry on to which is said by the police to provoke a special enquiry about the keeper. There is also a 'sensitive protected blacklist' category – where previous enquiries have led to 'controversy' or where special enquiries have been unsuccessful.[58]

Two former Lord Chancellors, Lord Gardiner and Lord

Elwyn-Jones, have attacked the extensive traffic in DVLC information as quite contrary to the undertaking in the 1975 Computers and Privacy White Paper. This White Paper claimed that 'administrative arrangements had been made to prevent information collected by one government department being transferred to a different department for a different purpose'. Lord Elwyn-Jones said the practice breached:[59]

> a long standing and salutary rule that information supplied by the citizen to a government department for one purpose is communicated for that purpose alone, and cannot be transferred for administrative or other convenience, to any other government department.

The government was unmoved.

By the end of the decade, British Telecom will have created a new – and unnecessary – means of surveillance. Under plans to introduce a customer service system (CSS) nationally, BT will automatically record, reproduce and store details of telephone numbers dialled by each subscriber. At present, telephone exchanges 'forget' this information immediately a call finishes. All that is retained is a record of the number of units to be charged for the call. Only by attaching a special recorder, called a 'printermeter', to a target line *in advance* of any call can investigators get information about numbers called. The new CSS system will automatically create data of considerable value for surveillance purposes. But since telephone numbers *per se* do not relate to identifiable individuals, information stored in CSS may not even attract the scanty protection of the Data Protection Act.

As may be inferred from their significance to the intelligence computer systems described in this and subsequent chapters, telephone numbers are simple but critically useful intelligence items. The information produced by the new CSS billing system is likely to prove an irresistible bait to security organisations who at present – even if they tap a target telephone line – have no way of discovering the origin of incoming calls. A search of CSS computers could provide this information – albeit at heavy processing cost, unless target numbers under surveillance were to be specially 'flagged' as details were supplied to the billing computers. But obtaining names and addresses from any telephone numbers recorded would be trivially easy.

Digital electronic exchanges, such as the new System X, automatically produce the information needed for CSS computers. But older exchanges will have to be fitted with individual 'call-logging' computers to convert the exchange's electrical signals into a form that the billing computers can interpret. It was originally intended to attach such call-logging computers to BT's old Strowger exchanges. But this plan has now been dropped because most of these exchanges will in any case be replaced by System X or other modern exchanges by the turn of the century.

After information is collated by the billing computers, an itemised bill sent to the customer (and retained also on BT records) will show the date, time, destination and duration of every trunk and international call listed. As for local calls, only their quantity will be printed out on the bill. An example of a typical itemised bill is shown in Plate 17. This sort of data will be stored by BT on microfiche.

Many customers will welcome a detailed explanation of telephone charges – until, perhaps, they realise the privacy implications. For BT, a major attraction of the new system is that it provides much more information about how the telephone system is being used, enables managers to adjust charging arrangements to maximise profitability and – in the longer term – could give the government the option to split up BT into smaller privatised units.

After a trial at Watford, 'live' customer experiments on a computerised billing system began in Bristol in April 1983. Rejecting the opportunity to write its own software, BT had decided to buy in a US-developed Customer Records Information System (CRIS) devised by the Cincinnati Bell telephone company. To produce the information needed for the CSS computers, a series of tests of suitable call-logging computers – each simultaneously monitoring the calls made from about 70,000 lines – began in 1985 in Edinburgh and Leicester, even though the plan to adapt the old Strowger exchanges had already been dropped.

Internal BT reports, marked 'in strictest confidence' but

obtained by the authors, indicate that BT is well aware of the threat to personal privacy that itemised billing creates. For important customers, they propose to suppress the recording of detailed information:[60]

> Certain select lines (for example, the Royal Household, and security installations) will have itemised calls output by the exchange with the telephone number part of the destination already translated into XXXXXXX for privacy reasons.

The CSS network of 32 computer centres and over 30,000 terminals may be fully operational, nationwide, by the early 1990s. Unless the privacy dangers posed by computerised billing information are now addressed urgently, the ability to 'sweep' vast numbers of bills held on CSS computers will enormously add to the power of the telephone tappers. We have already illustrated how even the humble telephone directory, when computerised, becomes a threat to privacy (see page 46).

BT is, naturally, computerising directory enquiry services (and has tested the powerful ICL CAFS storage system for this purpose), and may face commercial pressure to make a telephone directory searching service publicly available – perhaps via the Prestel teletext facility. In France, where a sophisticated system of this kind has already been tested, phones can be supplied with a small screen and attached keyboard to make automated enquiries.

The full administrative details of many other state services, and their associated databanks, are beyond the scope of this book – although many are listed in outline in Table 2, (pages 62-5) and shown in Figure 1 (page 66). Among the larger files not described above are Home Offices systems concerned with the prison and police services. There are about 300,000 records in the prison and parole indexes; and five million in the offenders' index, which is used to prepare criminal statistics. The smaller computerised government systems containing personal information include the Scottish Office's temporary pig subsidy scheme (17,700 names) and the 5900 names on the Central Office of Information's circulation list for *NATO Review*. The last occasion on which a full list of government databanks and their contents was published was in 1975;[61] the list was updated in 1977 as an annex to the Lindop report, and has not been revised or republished since.

For England and Wales, the Department of Education and Science maintains the Further Education Statistical Record (FESR) – containing about two million records on students at polytechnics and higher education colleges. The FESR system has been in operation since 1976; a parallel arrangement run by UCCA (the Universities Central Council on Admissions) records similar data for university students – the Universities Statistical Record. Uniquely, subject access to both FESR and USR has been available since 1970, at a charge of 50p. The subject also has the right to have inaccurate data corrected.

Local education authorities have charge of pupils' records through primary and higher education; in some authorities, this information is kept on computer. Parental access to these records has been a matter of increasing controversy. A 1975 survey found that only one in eight local education authorities at that time were willing to allow parental access to children's school records – and then only with the consent of the head teacher.[62] There are no plans and no reason to centralise school educational records above the local authority level. But in 1977 computer manufacturers ICL suggested an ambitious project to set up a national education network of computers linking schools, local authorities, further education institutes, universities and UCCA.[63]

In proposing the new system, ICL quoted its 'considerable experience of computer networking' – chiefly in setting up the central government general administrative network (GANNET), of which we have more to say in connection with MI5's computers (see page 28). But in this context GANNET was being hopelessly oversold. Technical problems dogged attempts to link one computer to another even a few miles away, let alone nationwide. The GANNET system was dropped by central government for civil computing, but was subsequently used to form a network between computers at Liverpool, Manchester, Salford and Lancaster universities. Like many other ambitious computer projects, this scheme failed because it was too radical for the available technology. But, a decade later, such computer networks are already commonplace.

7 Coming to Notice

According to fashionable new police jargon, espoused in different ways by both the police and their radical critics, policing is 'merely a sub-system of the total system of social control'. That description of 'the Job' was given in 1985 by Metropolitan Police Commissioner Sir Kenneth Newman, as the police and Home Office jointly promoted new multiple-agency ideas about crime control. Comprising the 'total system of social control' are central government departments, including the DHSS; employment, education and environment ministries; and local government agencies, including housing, education, planning and social services. Commissioner Newman's systems theory was a fair summary of the police approach to the search for a new role in the community during the 1980s.

Also included in the new scheme of policing is a much greater swapping of information and co-ordination of plans between agencies. Inside the force itself, this means continuing the trend towards pre-emptive police methods – and, in particular, the identification and 'targeting' of those whom the police think likely to commit crime. The first steps in this process were taken in the 1960s, when the 'unit beat' method of policing was introduced. A little-known aspect of this method was the introduction of local intelligence officers – originally called 'collators' – whose role was to collect all the information reaching the police, from whatever source, analyse it, and prepare indexes and retrieval systems for others to use. It is perhaps worth noting that such practices were in widespread use in Britain long *before* the army moved into Northern Ireland and began compiling card indexes on much of the population there.

The professional fortnightly *Police Review* noted in 1972 that:[1]

> Since 1966, the Service has had collators in most Police divisions and they have amassed information which in both quantity and quality would surprise most people on their books. Police intelligence is now forward looking, anticipating who is going to commit what, when and where ...

Much of this information, the *Review* said, was inevitably also quite inaccurate, 'frequently libellous' and 'tinged with the guesswork of the officer who provided it'. The information held was:

> Personal information [which] may seem a trespass on the freedom of the individual ... There is a serious danger that once a person is in the system he may remain there – there is no way of opting out until the Police consider he has reached the age of criminal ineffectiveness.

Every police force in Britain has established these local intelligence staffs and local intelligence indexes. Every medium-sized or large police station in the country now has a collator. Victims may go into the same card indexes as suspects and, depending on officers' whims and individual forces' standing orders, wide-ranging categories of persons or items of personal information may be recorded. Because intelligence officers examine most reports passing through a police station, their work means that virtually everyone who 'comes to notice' of the police goes on file forthwith. In practice, this is usually at least one in five adults living in the areas policed, and often one in three members of the economically active groups therein. These practices mean that, within a few years, a police computer file will frequently be opened on anyone who has *any* interaction with the police.

Many forces already have computerised intelligence systems, or store some information in computer networks whose primary function is to improve the efficiency of 'command and control' – the moment-by-moment assessment, marshalling and allocation of police resources to meet high-priority tasks. Those forces still lacking an intelligence computer system will nevertheless retain considerable amounts of information on card-index files. Local police intelligence files, computerised or not, are augmented by the Police National

Computer, described in the next chapter. The PNC holds national records (including personal criminal records) previously kept at Scotland Yard, and now provides this data rapidly, on-line, to patrolling police officers.

A typical local police intelligence computer now has the capacity to store 2 gigabytes of information (roughly 300 million words, or 3000 times the length of this book). Soon, most police forces in Britain will have their own information computer systems, with this size of databank available on-line – amounting to perhaps 100 gigabytes of computerised police records held nationally by the end of the decade.

There are two ways in which such stored information may affect police activities. First, in the general surveillance of the public at points of contact with the police system, information may be retrieved and used to guide police action. At the moment such opportunities to use stored information are often dependent on chance encounters, but the situation is likely to change as a result of new rules governing police behaviour towards the public. If the police are permitted to exercise general and complete surveillance – for example, by roadblocks or checkpoints, or compulsory identity cards – then their chances of encountering a wanted party are greatly enhanced. Second, information in police databanks may assist directly in the investigation of crime after it has taken place – either by offering leads from information already available, or through automated processing and analysis of information gathered during a major inquiry.

Police computer effectiveness depends on the police being granted powers to stop and question people about whom they are merely curious, and in a situation where no other course of action is obvious. Computer checks are of no value – and indeed could be a hindrance – in many serious incidents. To a police officer who has just witnessed a robbery, no computer information is needed to guide her or him to a decision to pursue and apprehend the robbers if possible. Nor can the PNC or local intelligence systems be used for directly alerting other patrols if the robbers escape (local 'command and control' computers are used for this instead).

Crucially, to obtain and use computer information, a police officer must be able precisely to identify a person or vehicle. In the case of vehicles, this has always been easy. It has not been so easy with individuals. But from the start of 1986, the police in England and Wales have had the power to create roadblocks of indefinite duration, to identify persons within a vehicle, and to search vehicles if they desire. All that is required for this operation is a written authorisation from a superintendent.

Individual forces' computer terminals are increasingly linked to and through the PNC, and to a small number of regional computer centres. This network will encroach on civil liberties in several ways. The most obvious danger is that, once an individual is viewed in some derogatory light by the police, his or her behaviour will attract increasing attention, and may then be subject to critical and adverse interpretation – further reinforcing police suspicions.

Although they are not sanctioned even in the new police laws (the requirement of 'reasonable suspicion', however hazy, remains a necessary factor), random stop-checks have long been standard police practice. Police internal documents obtained by the authors show the random-stop process in action. The City of London Police, for example, issue standard 'random vehicle check' forms to patrols, on which are entered details of any vehicle checked, the driver and all passengers – including their names and addresses, and where they were seated. Random means 'haphazard, aimless ... done without method or choice'. Random checks are the antithesis of responsive and responsible policing; they put society general-ly under suspicion.

An officer who does not report the results of a sufficient number of checks is regarded as underperforming. The PNC supports extensive random checking by providing a 'multiple vehicle check' facility – hundreds of vehicle numbers may be taken down in the vicinity of a demonstration, for example, and checked on the PNC in batches of six. Of course, vehicle checks need not actually be intrusive or objectionable, if they do not involve being stopped. But, for many, any obvious act of police surveillance is intimidating – particularly given the general demeanour towards the public of many urban police officers – and can provoke guilt and distress among those who have not committed any offence.

Police stop-checks, combined with rapid communications

and rapid data retrieval, draw a surveillance net across society. It is a quite novel situation when a police officer may stop someone to ask questions or carry out a vehicle check, not because of active suspicion about a particular crime, but to maintain policing norms for such checks, or on whim to see what information a computer may happen to retrieve. The rapid availability of data can itself encourage some kinds of abuse; for example, by the male policeman who used the PNC to discover the addresses of attractive women drivers.

Absolutely reliable personal identity checks would only be possible if national identity cards (which had to be shown on demand to police) were to be introduced. This is, in our view, still a remote (although increasing) possibility – barring the occurrence of major new terrorist activities in the UK which authoritarian politicians might choose to exploit. Nevertheless, new police powers produce, in effect, the same result in many circumstances. Powers are now generally available to enforce what are in practice non-judicial punishments, such as police detention without arrest (only permitted in Scotland at present).

Two new laws are responsible. In Scotland, the Criminal Justice (Scotland) Act of 1980 gave constables the right to demand the name and address of anyone who was either a suspect or a potential witness to a crime. Any person refusing to provide this information, giving false information, or refusing to wait while her or his identity is verified, is now liable to arrest and, on conviction, to a fine of £50. Constables in Scotland may detain anyone in a police station for up to six hours' questioning, without arresting them. In the 1984 Police and Criminal Evidence Act (generally applying only to England and Wales), the police were also granted general powers to stop and search any person or vehicle if there are 'reasonable grounds' for suspecting that stolen or prohibited articles will be found. Name or vehicle checks on computer will normally follow.

But police officers' suspicions or judgement of 'reasonable grounds' are wrong at least 90 per cent of the time. Official evidence suggests that, even in London, fewer than one in 50 police stops will lead to arrest and conviction. A 1983 Home Office study reported that, at best, 8 per cent of stops resulted in arrests; outside London, the comparable figure (measured in Luton and Watford) was 2 per cent.[2] Even within London, the researchers reported, it was 'estimated that up to one half of all stops made are not recorded ... this suggests that the percentage of prosecutions resulting could be as low as 4 per cent in London' (and 1 per cent outside). Since conviction does not necessarily follow arrest, it is probable that the percentage of innocent persons who are subjected to stop-checks lies between 96 and 99 per cent.

Another part of the 1984 Police and Criminal Evidence Act overturned a long-standing presumption about the role of the police – that their powers to use force were (in theory) no greater than those possessed by the ordinary citizen in common law. Section 117 now allows the police to use 'reasonable force' to enforce any other power in the Act.

During 1985, the PNC and other computers were used on at least 11.5 million occasions for personal checks. A few of these checks were used to update indexes; others were made in police stations during administrative or detective work. But most checks are made on the streets. Even if the percentage of stop-checks on innocent parties were to be as low as 90 per cent, it follows that over 10 million annual stops – and PNC checks – are made on innocent people. This was also the finding of a 1983 report on the policing of London by the Police Studies Institute (PSI), commissioned by the Metropolitan Police themselves. Moreover, some of the crimes 'detected' by stop-checks are actually *created* by the stop-check; prosecutions for obstructing the police or assault on a police officer reported after a stop-check are evidently the result of the initial police action, not its cause. The PSI researchers also noted that a police stop-check was in itself often offensive and punitive:[3]

> Most people stopped are innocent ... and they are unhappy about the way the police handle the incident ... Our observations produced examples of a number of cases where officers behaved rudely or abusively to people they had stopped and who were not shown to have committed an offence.

Being stopped in this fashion is in itself an infringement of liberty. The available evidence on police performance does not suggest that it is an infringement which can be justified in the

wider interests of society. Another analysis, prepared directly
by the Metropolitan Police, confirmed the low arrest results
from stop-checks found in the earlier PSI and Home Office studies. In 1984, 91 per cent of those stopped were not arrested.[4]

Some forces now use computers to collate information
gathered from stop-checks. The automatic collation of stop-
check records takes surveillance one stage further, by providing a historical police record of where people have been. Metropolitan Police standing orders require officers to complete a
crime intelligence/stop report form on every actual stop, as
well as on sighting or stopping 'suspects, known criminals and
their vehicles ... all forms will be passed to the Collator for his
information prior to disposal as confidential waste'.[5] This data
may even be used to generate further indexes of suspicion.
Suffolk Constabulary standing orders regard three successive
stop-checks at night in a four-week period of time as *prima
facie* evidence of suspicious behaviour on the part of the
person stopped – who is then permanently entered on the
computer as a 'suspect' (although no suspected crime is
specified).

To date, however, it has been impossible for Home Office
scientists to show that local computer networks improve
detection rates or other measures of police effectiveness. Since
any such computer project draws heavily on capital and
personnel resources, they may even have the opposite effect.
In computerising their local intelligence indexes at a time
when data protection has been under extensive discussion,
the police themselves have come under a certain degree of
community control. Some forces have been required to
exercise great restraint and caution as to what data they hold
on computer, compared to what they might have stored on
manual files and card indexes.

The appointing of police 'local intelligence officers' to supervise surveillance of the community, and to keep files on its
members, seems somehow to have an un-British air about it; it
is the sort of thing that 'does not happen here'. But it has been
happening for 20 years, since the newly created collators
of the unit beat system were given the task of systematically
transforming the street knowledge and observations once

made by individual beat police officers into a collective data-bank on people, property and events.

Although there has been no organised conspiracy of silence about the police local intelligence system, it is nevertheless remarkable that public material on the police – ranging from formal research studies to popular TV series – show a complete lack of awareness of the collator's fundamental role. But visit a police constable's working area in any police station, and you will usually see many reminders that handing in the day's information takings to the collator should be, for them, as routine as clearing the till at night is to a shop assistant. The collator system was an early attempt to do what, say, the 'whole person concept' does for the DHSS: to bring together in one place all information about an individual's dealings with the police.

One of the few official descriptions of the collator system is contained in an HMSO careers booklet for schoolchildren, which portrays the job in terms so bizarre and outdated as to be extremely funny. The career-seeking child is told of Policeman John the Collator, who works on 'building up a kind of "memory bank" ... Like a kind of "human computer", John stores this information and produces it on demand.' The information he collects, the booklet says, will be 'useful in helping the police to help the public'. The examples of a collator's work then given include providing enquirers with a list of vets or chemists open on early-closing days, or general information about local industrial production, or advice on social security entitlement, or even suggestions as to where to hire a hall for a public meeting (!).

The real duties of a police collator are described at length in a Merseyside Police document, *Functions and Duties of Each Rank*, obtained by the authors. The document contains a series of police job descriptions, including those for resident beat constables – often called 'area' or 'community' constables. Although Chief Constables can vary these duties as they desire, the similarities in the descriptions given across a range of forces are striking. The words about obtaining 'an informant in every street' which preface this book, for example, are drawn from the description of an area constable's duties in the Lothian and Borders Police. Similarly, a Merseyside resident beat constable is told that he should have 'a contact who is confident in him in every road and street'.

Merseyside area constables are also told to enlist the help of 'local officials, shopkeepers, tradesmen, garage proprietors and other reliable persons'. The instructions add that 'bus drivers and conductors, railway employees, taxi drivers and postmen are out at varying times throughout twenty-four hours' and can help 'in many ways'. But they are warned that 'the amount of information passed to the Collator will indicate the constable's effectiveness'.

Lothian and Borders area constables are told to enlist the help of 'local officials ... [and] shopkeepers, tradesmen, and garage proprietors who are always a good source of information'. The instructions add that 'bus drivers and conductors, railway employees, taxi drivers and postmen who are out at varying times throughout the day and night' can help too. But the constables are warned that their 'effectiveness to some degree will be judged by the amount of intelligence [they] feed into the Divisional Intelligence Officers [Collators]'. 'Local officials' are held to be of value because they have 'legitimate access to private houses and premises'.

The similarity of wording and phrasing clearly indicates a common origin in circulars and guidance issued either by ACPO (the Association of Chief Police Officers) or by the Home Office (and Scottish Office). In the new scheme of policing in the 1980s, community constables are not the benign and approachable local officers of the media myth – that image is, in a sense, 'cover' for the real job. They are expected, if need be, to exercise guile and deception in acquiring the information they seek. They are the collators' front-line information-gatherers in the field. In the last few years, the explicit intelligence-gathering role has been expanded by adding field intelligence officers to the collators' teams. Sometimes known as crime patrols, they are relieved of specific patrol or crime investigation duties and given the task of carrying out specialised surveillance in the streets.

Collators, according to these instructions, are expected to work only in a 'secure' office, to which other police officers do not have automatic access. The guiding principles of the collators' work are that:

All items, however insignificant, will be recorded and indexed, and will be available to all personnel at all times. The Collator will decide what information he considers could be of assistance to other intelligence sections … and ensure that such information is passed on … [Our emphasis.]

In the Merseyside Police, a collator is required to set up and maintain six card indexes:

(a) Daily Record Sheets [i.e., an event/date index of all information coming in]
(b) Intelligence Index [on people]
(c) Vehicle Index
(d) Local Modus Operandi Index [notable criminal methods]
(e) Street Index
(f) Miscellaneous Index

The intelligence index is a nominal card index:

giving details of all persons who have come to notice. This is an alphabetical index, and each card will contain full names of each person, their dates of birth, addresses, and any Daily Record number referring to information received regarding the person.

The intelligence cards would also cross-refer to all the other indexes. 'As much detail as possible' should be collected, the instructions say, and 'every effort must be made to keep this index up to date with all information received'.

Similar 'section intelligence–subject index' cards used by the Metropolitan Police provide space to record (racial) 'identity codes', descriptions, 'associates' and the name of any police officer who knows the subjects by sight.

The 'beat-street index' is used to identify houses and premises that a beat officer should keep under surveillance, or otherwise be aware of. The index is in alphabetical order of streets on the beat. Any information received concerning a person living at a particular address is used to generate a new entry. Other indexes, such as the vehicle index, have self-explanatory functions. Instructions are given for the regular weeding of the vehicle index of entries more than two years old, but none are issued for the regular weeding of the other indexes.

'The Collator's office,' the document says, 'should be an Information Bureau in addition to a Criminal Intelligence

Office.' Collators are also asked to display maps and charts of the crimes reported on each beat. Regular, force-wide collators' conferences are held, with similar regional inter-force meetings taking place quarterly. Another practice, which is standard throughout the country, is the circulation of regular collator bulletins, which are intended to 'inform police officers of items of intelligence', and which should not contain '[police station] domestic gossip ... stolen bicycles' or similar trivia. They should be serial-numbered and kept in conditions of high security. But the bulletin should be 'well set out and presented in a manner designed to make it interesting and easily readable'.

The latter requirement results in bulletins being written in (to put it kindly) a conversational manner and, often, the adoption of folksy titles and headlines. In London, for example, L (Lima) Division at Brixton has the 'Lima Lantern'; Shepherds Bush police have the 'Bush Telegraph'. Other bulletins may have more prosaic titles but more titillating headlines: for example, 'A Bad Case of the Benz' (Lancashire Police, regarding stolen cars of German manufacture); or 'Change of Partners' (Thames Valley Police, regarding some alleged drugs users' sexual lives).

On at least ten occasions on which information about local intelligence records or bulletins have been leaked, straight-forward fact has been found to be mixed with speculative observation – chatty but often sneering, sometimes bigoted and frequently highly prejudiced. Such 'raw' collator material does contain a great deal of apparently unexceptionable police reporting – 'unexceptionable' in the sense that *prima facie* many of the reports seem to have clear justification, such as reports of suspicious behaviour or of encounters with drug users administering injections to each other. But they also frequently contain highly derogatory comments whose accuracy is impossible to test without specific investigation.

Commonly, close attention is paid to the whereabouts and movements of known and (usually) convicted offenders – a practice which may often be justified, but when unsupervised carries the danger of reinforcing an unjust portrayal of a given individual. Another widespread pattern involves giving special attention to, or at any rate making special mention of, those in the community whom some in the police regard as less worthy than the ordinary citizen – 'druggies'; 'our African brethren'; 'homosexual types'; 'state benefit subscribers'; and so on.

The 'miscellaneous' categories in the indexes compiled can reflect other kinds of prejudice. A former Essex police officer wrote to the NCCL in 1975 that 'the collator at Brentwood kept an index file on "political" matters, although this was fairly sparse'. But it included communists and 'members of other subversive groups'. The collator at this station, the police officer wrote, had files not just on known and suspected criminals, 'but also on ordinary and innocent people who are about their normal work, or social affairs'.

Collators in the Manchester Police used red stars to indicate both sex offenders and others they regard as sexually deviant. A collator in the Thames Valley Police, the workings of whose office was studied by researchers, held an index of 'cows, queers, and flashers'. Daily record sheets in the same office gave further indications of general prejudices of this kind – stop-check records included such descriptive terms as 'effeminate appearance' or 'grossly obese'. This sort of data may also be put on the PNC (see page 242). In Lothians and Border Police collators' offices, 'indecencies' indexes include innocent homosexuals, on the absurd grounds that they are 'a danger to themselves'.[6]

In gathering this type of intelligence, Manchester Police were caught in October 1982 using a concealed camera to film men visiting a gay club in the centre of the city. This led to local protests, and in due course the police apologised for having secretly entered the offices of a nearby youth advice organisation, '42nd Street', to position and operate their camera. A disturbing demonstration of the vulnerability of such local records to leakage emerged in 1981. The Merseyside criminal records office passed information about the sexual preferences of a local man to an anonymous telephone caller posing as a police officer, telling the caller of the subject, 'He's a homosexual.'[7]

In 1982, one young man found that there was astonishing information about himself in a computerised Lincolnshire Police collator dossier. At the age of 18, he pleaded guilty to a burglary charge. Before sentence was passed, police officers attempted to show magistrates a 'criminal record' which alleged burglary at the age of 8 (before the age of criminal responsibility); and an 'indecent assault' on a female, at the age of 11. This 'offence', which the girl concerned had declined to pursue, was logged on the police computer as: PUSHED GIRL TO GROUND PUT HIS HAND UP HER SWEATER. Similarly prejudicial to a co-defendant on the same occasion was a police record from the criminal information computer recording that the subject had been stopped twice for 'namechecks'; there had been no offence alleged, arrest made, nor charge brought, yet, in the eyes of magistrates, the fact of recorded police checks might well attach suspicion to the person concerned.[8]

Despite assurances to the contrary, the case above is typical of many occasions on which computers have relentlessly disgorged years-old data highly prejudicial to the subject but of no contemporary policing value. When one Worcester man, Edward Winsbury, reported the theft of stereo and television equipment from his home, the situation rapidly turned into a long nightmare. After the end of the Second World War, Winsbury had left his unit without permission, and a 32-year-old allegation of desertion had been retained on permanent records and transferred to the PNC. Although suffering from a severe spinal injury, Winsbury was charged and taken into military custody for two days.

Not all police prejudices are quite so predictable as those described above. Some collator index cards lost by a Brixton detective said of their subject, a fruit and vegetable dealer: 'REMEMBER most receivers are greengrocers and most greengrocers are receivers??????????'[9] Other cards lost at the same time dealt with members of a particular family, the 'Wilsons' (who have asked for their real name to be withheld). Mrs Carol Wilson's card showed that she had been the subject of a dossier for four years, ever since her car was seen outside an address being watched by detectives of the Serious Crimes Squad. She was not there at the time, knew neither the householder nor the address, nor had she ever committed or been suspected of any offence. But the card was never weeded; on the contrary, it was updated with her new address and vehicle registration, based on information gleaned about her children. A card on her son Joe had recorded an informant's tipoff that the youth had been overheard talking about 'nicked stereo gear' three years earlier. No investigation took place, and the report could have been inaccurate or malicious. Anyway, the truth would be impossible to determine three years later. But the information was not weeded. Other cards on the Wilson family showed that three friends of another son, who had convictions, had become the subject of 'associates' files because they had been with him one day when he was stopped. On another occasion, this son was singled out for attention and searching by the Special Patrol Group while at home washing his father's car – probably as a direct result of his appearance on the collator's files.[10]

Inaccurate and maliciously provided information can enter and be disseminated in police records systems. A Plaid Cymru political activist, Robert Griffiths, saw part of his own files in 1982, when they were produced as 'antecedents' before magistrates who were considering a charge against him of 'conspiracy to damage property'. The antecedents included copious details about a teaching job he never had – specifying the period he was 'employed', the school, a note that he had left his previous job as a result of a 'difference of opinion', and a comment that he had been sacked from a subsequent post for 'extremist views'. All the information was untrue.[11]

Senior police officers have themselves suffered badly from malicious information entered on computer systems. Officers in one force placed an unpopular superintendent on the wanted/missing index of the PNC, adding in the 'warnings' section that the wanted man impersonated a police officer 'convincingly'. The superintendent was arrested and held overnight in London a few months later.[12] The head of the Merseyside Police computer team, Chief Inspector Gordon Fraser, in a review of European police computer systems, described a case in which one senior officer had been recorded as a mental defective who should be taken to the nearest mental hospital if found in the street; in another case an officer was described as disease-ridden, and there were instructions that he be fumigated if apprehended.[13]

The scale of collator recordkeeping has been demonstrated on a number of occasions. The Thames Valley Collator Project computer, for example, (described below) was designed to

hold information on about 10 per cent of the local population –
roughly double the number of people who would have
criminal records. Between one quarter and one third of adult
males in the Thames Valley area could expect to have records
on the computer. In Edinburgh, researchers have estimated
that one in three young working-class men will be the 'subject
of covert criminal intelligence reports'.[14]

Such estimates were fully confirmed when information
about police 'vetting' checks on a panel of prospective jurors
for the politically sensitive 'Anarchists Anonymous' trial was
leaked in 1979. It was found that over 20 per cent (19 of 91) of the
would-be jurors were the subject of police collator files. But
fewer than half (eight) had criminal records, of whom only five
were definitely identified. Five were recorded as the victims of
crime, three had family members who had been convicted, one
was said to be an associate of someone with a criminal record,
one had an address 'believed' to be a squat, and the remaining
person had gained a police record for having made a complaint against the police.[15]

The practice of mixing criminals willy-nilly with their
victims in police databanks is widespread and well established. So too is the habit of opening a file on anyone who
makes a complaint against the police. The Metropolitan Police
standing orders, for example, require that 'if a stop[check] is
resented, the circumstances are to be fully reported . . .'[16] They
also acknowledge that victims of crime 'may . . . but not
necessarily' go onto section intelligence indexes. There was, in
1979, 'no set procedure' for removing from records out-of-date
or irrelevant information.[17]

As the Lindop committee noted, 'the linking of factual
personal information with speculative data about criminal
activity could pose a grave threat to that individual's interests'.
The committee concluded that:

> It may sometimes be necessary, in special circumstances and in
> the interests of law and order, to do this, but we think it should be
> done with caution and subject to the most stringent safeguards.

They did not anticipate 'immediate grave dangers' from police
criminal intelligence computer systems, but did fear that:[18]

> There is a potential danger to the subject's privacy which could

increase with the extension of these applications over the next ten years.

This danger is evident from the collator bulletins we have seen. The most frequent type of entry urges police officers into stern action against the targets described therein. For example, according to the Lancashire Police, '[A and B] are worth every stop/check they can get', 'anyone using one of [C's] cars should be worth a stop/search'; 'it will be interesting to see who visits the new couple', 'he must be a good bet in the near future' (Thames Valley); 'this vehicle is well worth a stop', 'let us get him before he does anything more serious', 'both might be worth turning over' (Metropolitan Police). In all cases, if the targets are the threat police believe them to be, society is well served; if they are not, then such people have good grounds for grievance against the police.

Because of these contradictions, the solution to the problem cannot lie in banning the creation of records. Rather, it lies in making the police far more accountable than at present for the way they deal with the public, and for the way in which, in the longer term, they operate their records systems. It is clearly ridiculous to operate subject-access provisions which enable a local burglar or rapist to call on the police every Saturday to see if he has slipped up and the detectives are closing in; equally, it is intolerable that the police should have free rein to hold indefinitely *and use* the sort of information we have described above.

Incident after incident has demonstrated the extraordinary range and very variable quality of information which is now held on collator records and police computers. Over the last decade, for example, British police forces have collected and systematically compiled personal records on:

The membership of protest groups.

Anyone who protests about being stopped by police.

Those attending gay clubs.

The owners of vehicles seen parked near certain demonstrations or political meetings.

The owners of vehicles seen parked near the houses of suspected persons.

The victims of crime.

Those alleged to be 'associates' of criminals.

Parents and other family members of those with criminal records.

Those who have made complaints against the police.

Over 20 per cent of the adult population in most parts of Britain, irrespective of any involvement in crime, for 'local intelligence' purposes.

Cases in each of these categories are well documented; none is an isolated aberration. When, for example, former Devon and Cornwall Chief Constable John Alderson ordered a review of local Special Branch files, he found all but 20 of their personal records irrelevant to police purposes. Among other things, the Special Branch had recorded Tony Benn's lunch appointments when he was in the area. Animal rights' activists discovered that the membership of the Hunt Saboteurs Association was logged on the PNC, after three members of the organisation were stopped by police. The Cumbria grave of huntsman John Peel had just been desecrated. During the check, according to the prosecution in a subsequent case:[19]

> The car was checked out on the Police National Computer. [The police officer] was told that the owner was a prominent member of the Anti-Blood Sports League.

A month after this event, Hunt Saboteurs Association members observed police officers recording the registrations of cars at anti-hunt demonstrations. An Oxfordshire policeman also admitted in evidence that he regularly reported the registrations of vehicles seen in the driveway of the private home of one of the association's leading members.

Members of the Campaign for Nuclear Disarmament and most other lawful campaigning groups have frequently had similar experiences. In London, police now attempt to have all organisers of political meetings fill in a standard form giving details of key officials and speakers; the reports, passed first to Scotland Yard's A8 public order division, wind up in the Special Branch's extensive subject dossiers.

*   *   *

Police headquarters and control rooms have featured electronic equipment on a small scale since the 1960s. But the first police force computers, used for 'command and control', did not enter service until 1972. Four urban, or predominantly urban, police forces – West Midlands, Strathclyde, West Yorkshire and Staffordshire – were the first to obtain such computers. Their use spread rapidly and, by 1978, eight forces had them; all but two of these had direct access to the PNC through local terminals. By 1980, more than 25 forces had ordered or installed command and control computers. These computers, however, were in the main to be used for passing messages, checking and displaying the availability of police resources, or for map displays and similar tasks – not for criminal information or intelligence.

Storage systems for criminal information were slower to develop. After preliminary experiments in 1972, the Home Office offered to finance Thames Valley Police (TVP) to develop and test a computer for local intelligence records – the Collator Project. A Honeywell computer system was installed at TVP's Kidlington headquarters in 1975, and came into operation in August 1977. The system stores information about people, vehicles, 'occurrences' (events), crimes, and 'places' (public places or addresses). By the start of 1981, the computer held 135,000 nominal records, 114,000 occurrence records, and 111,000 house or place records. There were then relatively few records on actual crimes (about 22,000) or vehicles (25,000). Connected to the Kidlington computer centre were 35 terminals at 21 separate sites. Terminals at the force control centre and criminal records office were so arranged that four of six radio operators receiving incoming information requests had easy access both to the PNC and the Collator Project computer.

The number of personal dossiers on this system was growing at the rate of 700 new and 4000 updated records every week, according to statistics in a TVP internal computer feasibility study prepared in 1981. By mid-1986, therefore, 300,000 or more 'nominal' records could have been accumulated on the TVP computer – more than 15 per cent of the entire population of Oxfordshire, Buckinghamshire and Berkshire. In 1986, however, TVP stated that the nominal index held about 162,000 records; growth had slowed. TVP officers have since claimed that these raw figures can be 'misleading' and do not necessarily mean that 30 to 40 per cent of adults in their area are now on computer. Senior officers have argued that up to 30 per cent of the records held are on people living outside the immediate force area, while some other records could be 'distortions' such as multiple statistical entries caused by, say, 'one criminal with 15 aliases'.[20]

The latter claim appears spurious. Details of the TVP records formats published by the Home Office in 1976 show that a *single* nominal record has space for an almost unlimited number of aliases. The nature of these formats helps to explain the enormous growth in files, and shows that there are three equal reasons for a person's name to be recorded: 'offender in crime'; 'suspected in crime'; or *aggrieved* in crime' (our emphasis). People can be linked to houses or places as either 'frequenters' or 'occupants'. Standard spaces are also provided for everything from employment and postcode to driving disqualification, from date of birth to 'gait', 'manner' or 'habits'.[21] The police statistics also show that most computer checks were made on people (about 2000 to 3000 a week) and locations (500 a week). But many more personal checks are made on card indexes, which the computer updates daily. A card index provides both a back-up system if the computer fails and easier access to the information for station officers. Other records were checked only infrequently; most enquiries about vehicles, for example, were directed to the PNC.

The TVP computer was the first to use a full-scale 'database' system in which records could be interlinked in a great variety of ways. Each person's record was stored only once, although the same data about them would appear in response to any enquiries about vehicles, places, occurrences or associates. The database system, called IDS/II, employed 'pointers' to link records. Each person could be linked to up to 100 separate occurrences, addresses, and so on. But the Honeywell IDS/II system was known for its uneven performance, and there was subsequently no attempt to copy or repeat the Thames Valley project elsewhere. The Home Office pulled out of the project in October 1981, and their research moved in a different direction.

Nevertheless, after the Home Office's five-year experiment

had finished, TVP wanted to take over, continue with and eventually expand the Collator computer. In September 1981, the force sought and obtained the approval of their police authority to purchase a replacement computer, a Honeywell DPS8. The decision to do this, taken despite fierce opposition from some authority members, was made six months *before* the completion of a highly critical Home Office evaluation report on the project.

The Collator Project had proved controversial from the beginning. It had only been in operation for eight months when two American visitors from the FBI saw the system at the Home Office's invitation, and were 'horrified'. They told British newspapers that the computer had produced fourth-hand gossip about one man's alleged sexual tastes. This now well-known example of gossip and innuendo finding its way into police computers was revealed by the *Police Review* in 1978. During a demonstration of the system the US visitors happened to be shown a record on a local man who, it was claimed, 'fancied little boys'. The source of this extraordinarily damaging allegation was anonymous gossip in the village shop which had been overheard by a policeman's wife, reported in an occurrence book by the policeman, extracted by the collator, transferred to the computer, and would now be regurgitated if any enquiry were to be made about the man via police computer terminals. The allegation was untrue, the magazine reported, and typical of the 'substantial proportion [of] unchecked bunkum' on local intelligence files.[22]

Because of events like this, the force's 1981 feasibility study predicted that their computer would fall foul of then strict Home Office guidelines about linking police computer systems. The study said, 'It is unlikely in our case that a link [with the PNC] would be allowed to the criminal intelligence computer.' But the new computer came into operation nonetheless in 1984. The £800,000 system has 75 on-line terminals, and 800 megabytes of on-line data storage – a substantial increase on the size of the previous disc store, and enough in theory for 100 words of description on every one of the area's 1.77 million inhabitants. A separate command and control computer system has also been installed.

All this occurred despite the Home Office research report,

published in March 1982, which should have been the Collator Project's obituary. The project was found to have had 'no effect' on crime, according to two internal Home Office studies. It was said to be impossible to show that police 'criminal intelligence' computer systems have any value in fighting crime. The evaluation team commented bluntly on the effectiveness of the criminal intelligence computer in combating crime, 'It is impossible to detect any change in the crime statistics that can be unambiguously attributed to the presence of this system.'[23] No 'strong direct effect' in reducing crime had resulted from the use of the intelligence computer, the researchers reported, adding that 'if [such an effect] existed, it is unlikely that it would have been overlooked during ... an extended period'.

According to official figures, the crime detection rate in the Thames Valley area in 1975 was 45 per cent. In 1979, after the computer had been in full operation for 18 months, the detection rate was actually *worse*, at 44.8 per cent. This is not a significant difference – but the figures demonstrate that the computer was not helping.

The Home Office report pointed out that many 'police forces seem to place great emphasis on indirect retrieval' – where the computer is asked to search for some unknown person or event with specified features. This is the facility provided by 'searching on multiple keys', or by using free text retrieval systems (see page 42). But the research team found that as few as one in 3000 crimes were solved in this way – and only then in cases where the offender had been seen at the time of the crime. Moreover, such searches were hampered by the 'inaccuracy and incompleteness of the recorded data' against which checks could be performed. They also found that many Thames Valley police officers were anyway sceptical about the value of the computer. More than one in three officers told the Home Office that, in their view, 'no use would be served by using the system'.

Ironically, and despite the huge growth in personal records held on the Thames Valley computer, and its likely exemption from subject access provisions under the new Data Protection Act, the Home Office's internal report claims that putting police intelligence files on computer may actually prevent the police from recording unverified or inaccurate and damaging personal information. Because it is computer-based, 'the system seems to carry less unsubstantiated information and more matters of public record'. The researchers found that the system had 'shifted somewhat from being an intelligence system':

> It is believed that this is partly because users are less likely to risk inserting sensitive or potentially embarrassing data which might be seen by a large number of police officers ...

Members of the Thames Valley Police Authority were eventually provided with copies of the Home Office's evaluation report. But they were not permitted to discuss the report's findings until after they had voted to buy the new computer system to keep the Collator Project going. The problem of proving criminal intelligence computers to be of any value to the public in clearing up crime was, said the report, 'intractable'. The 1984/85 Home Office annual report on the police research programme added that, so far as 'crime and criminal [information] computer systems' are concerned, 'quantitative measures of benefit are as elusive as ever'.

Before these cautionary words had been written, however, the Home Office's Scientific Research and Development Branch had already embarked on a second phase of police intelligence computerisation. The chosen police forces on this occasion were Kent and Humberside. It took three years of Home Office persuasion, until 1980, to get the two constabularies to work together, and a further three years for all parties to join with the government Central Computing and Telecommunications Agency and agree on suitable computer and software suppliers. In 1983, a contract was awarded to Software Sciences Ltd, and to Burroughs for the supply of four Burroughs B5900 computers and 200 terminals for the two forces (132 for Kent, 70 for Humberside). Each computer would have 2 gigabytes of storage for 'crime and criminal information' data. The project was announced as 'an important step towards nationwide standards' for such computer applications; it was 'envisaged that the detailed specification may be adopted in part or in whole by other police forces'.

In Kent the police converted 60,000 of 130,000 existing

collator records to computer file. Twelve unemployed people were specially taken on under the Community Enterprise Scheme to do this work. Direct computer-to-computer PNC links were also provided for both installations, which entered service early in 1986. The functions of each computer are to store crime intelligence (nominal collator records and details of convictions), to maintain an incident record on crimes and occurrences, and to transfer messages between police stations. Free text searches can also be carried out. Police representatives have stressed that the criminal information application will only store details of those 'convicted of a recordable offence'. But details of victims of crime, and of suspects, will still be recorded in the 'crime reporting' databank.

Merseyside Police had intended to adopt a similar system, having in 1980 purchased a single identical Burroughs computer from Software Sciences to run their command and control systems. A crime and criminal information system, storing both criminal records and criminal intelligence, was planned by the police as a second phase. But, late in 1982, the Merseyside Police Authority refused to pay for the computer unless the police agreed a data protection code of practice for criminal information going into the system. Among the safeguards required was the exclusion of intelligence information and the appointment of an outside supervisor to oversee the storage and use of personal data. After the police had agreed to seven safeguards in April 1983, the Police Authority agreed to buy the £1.5 million computer.

But a further row broke out a year later when the authority discovered that most of the facilities they had agreed to pay for were in any case due to be provided nationally by the PNC; they became extremely suspicious about the honesty of the police in stating their intentions for the system. The police also reneged on their commitment to allow independent monitoring, claiming during 1984 that the job could be done by the Data Protection Registrar instead. In consequence, the scheme was held up indefinitely.

West Yorkshire Police Authority expressed similar concerns, and in 1982 refused to fund a £1.7 million computer until the data protection and privacy questions had been considered. West Midlands Police anticipated rows on this issue when, in

1983, before the passing of the Data Protection Act, they adopted their own code of practice. They decided not to link a planned new £3.5 million criminal information system to either the PNC or local command and control computers.

By 1985, however, a stream of other police forces less constrained than Merseyside had embarked on wholesale criminal intelligence computerisation. In Edinburgh, the Lothian and Borders Police had purchased a dual Honeywell computer, 2 gigabytes of data storage, 130 terminals and the Status free text retrieval system. By November 1981, the Lothian and Borders computer held 70,000 crime reports and over 30,000 other records; the police refused to divulge how many personal records were held on a 'nominal file'. But the number of manual collator records held by the force before computer-isation is known – some 80,000, or roughly one for every ten of the local population. These figures, moreover, cover only the central intelligence records; other records are compiled by divisional and sub-divisional collators.[24]

The nominal file holds details of 'criminals of active interest to the police, their personal details, associates and vehicles used. It is also hoped to include a "stop-check" facility to record their movements.' There is a free text 'scratch pad' facility into which officers can enter unstructured data. Although the most frequently given example of a possible scratch-pad entry is a nickname for a public house, it will be apparent that any type of data, including personal or political information, could be included in a databank of this kind.

The Lothian and Borders Police computer is linked to both the PNC and the Scottish Criminal Records Office (SCRO). An enquiry about a name or vehicle is automatically checked against all three computers. The SCRO is another Honeywell computer centre, located in Glasgow, with 1.4 million records on file. It provides a regional criminal records and information office, serving Scotland. The computer's attributes include a 'multi-search facility on information relating to convicted criminals'.[25] Another Honeywell police computer system was ordered by South Wales Constabulary in June 1983. It will have 70 terminals operating an incident and resource information system, and is due to come into operation in 1987.

*   *   *

Manchester Police ordered another major computer system, whose original specification gives it a dramatically intrusive potential. As part of a 'computer-assisted policing' (CAP) scheme, the Manchester Criminal Records Office (MANCRO) willl hold records on some 300,000 people. It too has a 2 gigabyte storage capacity. The Manchester computer system was the result of a design study by outside consultants PACTEL during 1978 and 1979. They recommended the computerisation of the MANCRO criminal records, and the installation of an 'information support' system, which would computerise divisional collators' records:

> Collators' manually maintained information should be so organised as to be readily available to support enquiries placed upon it (latterly through pointers in the computer-held MANCRO nominal records), pending any possible future changeover to a computerised system for collators' records.

There was, suspected PACTEL:

> [a] strong latent demand for access to collator-held information ... A major characteristic of these demands is that they largely arise in the field and should, ideally, be met there within seconds if the information is to be fully effective ... Any officer on patrol [should have] access by radio to a facility ... that is equipped to retrieve and relay the information pertinent to his enquiry.

In other words, all collator information, of whatever quality or reliability, should be instantly available to a patrolling police officer who happens to encounter the subject of the data.

PACTEL estimated that, if their suggestions were adopted, computerisation would produce a tenfold increase in checks on collator records over a ten-year period. This would imply that, by 1995, there would be some 36,000 checks a day, or 13 million stop-checks a year, on the streets of Manchester: an immense extension of surveillance and intrusion into the lives of ordinary citizens. It was an extraordinary claim to make without further comment. The consultants, whose report was prepared 'in close consultation' with Home Office scientists, nevertheless went on to suggest new computer link-ups, including:

> Further cross-referencing of vehicles and persons, including possible access to DVLC information.

Cross-indexing ... to permit inter-force enquiries on persons' names.

But the report, written in 1979, notes that 'the present political climate is not favourable to the retention of such data [collators' records] on police computers'. The police were also advised to install the computer in 'hardened' facilities to ensure survivability under physical attack. Portraying the Manchester Police and their computer centre almost as though they were an alien occupation force fearing a popular uprising, the consultants warned that:

> The time when the full power of the Force's CAP (Computer Assisted Policing) may most be required could be under conditions of the severest threat.

This paranoia-tinged vision culminated in the suggestion that even police officers should not be allowed near the computer or its terminals except subject to 'positive personnel clearance'.

The Manchester contract went to computer software company Logica, but was not, according to reports, profitable or successful for the company. Both the Manchester project and a similar criminal information databank for Northumbria Police ran well over time and cost for the suppliers. Logica, and Northumbria contractors SPL, were both reckoned to have lost millions of pounds on the deals. The £2 million Northumbria Police system, now installed at the force's Morpeth headquarters, has a 2 gigabyte database, is linked to the PNC and 111 local terminals and uses American Tandem computers.

An alternative to free text retrieval software is ICL's Contents Addressable File Store (CAFS). Eager to make its entry on the police computer market, ICL sold a type 2955 computer with a 800 megabyte CAFS and 70 terminals to North Yorkshire Police at a bargain price in 1982. The system allows for wide-ranging searches of unstructured information held in the CAFS disc store. The officer in charge of the system, Chief Superintendent David Severs, said, 'It is possible to search unformatted with very little training. It's very exciting for us.' He later asserted that the North Yorkshire computer was 'an incident logging system ... not an intelligence system'.[26] In fact, in the case of CAFS, the distinction is meaningless, since reports of incidents are about people, and that information – including details of victims and suspects – is held on computer. In one 'live' demonstration, the CAFS-equipped computer found 120 references to 'window cleaners' in the files in eight seconds – a much faster performance than a 'software' text retrieval system.[27]

Tayside, Hampshire and Cheshire Police have all stored criminal intelligence information in computers shared with their local authorities, a procedure that is now widely regarded as unacceptable. Other, smaller police computer information systems have been installed by police forces in Durham, Dorset, Devon and Cornwall, South Yorkshire, Lancashire, West Mercia and Lincolnshire. The Suffolk Police criminal information system was one of the first to be installed, in 1977. By 1983, it held over 93,000 entries in its nominal index, corresponding to about one in six of the local population. Sussex Police ordered a £1.2 million criminal information and incident logging system in 1981. Other systems have been or will be installed by all the Scottish police forces, by West Yorkshire and Essex Police, and by the Royal Ulster Constabulary.

The largest computer network of all is that being installed by the Metropolitan Police, the first phase of which opened in October 1984. A £24 million computer complex at New Scotland Yard, used to log emergency calls and incident reports, is linked to 800 terminals at police stations throughout London. The new system, operated by dual US-made Sperry computers, is essentially a command and control system – although, as might be expected, the incident log automatically stores information about the victims, witnesses or suspects of crimes. During 1984 and 1985, however, the Metropolitan Police were formulating a 'user requirement' for a crime and criminal intelligence system. With between 800,000 and one million names in the Metropolitan Police's present manual collator indexes, an intelligence computer for the force, if one is commissioned, would probably be the largest such local police installation in the world. The London force already has a comprehensive intelligence-gathering network, including area crime units, a 'central information unit' concerned with public order, and 24 District Intelligence officers. One of the area's crime teams already uses the facilities of the C Department computer (see Chapter 9).

*   *   *

Present trends in police computing show an explosion at the local level – a process constrained only by cash limits and some urban police authorities' desire to enforce proper data protection safeguards. In a series of separate but closely related developments, many local police computers have been linked to the PNC. The work of collators and criminal intelligence teams has been co-ordinated, and regional criminal intelligence offices have been set up to cover several police force areas. The growth of a national network of linked police computers has been made possible by the development of a standard PNC 'interface module'. The first test of this took place in Birmingham in 1975, when West Midlands Police linked their subdivisional stations to the PNC through the command and control computer. By April 1979, about 600,000 PNC enquiries a year were being routed through the Birmingham computer. The force found that the availability of extra terminals multiplied several times over the extent of its PNC use.

Certain forces have spoken of an 'operational requirement for the development of a local criminal index system to extend and complement the national files maintained by the PNC'. In such a system, if no data were found on a local computer, a search would be referred to the PNC. 'Pointers' on the PNC would then indicate which local or regional computer centre held information on the subject of the enquiry, and the PNC would be used to retrieve and relay this information from local records to the enquirer.

Although such a system has yet to be sanctioned or designed, the PNC is fast becoming the focus of links between national, regional and local crime information and criminal intelligence records. The Merseyside Police computer specialist, Chief Inspector Gordon Fraser, undoubtedly spoke for many technology-orientated officers when he suggested in 1978 that 'a national computer network of criminal information systems, incorporating the PNC, is the answer'.

By May 1985, 31 police forces had either planned or begun to operate a PNC interface. Those then operating a PNC interface were Sussex, the Metropolitan Police, Suffolk, Northampton, Cambridge, Lincoln, West Midlands, West Mercia, South Wales, Warwick, Wiltshire, Bedford, Nottingham, Durham,

North Yorks, Cleveland, Stafford, Merseyside and Cumbria, and Grampian and Fife Police in Scotland. The police forces then *planning* a PNC interface were Kent, Essex, Avon and Somerset, Hertford, Humberside, South Yorks, Cheshire, Northumbria, Lothian and Borders, and the Scottish Criminal Records Office in Glasgow.[28] It is intended eventually to extend such links to every police force in the country.

For police patrols, PNC information is obtained by radio from an operator at force or divisional headquarters. At the time the police personal radio networks were set up, it was not widely appreciated that their major purpose was to provide a direct link from PNC to police patrols, rather than, say, to facilitate emergency calls for assistance. The purpose and effect of a national criminal intelligence network would be to make intelligence data available equally speedily to patrol officers.

The PNC 'cross-reference' system, called RX, may be the harbinger of extensive future linkage between personal records. The RX index provides 'pointers' to criminal information held in regional or local files. Criminal records files on about a million people are cross-referenced in this way. Criminal intelligence files, as such, are not yet included in this system.

The Lindop committee distinguished between criminal 'information' and 'intelligence'. Information, it said, was '"hard" factual data, such as name, date of birth, physical description, and criminal convictions' – all of which could be verified by observation or from records not held primarily by the police. In contrast, criminal intelligence 'may be speculative, suppositional, hearsay and unverified, such as notes about places frequented, known associates, suspected activities ...'. The Home Office did not find this distinction difficult to draw when it gave evidence to Lindop in 1977:[29]

> In considering whether to link criminal intelligence and criminal information records, the protection of privacy had to be weighed against the need to collate such information for the maintenance of law and order ... it was thought desirable to postpone such a linkage for about ten years while the public debate on privacy proceeded.

Ten years have passed, the debate is officially regarded as concluded, and the Home Office says it does not now choose to distinguish between criminal information and criminal intelligence on computers.[30] It defines 'computerised criminal information systems' as those 'which hold records hitherto kept on paper relating to crime, criminals, and criminal activities'. All such records, if they are not already on computer, are beginning to migrate to computers, in ever-larger quantities. The Lindop committee foresaw this process:[31]

> If police applications devoted specifically to intelligence proved ... to be really useful to individual police forces, pressure could build up to have [local criminal intelligence records] linked together into a single system or a set of large regional systems, for the more efficient use of police resources.

This could lead to a 'potential danger to the subject's privacy which could increase with the extension of these applications over the next ten years'.

In fact, despite the arguments about law and order, the utility of criminal intelligence computerisation to police efficiency is, as the Thames Valley experiment showed, highly questionable. A Home Office working party, the Pearce committee, reported in 1979 that there was no point in planning a national computerised police intelligence system. One of the committee members, Merseyside Chief Constable Kenneth Oxford, described such plans (somewhat hypocritically, in view of Merseyside's own subsequent proposals) as having 'inherent dangers'.[32] The Pearce committee recommended, however, that a national 'central, definitive record' be established. At the time, this was to be the National Identification Bureau's microfiche files; in the future, it will become the PNC's 'conviction application', described in the next chapter.

Four months after Pearce reported, newly appointed Home Secretary William Whitelaw told a police superintendents' conference that 'the most pressing need is ... to develop criminal information systems'. The Manchester, Kent and Humberside projects, among others, were urged on, as part of a national strategy to test and develop the new systems. But the discouraging Thames Valley Police project report soon followed. In 1981 other Home Office scientists reviewed the value of free text retrieval systems, and found evidence that 'the inherent [and expensive] sophistication of this type of information retrieval system ... not only makes it difficult to operate but ... is not justified by its operational use in the investigation of crime'.[33]

Since then, the Home Office has (not entirely effectively) urged police forces to exercise caution before seeking to spend millions of pounds on criminal information systems, none of which have produced any tangible benefit to the community in terms of personnel savings or improved clear-up rates, and have usually had the opposite effect.[34]

The latest developments in this area are special computers for the investigation of major incidents and clever systems used to enhance surveillance methods. The first major incident investigation experiment, known as MIRIAM (major incident room index and action management), was planned in 1976, but began only several years later.

In major inquiries, large teams of detectives may take tens of thousands of statements from people they interview or receive messages from. If the information gathered is not systematically examined and analysed, important clues to the identity of the miscreant may be missed. This was emphatically the case in the Yorkshire Ripper inquiry. Over a period of nearly five years, mass killer Peter Sutcliffe was interviewed nine times by police, and his car was seen 36 times in red-light districts. In retrospect, a profusion of police professional and clerical errors were recognised and admitted. If senior police officers' judgement had been better, many of Sutcliffe's victims would not have died.

The catalogue of errors during the Ripper inquiry had a profound effect on many senior police officers. Extensive computerisation of major incident inquiries was seen as essential to avoid future catastrophes, while senior officers from Chief Constables downwards were dispatched to special training courses. When the MIRIAM computer experiment (located at the Essex Police headquarters in Chelmsford) did not get under way until 1983, police impatience to start using computers opened the floodgates for a host of different major incident investigation systems.

Surrey Constabulary was given permission to use the 'auto-index' retrieval system on the PNC during the hunt for a rapist in January 1983. South Yorkshire police started using auto-index too, on locally installed Burroughs computers. Lothian and Borders had recourse to their new computer's free text retrieval facilities during a joint hunt for a multiple child killer with Leicestershire Constabulary. In the same year, West Yorkshire Police tried out a new and similar system, called Mica. Mica was later used, successfully, in the hunt for 'the Fox', a multiple rapist in the Bedford area. In January 1984 the Association of Chief Police Officers introduced their own specification for computerised investigation indexes.

The MIRIAM experiment involved two Honeywell DPS6 minicomputers and Status free text retrieval. The MIRIAM computers were taken over by Essex Police in 1985, and converted to serve also as a command and control system. The final result of the project, christened HOLMES (the Home Office large major enquiry system), specifies standard data formats for such investigations; each HOLMES computer may operate three software programs, or 'modules', including automatic indexing, free text retrieval and special data entry methods. Police forces have since rushed to purchase mini-computer systems suitable for HOLMES.

But HOLMES computers have been criticised on two counts. When, in 1982, HM Inspector of Constabulary, Sir Lawrence Byford, a strong computer enthusiast, sang the praises of the 'all singing, all dancing' HOLMES, and urged the government to fund their purchase, a leading forensic scientist pointed out at the same time that government cuts in other areas were threatening to cripple the forensic pathology services on which police detective work primarily relied.[35]

Second, the ultimate use or disposal of the information which is collected during major inquiries is a matter of particular public concern. It is usually the case that records (of both factual and highly speculative varieties) are assembled about thousands of innocent people – including those who have volunteered their time or information to assist the police. During the Ripper inquiry, the police systematically and secretly recorded the vehicle numbers of 21,000 men who were seen in Manchester and Yorkshire's red-light districts. Had they used the information effectively, they would have found the Ripper. But such information should properly have had no existence after the arrest and conviction of Sutcliffe.

Because of the odious nature of the crimes which usually provoke such major inquiries, during questioning some people may impart information which they would not wish to see form part of permanent police records. But special Home Office guidelines for HOLMES computers, issued in 1985, do not recognise this fact. These say that the police may gather data 'from any source' and that it should 'so far as possible, be adequate, relevant and not excessive in relation to the purpose of the enquiry'. (But the guidelines acknowledge that the 'not excessive' restriction is virtually meaningless.) When the inquiry has concluded, none of the data should at any stage be destroyed, but should be 'archived securely so that they are preserved and available for examination'.

The guidelines 'recommend' that data be used only for: 'investigation of the main or subsidiary offences or any related prosecution'; enquiries into alleged miscarriages of justice; or to assist 'anyone who is legitimately concerned with the investigation of ... a recordable offence, and who has good reason to believe that relevant data are held on the major crime investigation system'.[36] The police are cautioned that, before data is released for the latter purpose, the approval of an Assistant Chief Constable should be obtained; however, no need is acknowledged for outside supervision – for example, by reference to the Data Protection Registrar.

Fears that the capabilities of police computers might be extended to include expert systems performing automated 'social control' tasks are, given the present stage of police computerisation, a long way from realisation. Despite the advocacy of technocratic enthusiasts, many police forces will still be grappling with the simpler aspects of information technology towards the end of the 1990s. Only if and when giant, uncontrolled databanks become commonplace within the police service will the possibility of new experiments in expert systems and advanced analytical methods become probable.

In contrast, pattern recognition systems have made rapid progress. Automatic vehicle-numberplate scanners for use with the PNC have been field-tested twice since 1980. Both the Metropolitan Police laboratory in London and the Home Office research centre at Sandridge, Hertfordshire, now offer

sophisticated photographic, video and audiotape enhance-
ment and authentication services. Further research is under
way in computerised photographic processing, including
attempts to develop automatic facial recognition systems. The
police laboratory is also attempting to develop an electronic
photograph album, based on optical digital storage methods.
But the Home Office Scientific Research and Development
Branch annual programme report says that the provision of
such services is severely restricted by government cash limits.
They were, in 1985, 'unable to cope with all demands'.

The growing scope and accessibility of computerised police
information is a matter of serious concern, which the Data
Protection Act largely fails to address. The Home Office,
commendably and unusually, has not endorsed a minimal
interpretation of the Act, under which police forces might seek
widespread exemption for criminal information or intelligence databanks.[37] The databanks described in this chapter
will all be registered. But registration is of limited value,
because subject access is severely constrained. Transfers to or
from police computers need not be registered at all. The
possibility of unregistered transfers to and from police files is
intolerable; if on any occasion an overwhelming need is found
for such a transfer, the fact that the transfer has occurred
should be recorded, and be discoverable and challengeable by
the subject after the period of investigation. Subject access provisions should at least require the police, after a suitable
period, either to destroy non-verifiable 'intelligence' data (by
Lindop's definition, see page 218), agree its disclosure to the
subject, or justify its retention without disclosure to an outside
agency such as the Data Protection Registrar.
    Such safeguards are needed, first of all, because of the
potency of information from police databanks in relation to
individual liberties. Information given in response to a radio
enquiry helps determine a police officer's course of action. If
the message is that someone should be arrested for an offence,
then the course of action to be taken is obvious, and the fact of
passing the information unobjectionable in principle. But
where a previously 'spent' conviction or, for example, a record
of political or trade union activity is indicated, and when no

offence has been committed, it is both offensive and unnecessary that such information should be readily available to encourage discriminatory treatment.

Many subjects of collator files have not committed nor – often – have even been suspected of committing crime; as explained above, the files in question normally record the *victims* of crime together with criminals who 'come to notice'. Statistics show that most checks made on the PNC or other police computers do not concern people who have committed any criminal offences.

The police say of many of their criminal intelligence or information systems that they are restricted to holding details of 'convicted criminals'. This is not the justification it might seem, containing as it does the implicit judgement that once someone has one 'recordable' conviction to their name, their right to personal privacy is abrogated. Such a notion marginalises offenders, rather than reaccommodating them within society. It is also quite contrary to the principles of the Rehabilitation of Offenders Act 1974, which provides that a 'rehabilitated person', whose conviction is spent, 'shall be treated for all purposes in law as a person who has not committed ... or been convicted of ... the offence or offences'.

There are clearly defined circumstances in which information about criminal records may be passed on, largely in matters concerning convictions of members of the professions and others with special public responsibilities, such as foster parents. The list of those whose professional bodies will be informed of convictions includes doctors, nurses, midwives, teachers and others supervising children, barristers, solicitors, magistrates and civil servants.[38] There are also criteria for 'weeding' national criminal records, although these are highly restrictive. So far as the national criminal names index of the PNC is concerned, the names of offenders (except in cases of murder or other crimes 'of special interest') are removed after 20 years, provided there have been no new convictions, and the person concerned is over 40. For those aged under 40, weeding does not take place unless the offences concerned occurred before the person was 14 years old. For persons over 70 years old, their names are removed after 10 years, if there have been no new convictions during that period.

In conclusion, the problem of obtaining information to 'clear up' crime will not be solved by using larger computers; for it has its roots in the lack of police accountability to the community (particularly in London) and the force's failure to respond to the community's policing priorities. It should be obvious that no increase of police personnel, computers or surveillance machinery can compensate for the loss of information that an alienated community has refused to provide.

8 PNC

Housed in secure and well-protected premises in Hendon, north London, the Police National Computer (PNC) is the focus of a national information and communications system that has been growing dramatically in extent and effect for more than ten years. The PNC stores nearly 50 million records on vehicle owners, stolen and 'suspect' vehicles, criminal names, fingerprints, convictions, wanted and missing persons, and disqualified drivers. These databanks are used more than 70 million times a year. Among other facilities, the PNC provides a nationwide communications 'broadcast' network between every police force in the country, and cross-references records at regional and national level.

The PNC's information store has become increasingly central to routine police work, augmented by a rapid communications system designed to link the PNC to every police officer on patrol. New legal powers and the rapid availability of information, taken together, provide a potent system for checking individuals who may not have committed any offence but are nonetheless required to account for their identity and presence in public places.

The second decade of PNC operation will encroach further on civil liberty. Since 1974, when its most widely publicised early applications – the register of vehicle owners and the stolen (and suspect) vehicles list – appeared relatively uncontroversial, the PNC has become pivotal in emergency operations. During the 1984/85 strike by the National Union of Mineworkers, police chiefs at the Scotland Yard National Reporting Centre used the PNC as one hub of their communications network with provincial police forces and their command centres.

Current trends point to the eventual integration of personal records held by the police into a three-level computer network. The PNC forms the national centre, to which regional criminal records and crime intelligence offices are already linked. The bottom tier consists of individual police force computers. The Home Office, in a 1984 internal circular to police forces,[1] has referred to a continuing 'upwards growth path' planned for the PNC. This does not as yet formally include national intelligence records, but PNC staff and senior police officers are in no doubt about the ultimate intention. In a 'deniable' and 'off the record' talk before an official visit by the Data Protection Committee in 1976, the then Director of the PNC told his staff that their long-term 'main function . . . is to set up a national criminal intelligence centre . . .'.[2] There may be some caution in integrating intelligence records, given the Data Protection Act. But it is quite clear that – whatever promises may have been given in the past – a national police intelligence network must lie at the end of the present path of computerisation.

The major indexes on the PNC are now reasonably well known. The government – believing that the computer has gained acceptance – is much more open in its statements to Parliament, the press and the public about PNC facts and figures than when operations began in 1974. Much other information has emerged, however – some of it in breach of official secrecy – which indicates that many unconvicted, innocent and unsuspecting people are put under surveillance or recorded on the PNC. The PNC is permitted routinely to store some data on the sensitive subjects for which in other circumstances the Data Protection Act prescribes particular safeguards – specifically, racial origin, political opinions or beliefs, physical or mental health or sexual life, and criminal convictions. Careful analysis of information about PNC operations shows that:

Eleven million people are checked against the PNC every year, most of them on the street. New applications of the PNC will store personal details about witnesses and victims, as well as suspects and offenders.

Nineteen million vehicles are checked against the PNC every

year; more than 99.5 per cent of these vehicle checks are on vehicles which are neither stolen nor wanted.

Despite this, 250,000 vehicles are recorded on the PNC every year as being 'seen in noteworthy circumstances' – often for such political reasons as presence at demonstrations or strikes.

At least 70,000 individuals are under surveillance in special sections of the wanted/missing index or as users of stolen/suspect vehicles recorded as being 'of long-term interest to police'. But the people and vehicles concerned are neither wanted, missing, nor suspected of having committed or being involved in 'any offence'.

Vehicles may be recorded on the PNC stolen/suspect vehicles index because of 'unsubstantiated suspicion about an unconvicted person' or to record 'sightings which do not necessarily imply suspicion at all'; even if criminal involvement is suspected, it may be 'actual or *potential*' (our emphasis).

The wanted/missing index, which can be accessed from all 1500 PNC terminals, includes grossly over-simplified 'warning' signals and highly prejudicial and subjective descriptive personal information in PNC personal records – routinely castigating people as 'liars', 'effeminate', female impersonators, makers of 'false allegations against police', 'drugs' possessors (no distinction is made between lawful drugs on prescription and illegal drugs); or referring to such traits as 'arrogance' or 'physical abnormalities'. Such descriptions may obviously adversely influence police behaviour towards the subject.

A special facility exists to notify senior officers or the Special Branch when an enquiry is made concerning a person of interest – without necessarily notifying the enquiring policeman that the person is so identified.[3]

PNC surveillance has been extended by the experimental development of an automatic vehicle-numberplate reading system, which scanned the numberplates of cars entering London.

PNC vehicle indexes have been used to record political information about 'association with an organisation' – which has been shown to have included information about civil liberties groups, animal rights organisations and gay activists.

A 'blocked' facility on the PNC protects MI5 operations and vehicles *against* police interference, by withholding data from police enquirers.

Frequent leaks of PNC information have occurred, and information on vehicles or criminal records has routinely been passed to unauthorised users, including private detectives and for payment.

PNC information has been used privately by some policemen for such purposes as contacting or harassing women.

The PNC was first presented to the public as a system concerned primarily with factual information. But 'intelligence' information is also stored, as the Lindop committee pointed out in their 1978 report.[4] The committee noted that:

> The file of stolen or suspect vehicles can include vehicles required to be kept under surveillance; the file of wanted or missing persons can include persons required to be located, even if they have not been reported missing and warrants have not been issued for their arrest; both files have scope for the inclusion of free text comment by police forces about the entry.

The PNC's computers provide rapid access to information of a speculative nature, as well as so-called 'hard' data about vehicles and people. The largest and most important databases on the PNC are the lists of vehicle owners (registered 'keepers'), stolen and suspect vehicles, the names and descriptions of people with criminal records (or awaiting trial), and also the names of wanted or missing persons. During 1985, a major new PNC database, intended to hold full details of criminal convictions, also came into use.

Minor PNC databases hold details of stolen plant and vehicle engine and chassis numbers, disqualified drivers, crime patterns and fingerprints. Following experiments in 1983, the PNC can also store and index all the information acquired in police major incident investigations, using a system called Auto-Index. The inclusion of this system as a standard facility on the PNC creates the risk that at least some of the information volunteered by the public in the course of a major incident inquiry would be retained and transferred elsewhere for other purposes – finding its way onto both PNC indexes and linked regional or local intelligence files. This is a direct violation of the third data protection principle (see Table 1, page 32).

The PNC's raison d'être has always been that it should stand at the centre of a national communications network, which allows the patrolling police officer direct and speedy access to the data stored. Ideally for the police, the spread of its data would eventually cover the entire population. Its function is expeditiously to guide a police officer as to his or her course of action.

It was appreciated from the beginning that the PNC would be of little value or effect unless close attention was given to the means of access and the means of passing data from the databank to the data user. There are about 1300 video display terminals installed at police force headquarters (and often, in addition, at divisional and subdivisional stations) throughout the country. The PNC's specification calls for searches for names or vehicles to be completed within a target of five seconds from the time the information is entered on the VDU. As anyone who has ever accidentally overheard police VHF radio can testify, the speed at which PNC data is supplied is indeed remarkable. It would be unusual for the PNC to take as long as 30 seconds to find a 'trace' on an individual (if a record existed).

In situations where powers to check everyone's identity exist, there is evidence of proportionally rather greater use of the PNC to make enquiries about individuals. A good example of this has been given in recent (public) annual reports by North Wales Police,[5] whose Special Branch supervises the port of Holyhead, Anglesey, carrying tourist traffic to the Irish Republic. North Wales Special Branch have used the PNC three times more frequently than their uniformed colleagues. In 1980, they carried out 14,634 personal checks, an average rate of 670 checks per officer per year. The North Wales criminal intelligence section were also relatively heavy users of the PNC, according to the force's official report.

Despite the present scale of PNC use, there is considerable scope for growth. Averaged over the country's 120,000 police officers, the 30 million PNC checks on non-offenders mentioned above amount to only 250 checks per officer per year – one per working day. Allowing for the many police officers not available for patrols, the average still remains as low as two to three PNC checks per working day.

Extensive nationwide training for all new police recruits in the use of computers, together with the effective communications network available, has promoted vigorous growth both in PNC information records and in the frequency with which these records are accessed. This growth is expected to continue. By 1985, apart from the 11.5 million checks on named individuals, there were 19 million checks on vehicles. About 40 per cent of the name checks provide a 'trace', and the name may then be found on the criminal names or wanted/missing indexes. *All* vehicle checks on a valid registration are normally successful in producing information about the owners, but only about one in 500 checks produces a trace from the stolen/suspect vehicle index.[6]

Much of the growth in size of the PNC is accounted for by new vehicle registrations. (The PNC also retains details of void registrations and scrapped vehicles for a fixed period, thus holding particulars of rather more vehicles than are actually on the roads.) But the rest is personal data. By 1987, five million more personal records will have been put on-line, as a result of the new conviction and criminal pattern analyses applications of the PNC.

Figures were provided to Parliament in 1983, and directly to the authors in 1985, showing the rate at which each index is used (see Table 6, page 239). Most PNC checks (about two thirds) concern vehicles. The different indexes have been linked in such a way that, for example, all PNC vehicle enquiries automatically search both the vehicle owners' and stolen/suspect vehicle lists. Name enquiries can still be made to separate indexes (criminal names, wanted and missing persons, disqualified drivers, and cross references), but the most commonly used procedure is now to search all four indexes at one time.

By June 1985, some 526 terminals (keyboards and video display screens) and 171 dataprinters (which print information on paper as a permanent record instead) were coupled directly with the PNC. At first, these terminals were the only means of consulting PNC records.

Of all police computer projects, the PNC has the earliest roots. Plans for the PNC first began to take shape in 1968, four years after the 1964 Police Act had consolidated existing county and county borough policing into 43 forces in England and Wales, and eight in Scotland. Regional criminal records offices and regional crime squads were introduced at the same time. Prior to this, only Scotland Yard's Criminal Records Office (CRO – but now known as the National Identification Bureau, or NIB) maintained a collated national set of records on criminal convictions. The subsequent rationalisation of police records was the first step towards creating the present three-tier information system.

Early work for the PNC was done by a joint Home Office, Metropolitan Police and Prison Commission organisation called JADPU – the Joint Automatic Data Processing Unit, which carries out routine administrative computing work for the parent organisation. Perhaps the most familiar JADPU application – to Londoners, at least – is the processing of parking tickets. JADPU computers also undertake a wide range of routine tasks ranging from police payroll to equipment records.

In 1968, Surrey Police at Guildford experimentally used a JADPU computer terminal to log and search for stolen cars. The Home Office then allocated funds to JADPU to establish the Police National Computer Unit (PNCU), to examine and report on the possible applications of a national police computer. Their report, published in 1969, concentrated on the possibilities of computerising the existing central national 'indexes' – in fact, full police records – maintained at New Scotland Yard. The JADPU report identified the major future applications as concerning stolen vehicles, vehicle owners, fingerprints, wanted or missing persons, criminal names, persons under suspended sentences, *modus operandi* used in crimes, stolen cheques, stolen property and stolen bicycles. Approval for the construction of the PNC was given later that year by Harold Wilson's government, and construction began at Hendon. PNCU became, and remains, an autonomous unit within the Home Office's Police Department. The first two of an eventual three Burroughs B6700 central processors were delivered to Hendon late in 1971.

Apart from the central processors, the Hendon complex includes a communications network control centre from which British Telecom cables radiate to terminals and data-printers throughout the country. To save money, many police terminals share a single line to the computer, and the network control 'polls' each terminal in turn to see if any transactions are waiting. In order to provide for a rapid response, all PNC data is stored on banks of disc files, to which the central processors are connected. The first PNC installation had 2000 megabytes of disc storage – roughly equivalent to, say, 30 words of information on each of 10 million people. To prevent electric grid failures affecting the service, an 'uninterruptible' power supply and generator are installed at Hendon. More-over, backup magnetic tapes – containing complete copies of all files – are held both at Hendon and at a separate and secret high-security location, which is said to be resistant to bomb attacks, whether conventional or nuclear. Despite all this, computer tapes have gone missing from the PNC on at least one occasion.[7]

Home Office programmers and a private consultancy (Hoskyns Systems) jointly developed the PNC programs, known as the central system. To the central system are attached program 'modules' dealing with each of the major applications, such as fingerprints or vehicle owners. Initially, the PNC was designed to hold 40 million records and permit a peak transaction rate of about 21,000 enquiries an hour. The first part of the central system was completed in 1974; the PNC then went 'live' and began making use of the stolen/suspect vehicles index and the vehicle owners' index.

Developing PNC software was a major undertaking. In 1975, advertisements for staff described the PNC as 'one of the most powerful real-time computer systems in Britain ... a linked data-communications network will eventually contain up to 1000 VDU and Dataprinter terminals'. But it would be confined to 'factual' data, officials claimed. The Home Office gave an unequivocal assurance: 'Criminal intelligence is not going into the national computer. That is categorical.'[8]

In January 1978, the Home Office announced that the present capacity of the PNC was exhausted, and that new processors were being purchased. They also argued that the (existing) processors were 'incapable of dealing with the sheer weight of numbers of enquiries being received'. It appears that it was necessary to expand both the storage and processing capacity of the PNC. There was then allegedly no storage space left for the wanted and missing persons application or the disqualified driver index to go 'live'.

The original PNC central processors were replaced on 30 July 1978, after four years of operation. Senior police officers already saw the network as quite indispensable to their work. Scotland Yard Deputy Assistant Commissioner Peter Nievens wrote to Fleet Street editors asking that nothing be published until the changeover was complete, warning that:

> There will be a risk of unplanned breakdowns in the computer service ... I should be grateful for your co-operation in refraining from publishing anything about this temporary loss ...

Displaying a quite extraordinary sense of priority and insecurity, Nievens added, 'There is a slight risk that some *subversive elements* or criminals might attempt to take advantage of the reduction of this facility.' (Our emphasis.) He did not further elaborate on his fears. After the processors were changed, the Home Office trebled the original PNC disc storage capacity to 6000 megabytes, and then enlarged it again to 9000 megabytes. By 1985, the PNC disc store was 12,200 megabytes – or 12 gigabytes. There are now three PNC central processors, Burroughs B7700s, and six other computers controlling the communications network and the memory stores. By 1988, the PNC's main processors will have been in continuous operation for ten years, and it is expected that they will be replaced. At the time of writing, however, the government had not made any definite plans about when and how to replace this hardware.   *   *   *

Table 5
PNC applications and indexes[9]

Index/application	Date 'live'	Number of records				
		1977	1979	1983	1984	1985
Stolen/suspect vehicles						
– registrations	1974	120,000	260,000	298,000	313,000	380,000*
– search by description	1974	—	—	—	—	—
– engine/chassis numbers	1974	—	100,000	407,000	451,000	543,000
Vehicle owners	1974	17.7 m	23.25 m	30.48 m	32.76 m	35.61 m
Broadcast system	1975	—	—	—	—	—
Fingerprints index	1975	2.20 m	2.05 m	3.15 m	3.31 m	3.51 m
Criminal names	1977	3.80 m	4.00 m	4.64 m	4.78 m	4.97 m
– conviction records	1984	—	—	—	—	467,000
Cross reference	1977	—	×	927,000	930,000	984,000
Wanted/missing persons	1978	50,000	100,000	116,000	107,000	109,000*
Disqualified drivers	1980	—	170,000	255,000	290,000	298,000*
Crime pattern analysis	1983	—	—	—	—	11,500+
Major investigations	1985	—	—	—	—	58,000
TOTAL RECORDS		23.92 m	30.38 m	40.56 m	42.93 m	47.33 m
[TOTAL ENQUIRY RATE (PER ANNUM)		18.0 m	58.3 m	61.1 m	—	72.95 m]

× Information not available.

+ First used in May 1983, but available to police forces only 'on an experimental basis, pending evaluation'.

* The Home Office also supplied figures suggesting that the number of separate vehicles or 'individuals' in the stolen/suspect vehicles index, the wanted/missing index, and the disqualified drivers index were respectively 10, 10 and 25 per cent lower than the number of entries shown above.

The present scale and recent growth of the major indexes on the PNC are shown in Table 5 (above) and depicted in Figure 4 (pages 236–7). The indexes are generally named after manual record systems at Scotland Yard. After the first 100,000 records on the stolen/suspect vehicle index went 'live', in March 1974,

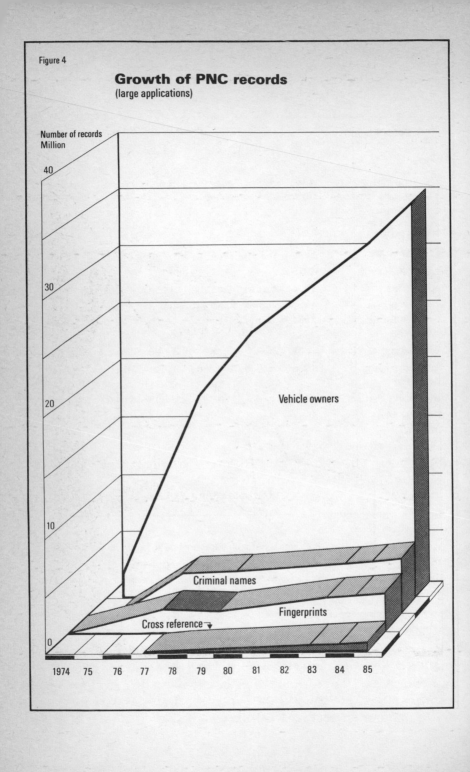

Figure 4

Growth of PNC records
(large applications)

Number of records
Million

40

30

20

10

0

Vehicle owners

Criminal names

Fingerprints

Cross reference

1974 75 76 77 78 79 80 81 82 83 84 85

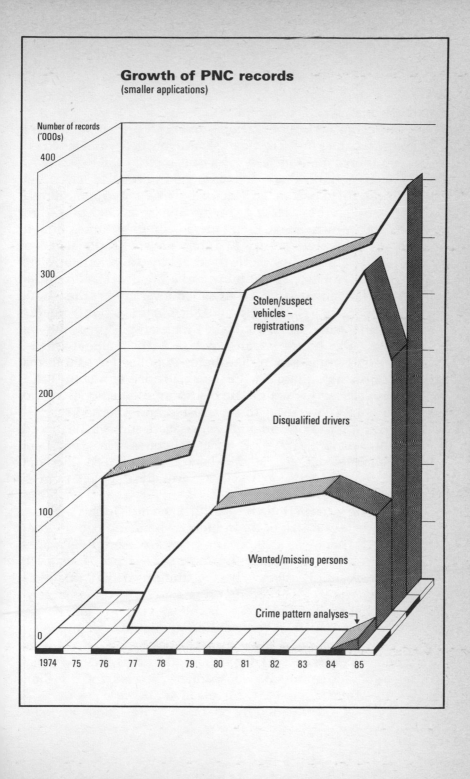

Growth of PNC records
(smaller applications)

Number of records
('000s)

400

300

200

100

0

Stolen/suspect
vehicles –
registrations

Disqualified drivers

Wanted/missing persons

Crime pattern analyses

1974 75 76 77 78 79 80 81 82 83 84 85

details of vehicle registrations were gradually transferred from the Department of Transport Driver and Vehicle Licensing Centre (DVLC) in Swansea. The PNC vehicle owners' index began operating six months later.

The computerisation of the central fingerprint index and the criminal names index of the then Criminal Records Office (now the National Identification Bureau) rapidly followed. From early 1975, individual police forces were also given the opportunity to use the PNC as a rapid inter-force communications system, by selecting the 'broadcast' facility from their terminals. Any message then entered would be transmitted to all, or a selected group, of other police headquarters or terminals. This is not a rarely used facility; as early as 1976, the PNC was handling 32,000 messages annually. The broadcast system has since also been assigned a variety of other exotic and emergency tasks; Home Office circulars on *Satellite Accidents* issued in 1979 and 1985, for example, prescribe that the PNC will be the means by which the Cabinet Office's emergency organisation distributes to police forces information on an impending satellite crash. In crisis or war, the PNC's role is believed to include the distribution of national 'round-up' lists of 'subversives' to be arrested and interned.[10]

Some applications originally envisaged, such as the recording of stolen bicycles or stolen cheques, have not been implemented at all. Yet between 1977 and 1985, the total number of records on the PNC virtually doubled from 24 million to over 47 million.

Over the same period, the growth of the individual databases was varied. The size of the vehicle owners' index more than doubled. There was a 30 per cent increase in criminal names, and a 60 per cent rise in the number of fingerprints recorded. This may simply reflect the registration of new offenders, although the PNC's 'weeding' criteria, described in Chapter 7, mean that much information is unnecessarily retained.

The stolen/suspect vehicle index, which has multiplied in size almost threefold since 1977, has been used to log the car numbers of strikers and demonstrators and has been coupled to automatic numberplate scanners; it also records both vehicles under long-term surveillance and vehicles used *for* undercover surveillance by police and intelligence agencies.

Table 6
Enquiry rates on the PNC[11]

PNC index	Enquiries made annually	
	1983 (based on four-week sampling period)	1985 (based on one-week sampling period)
Stolen/suspect vehicles	(37.77 m (2,898,699)	19.76 m (380,000)+
Vehicle owners	(	19.76 m (380,000)+
– engine/chassis numbers	N/A	1.0 m (19,000)
Fingerprints index	0.28 m (21,148)	1.06 m (20,500)
Criminal names	7.67 m (589,634)	8.68 m (167,000)
– conviction records	—	not on-line to police
Cross reference	0.30 m (22,722)*	8.87 m (170,500)
Wanted/missing persons	6.77 m (521,142)	8.84 m (170,000)
Disqualified drivers	5.59 m (429,798)	6.70 m (129,000)
Crime pattern analysis	—	52,000 (1,000)
Major investigations	—	0.91 m (17,500)
Transactions on individuals	N/A	13.22 m (254,000)
TOTAL ENQUIRIES – ALL INDEXES	58.29 m (4.48 m)	74.63 m (1.44 m)
TOTAL TRANSACTIONS	30.82 m (2.37 m)	32.30 m (600,000)

† The vehicle owners and stolen/suspect vehicles indexes are now searched simultaneously for information; separate enquiries are no longer made of each index.

* The cross reference index is now checked on all criminal names index enquiries. The number checks made on this index only were approximately 182,000 in 1985.

The second PNC list with direct intelligence and surveillance applications, the wanted/missing index, has not shown comparable growth.

PNC information is structured in accordance with the specific spaces in each record for prescribed items of information. But in the case of the wanted/missing persons and the stolen/suspect vehicle indexes, a space is included for a short 'free text' item, which may be used to hold general comments and personal data about an individual or vehicle owner or user. On a stolen/suspect vehicle entry, 120 characters (about

20 words) are allowed; on the wanted/missing index, 100 characters are available.[12]

The five-million-strong criminal names index includes standard personal details such as name, alias, date and place of birth, a description, CRO number, special 'warning signals' and 'descriptive details'.[13] Also given are the 'date first came to notice' and the date and time when the record was last amended. The PNC can search for either aliases or true names – both are produced by the computer if a 'trace' is found. Only the National Identification Bureau (NIB) can enter, change or delete information from the criminal names index. This is done by means of a form – a 'CRO74' (to be redesignated NIB74) – which is one of the most commonly used and standardised police information documents.

After an arrest, a CRO74A is sent to the NIB, and a PNC computer record created, even though charges may yet be withdrawn or an acquittal result. The CRO forms are micro-filmed, and retained at Scotland Yard as microfiches, together with fingerprints, photograph (*after* conviction), 'descriptive forms' and 'antecedents' (which may give details about the crimes committed), and notes on the subject's employment, family and friends (logged by the police as 'associates') and social circumstances. Extremely carelessly, according to police standing orders the criminal names records 'do not specifically distinguish between convicted and unconvicted persons',[14] and thus give no warning at all to an enquiring police officer that a court may yet acquit the person before them, whom they have been told has a criminal record. The criminal names index went live in August 1977, with 3.5 million names on file, and has since grown by over 30 per cent. Building up the index took four years of data preparation.

The type of warning signals and descriptive details which are entered on CRO74 forms and then indexed on the PNC, and the manner in which they are phrased, are often gravely pre-judicial. Standard NIB instructions for completing CRO74s invite officers to enter such 'personality types' as 'excitable, brash, arrogant, effeminate, a liar, requires to be dealt with firmly, responds to sympathy...' This information is sought on the basis that it 'may assist an officer in dealing with the subject in the future'. But there is no way in which cursory

Table 7
Wanted and missing persons index – categories[15]

PNC category	Meaning	Number recorded
Locate	'Sought, or whose whereabouts need to be established' by police in relation to unresolved enquiries	39,300
Wanted	'Wanted for specific offences where there is sufficient evidence to charge the subject' or 'legally prohibited from entering the United Kingdom'	29,000
Missing	'Missing and may be vulnerable to harm, or believed to be in company of such a missing person'	2,000
F T A	Failed to appear in court	19,300
Deserter	Deserter from armed forces	10,300
Suspect	'Suspected of a specific offence but where there is insufficient evidence to charge immediately'	3,700
Found	'Found, and unable by age or illness or other circumstances to establish their identity' (incl. corpses)	173
Lifer	Released on licence from life sentence	1,175
Custody	Notify to another force if held in custody	162
Impending	Subject to an impending prosecution	137
A. Care	Absconded from care	639
A. Hospital	Absconded from hospital	55
A. Detention	Absconded from detention	2
A. Borstal	Absconded from Borstal (youth custody)	90
A. Prison	Absconded from prison	365
A. School	Absconded from school	117
A. Remand	Absconded from remand	35
R. Detention	Recalled to detention	2
R. Borstal	Recalled to Borstal	2
R. Prison	Recalled to prison	226

judgements of this kind entered by one police officer once onto a CRO form can remotely be held to be objective; they are manifestly not 'factual data'. Such invited comments as 'a liar', 'arrogant', or 'effeminate' (doubtless intended to imply homosexuality and invite further prejudice from many officers) will no doubt adversely affect the subject's treatment by police in any encounter. Form CRO74A also solicits information for the PNC on a numerical 'racial classification' (whose categories are listed in Table 9, page 244) and such 'marks/scars' as 'moles, warts, physical abnormalities . . . amputations, limps, deafness, defective speech, etc.'

Many of the formal 'warning signals' – which are held on disqualified drivers, as well as on both the criminal names and wanted/missing indexes – are no less derogatory (see Table 8, opposite). These were described in Parliament as 'extra information of which a police officer should be aware'.[16] Some of the warnings are clearly sensible and would provide worthwhile assistance (*if* true), but it is not immediately apparent why categorising individuals as alleged male and female impersonators (impersonation of this kind is, of course, no offence) should be thought helpful. If a police officer has given the wrong sex when asking for a PNC check, the computer will return NO TRACE.

Some of the warning signals are also dangerously misleading. The 'alleges' warning – asserting that the subject 'makes *false* allegations against the police' (our emphasis) is subject to no test of accuracy. No process has been established whereby such a comment might be deleted if the subject had in fact made a *successful* (or even 'not proven') complaint against the police; and it would be entirely possible for such a derogatory comment (implying that the subject is a liar and thus inviting, to say the least, less than courteous treatment from some officers) to be recorded against someone who was in fact the victim of unlawful police behaviour. A 'drugs' warning is also dangerously ambiguous; it can mean either that the subject is in medical need of special drugs or that she or he is a known or suspected user of illegal drugs.[17] Similarly, the 'ailment' warning can indicate a carrier of hepatitis or other infectious diseases – or that the subject is medically vulnerable because, for example, of a heart condition. Such

Table 8
Warning signals used on the criminal names, wanted/missing and disqualified drivers' indexes[18]

Warning signal	Meaning
Dead	Reported dead
Violent	Assaults police
Weapons	Carries weapons
Mental	Mentally disordered
Escaper	Potential escapee [from cell, prison, etc.]
Ailment	May suffer from a physical ailment
Drugs	May possess drugs
Explosives	May possess explosives
Alleges	Makes false allegations against police
Refer/file	Refer to file [held at a specific police station]
Deportee	Deportee (subject to deportation order)
Alien	Alien (non UK citizen)
M/Impers	Impersonates male
F/Impers	Impersonates female
F/Appear	Fails to appear
Alcoholic	Alcoholic
Epileptic	Epileptic
Suicidal	Suicidal
Off/Bail	Commits offences on bail

ambiguity is clearly foolish as well as dangerous. Additionally, according to the Lindop committee, other and separate indicators may show that 'the Special Branch has an interest in the subject'. This can be done by including an 'RX' cross reference to Special Branch files.[19]

Once a case comes to court, another form (CRO74B) is sent to the NIB and the results of the case entered on the PNC. If the person is acquitted of all recordable offences (and has no prior recordable conviction), then both the NIB and PNC records must be deleted and destroyed – except in the cases of a few sexual or theft offences.[20] But in 1985, the Home Office admitted that criminal names records deleted from the PNC were retained on microfiche – a practice which defeats any safeguards for *computer* data in the Data Protection Act.[21]

Table 9
Police racial identity codes[22]

'Race code'	Ethnic type
RC 1	White-skinned European
RC 2	Dark-skinned European
RC 3	Negroid
RC 4	Indian or Pakistani
RC 5	Chinese or Japanese
RC 6	Arabian or Egyptian

The criminal names and wanted/missing indexes are searched using available details of name, age, sex, colour and height as 'search factors'. Either the subject's name or CRO number is required to make the check, but the other factors are optional. Names are indexed on the PNC using SOUNDEX, a programming system which allows the computer to recognise similar-sounding names, despite widely varying spellings. Even if full information is fed to the PNC, it will allow automatically for a range of errors by checking a band of ages, a group of similar names (using SOUNDEX) and a small range of similar heights.

The PNC holds only 'serious' recordable crimes – but this of course includes many minor offences, including offences against public order. The NIB's 'weeding' criteria are extremely minimal, with predictable results. In one incident in the early 1980s, a teacher in his late thirties offered to stand bail for a friend at a magistrates court. A PNC check on his 'antecedents' by the police unearthed a 22-year-old conviction as a youth for minor criminal damage. Nor is the removal of records after acquittal a uniformly reliable process; in 1978, Christopher Price MP cited the cases of two demonstrators at the Grunwick strike against whom public order charges were dropped. Some time after this, Price revealed, information on their charges was still available.[23]

The 'wanted/missing' index holds about 100,000 names broken down into twelve categories (see Table 7, page 241). At first, these categories were secret, although it was well known that, besides the genuinely wanted, there were lists of people on whom surveillance and reporting only was desired, in a category called 'Locate'. Asked by one of the present authors in 1979 to supply details of the categories included on the wanted/missing index, the Home Office refused, claiming that this information 'although not classified in a formal sense, would jeopardise the security of the PNC'. When it was pointed out that details of the wanted/missing categories could be extracted from a photograph of a training course in a published Home Office booklet, the ministry's then Director of Information, Donald Grant, claimed that the photograph concerned was 'deliberately left unclear' and refused to confirm the details.

Most of this information was in fact provided to Parliament four years later, together with the numbers recorded in each category. A complete list of categories was published in 1985.[24] But some key aspects have been omitted. For example, the largest part of the index – nearly 40 per cent – concerns people in the 'Locate' category, which Home Office minister Patrick Mayhew outlined to Parliament as dealing with people 'sought, or whose whereabouts need to be established, by police in relation to unresolved enquiries'. The full description of this category, however, was given in the less public Home Office code of practice for the PNC, which added the words 'although they are not suspected of having committed an offence'. The minister had deliberately concealed from the parliamentary record the fact that this major part of the index concerned people neither wanted nor missing, nor even suspected of any offence. The title of the wanted/missing index is a striking piece of civil service or police sophistry. Many entries on the index are neither wanted nor missing persons. Forty per cent are under surveillance – Locate – and another 10 per cent are among the 10,400 described as deserters from the armed forces. As is apparent from the example given in Chapter 7 (page 202), these entries may be as much as 40 years out of date, and those whom they describe may be completely unaware that they are vulnerable to arrest if checked on the PNC. The failure to weed such records of other than recent offences is a remarkable example of vindictive bureaucracy.

The wanted/missing index holds further, explanatory details about the reasons for a subject's inclusion, descriptive details and warning signals, a date for the entry to be weeded and information about powers of arrest. There are also spaces for up to 100 characters of 'free text'. Entries in the wanted/missing index can be cross referenced to associates – in the sense of others being sought in connection with the same matter. Data can be retrieved from the index using reference number, name and descriptive details, or by type of entry or offence. The Metropolitan Police newspaper, *The Job*, reported in August 1977 that the national CRO wanted/missing index then amounted, pre-computerisation, to some 65,000 records. But the paper anticipated – accurately – that this total would 'virtually double overnight as provincial forces feed in their own indexes'. Unlike the criminal names index, most information on the wanted/missing index is fed in directly by officers in provincial police forces, on the authority of inspectors.

As well as national (NIB) criminal records at New Scotland Yard, individual forces maintain their own criminal records, and additional personal records are held at regional CROs. The PNC's cross reference system, holding about a million names, links these separate records – and automatically responds to any names enquiry with a reference number to local files (if any have been noted). For local police forces, the cross reference index will produce the national CRO number when the local number is fed in, facilitating searches of the criminal names and wanted/missing indexes. The application may also be used in reverse, so that a list of local files on an individual may be obtained. The new convictions application extension of the criminal names index will hold details of both convictions and 'impending' prosecutions, including CRO reference number, local references and details of whether photographs and fingerprints are available. Eventually, further personal details may be put on the index, and arrangements made for searches by 'personal description'.[25]

Like the other nominal indexes, the disqualified drivers' index holds name, age, sex, racial classification, height, 'warning signals' and 'descriptive details', and a CRO number (if any).[26] The driver's address is also recorded, together with a PNC identity number, details of up to two disqualification orders, and her/his DVLC driver number. According to the PNC code of conduct,[27] entries on this index should be removed 'on expiry of the period of disqualification'. But, on at least one occasion, senior police officers have claimed that 'once a [disqualified] driver's name is on the index, it will remain there regardless of the length of the ban'.[28]

Some 36 million vehicle owners or 'keepers' form the largest single group recorded on the PNC. The vehicle owners index records the keeper's name and address, together with a description of the make, type and colour(s) of the vehicle. There are also (unspecified) 'indicators which provide additional information of use to the police'.[29] Apart from these extra indicators, the index is entirely derived from the full vehicle registration information, held by the DVLC computers at Swansea. This index can be used from four PNC terminals outside the police, two at the DVLC in Swansea and two at the Customs and Excise Special Investigation Branch in central London. The users of these terminals cannot use any other PNC index.

With almost 20 million vehicle checks a year, the vehicle owners and the stolen/suspect vehicle indexes (now linked) are responsible for two thirds of the PNC's workload. Using the facility for multiple checks, patrol police officers are officially invited to carry out 'useful' general checks on groups of vehicles seen in 'car park, service areas or road check situations'.[30] This facility is also used to check vehicles seen near public meetings or demonstrations. In investigating major incidents, possible suspect vehicles can be searched for by description rather than by registration. This allows the police to obtain a list of vehicle owners, possibly in a defined geographical area (using the postcode system, see page 57) who own vehicles matching a partial description provided by witnesses. The description can include some or none of the vehicle registration. The information in the PNC vehicle owners index is also available to the public from the DVLC itself on payment of a small fee, and on showing reasonable cause (e.g., involvement of the vehicle in a minor accident). Such a DVLC enquiry, however, takes several weeks.

The stolen/suspect vehicles index is rather more controversial. The twelve categories for inclusion on this index go far beyond vehicles which are actually stolen or suspected of involvement in crime. The categories, and the numbers of entries in each, are listed in Table 10 (opposite). The stolen vehicles index replaced a manual central vehicle index kept at the Information Room at New Scotland Yard, which then covered vehicles lost or stolen, removed by police or repossessed by a finance company, and those 'seen under suspicious circumstances'. Contrary to the oft-repeated and disingenuous claim that the PNC and similar computers have done no more than replace earlier manual record systems, the new categories, such as 'seen in noteworthy circumstances' or 'long-term interest to police', did not previously exist on Scotland Yard records. These categories, aimed at general surveillance rather than the apprehension of known offenders, were first invented for use by the PNC.

The most politically sensitive use yet known to have been made of the PNC was its direct application to restricting industrial action in the 1984/85 coal industry dispute. Soon after the beginning of the strike, in March 1984, police officers began regularly recording the numbers of cars used by striking miners (as well as those of NUM officials and journalists covering the strike[31]). Soon after this, Kent Police set up roadblocks at the Dartford tunnel, quickly to be followed by similar actions throughout the East Midlands and Yorkshire coalfields. These operations were intended to prevent pickets from travelling to pits. Three months later the government admitted that miners had been put under PNC surveillance. Then Home Office minister Douglas Hurd acknowledged that:[32]

> Registration numbers of some vehicles used by pickets in the current dispute have been entered in the stolen and suspect vehicles index in the category of vehicles seen or checked in noteworthy circumstances.

Hurd pointed out that this category, which is often used for recording vehicle stop-checks, was 'regularly weeded' of records after 14 days. But he did not claim that this weeding was in fact taking place in respect of pickets' vehicles. In this case, it is rather more likely that such records were retained on the PNC for the currency of the dispute.

Table 10
Stolen/suspect vehicles index – categories and usage[33]

Lost or stolen	(LOS)	194,781
Obtained by deception	(OBD)	498
Found or apparently abandoned	(FOU)	25,534
Repossessed by a finance company	(FIN)	92
Suspected of being involved in a crime or other incident	(SUS)	2,296
Of long-term interest to police	(INT)	41,077
Removed to police pound	(REM)	11,351
Removed by police from one street to another	(STS)	171
Owned or used by police	(POL)	8,666
Blocked (details not to be passed over open radio channels)	(BLO)	4,097
Seen or checked in noteworthy circumstances	(SEE)	9,345
TOTAL (Index entries, including multiple entries for the same vehicle)		297,908
(Vehicles recorded)		283,000 (approx.)

Many of the terms used in Table 10 (above) are self-explanatory. But the SUS 'suspect' and INT ('long-term interest') categories bear further examination. SUSpected or INTerest reports are 'intended to inform enquirers of suspicion about the user's actual or potential criminal involvement'.[34] The SUS category is relatively small (about 2300 records in 1983) in comparison to the long-term surveillance INT category (41,000 records), and the action to be taken on finding a SUS vehicle is clear. In the INT category, however, there is no requirement that the interest have anything to do with criminal activity. According to the PNC code of conduct, INT entries may 'seek [unspecified] action to be taken on sighting a vehicle', with the PNC providing 'such particulars of the user as are needed to enable officers to act appropriately'.

A leading member of NCCL, and gay activist, Roland Jeffrey, noted in the late 1970s that his NCCL membership had found its way onto the PNC vehicle indexes, when he called at a London police station to report a minor accident. The PNC terminal was just out of sight, but well within earshot. After making a routine check on his registration, the terminal operator warned his colleague, 'You want to watch out here. We've got one of these civil liberties types.'[35]

The PNC code of conduct contains an apparently reassuring but actually misleading note of caution: 'Vehicles must not be recorded as suspect simply because the user belongs to a particular group or organisation.' This qualification would appear to result from a row in 1977, when Home Office minister Shirley Summerskill implicitly acknowledged in Parliament that information about the membership of protest groups had been entered on the PNC (in the 'free text' space available on the stolen/suspect vehicles index). Mrs Summerskill told questioners that 'information about political beliefs and activities is not held on the Police National Computer'. But she added:[36]

> Information about association with an organisation has been held for a limited period in the index of suspected and stolen vehicles when a police officer has judged it relevant when reporting a vehicle as suspected of being used in connection with crimes.

The caution in the code of conduct does not hinder police officers from continuing their common practice of logging and entering into permanent records the numbers of vehicles seen outside political or protest group meetings or demonstrations. For the code puts no bar on the uninhibited inclusion of such information in the much more frequently used INT or SEE categories. Nor is the Home Office's reference to a 'limited period' of time for the storage of such records of much avail to civil liberties. The INT category is specifically described as being 'long term'. In any case, the standard retention period for stolen/suspect vehicles index entries (except SEE) is three years, and the record can be retained beyond this time on request. Plenty of space on the PNC is available for police officers to enter their lightest suspicions; Merseyside Police standing orders note that 'None of [the] rules is intended to preclude the use of the system to record purely circumstantial suspicion.'

The SEE category, according to the same standing orders, 'was introduced to record sightings which do not necessarily imply suspicion at all'. This category was used to hold the details of miners' cars during the 1984/85 strike. The code states that information in this category 'should be limited to a description of the vehicle and details of the occupants'. Currently, at any given time, there are about 10,000 SEE records. Since these records are normally held only for two weeks, this implies that over a quarter of a million such police observations are noted on the PNC every year.

More intriguing is the blocked (BLO) category of entry, which is available to protect undercover police operations, as well as the activities of Special Branch and MI5, *against* ordinary police interference. Details of MI5 vehicles, which are officially registered as belonging to a small mews garage in Mayfair, are BLO entries on the PNC. During 1982, a couple in Talysarn, a small North Wales village near Caernarvon, observed two men behaving suspiciously in a telephone box outside their house. After the men left, the couple checked the telephone box, found an electronic listening device planted behind a panel, and removed it. As they left the box, a car was driven at them, mounting the pavement, and blocking their way. One man demanded, 'I'll take that,' and threatened the couple. His colleague added, 'It doesn't matter if you do report me to the police. It would just make no difference.' The device was handed over, under duress. A local policeman was called, and made a PNC check on the vehicle's registration, only to be told over the radio, 'No details of the vehicle by request of the Home Office.'[37] After subsequent parliamentary protests about the Talysarn incident, the Home Office released their guidelines to Chief Constables on the 'use of equipment in police surveillance operations'. But the Home Office refused to reveal the identity of the undercover agents. We have established that they belonged to No. 4 Region Technical Support Unit, based in Birmingham.

Merseyside Police standing orders say that the BLO category can also be used 'to record unsubstantiated suspicion about an unconvicted person'. This facility is particularly intended to avoid terminal operators radioing PNC information to patrols who 'may be within earshot of the suspect'. The Home Office has said that the category may also include 'police vehicles used in observation duties'.

According to Home Office scientists, when the stolen

vehicles index was first introduced, only a minority of its records – one quarter – concerned vehicles which were actually stolen.[38] Reporting that in 1976 there were then about 120,000 entries on this index, the scientists explained to an international conference on police computers that the number 'having been stolen' was 'about 30,000'. The number of vehicles recorded has since almost trebled; by 1985, there were 350,000 entries on this index, nearly one in five of which were described as SEE, SUS or INT. The free text entry (about 120 spaces) can hold any 'appropriate' personal or criminal information, details of vehicle users, or other personal details 'needed to enable officers to act appropriately'.

A smaller, subsidiary index records the chassis, engine or serial numbers of stolen vehicles and other property, including contractors' plant. No personal information is held in the chassis/engine number index.

Like the criminal names index, the fingerprint system on the PNC is under the sole custody of the National Identification Bureau at New Scotland Yard. The fingerprint records are a backup method of identifying an arrested person if there is no trace of the name given on the PNC or NIB manual records. About 5 per cent of arrested people are identified in this way, using the 3.5 million fingerprint sets now indexed in Scotland Yard's National Fingerprint Collection. The fingerprint records themselves are stored in a separate computer system, called Videofile. The PNC holds a numerical index derived from the famous Henry system of classifying fingerprints.

PNC and Videofile work together. Fingerprints are either taken from an arrestee or may be found at the scene of a crime, and are then sent to Scotland Yard, to be encoded by specialists. A four-digit code identifying the pattern and number of ridges on each finger is passed to the PNC. As a background, 'batch' task, the PNC searches for possible matches, which are then fed to the Videofile installation. The Videofile automatically retrieves the possible matches on a split screen, for comparison with the new print for a final, manual identification. When first introduced in 1976, the fingerprint application took up one quarter of the PNC's storage capacity.

The fingerprint entries are cross referenced to criminal records numbers and to entries in the criminal names index. According to the PNC code of conduct, 'limited personal data may also be held' on the fingerprints index. This may include places frequented, or distinguishing marks. Clever systems which can automatically recognise and encode each fingerprint recently became available. Home Office scientists had been working on developing a recognition system for more than 20 years, but an early series of projects with Ferranti Ltd was unsuccessful. In July 1984, however, the Metropolitan Police took delivery of a £2 million system developed by the Logica computer consultancy; if successful in operation, it may be installed at eight British regional fingerprint centres, in Birmingham, Manchester, Bristol, Cardiff, Durham, Preston, Wakefield and Glasgow. These centres, with New Scotland Yard, are the exclusive users of the PNC fingerprint index. At the time of writing, the Home Office were considering transferring fingerprints information entirely to New Scotland Yard.

According to information given to Parliament, the new crime pattern analysis (CPA) application of the PNC stores details of offences, including location and date, 'modus operandi',[39] details of property stolen, and a 'free text section for any additional information'.[40] The PNC's code, however, gives a different description, implying that much broader categories of information will in fact be held, including:

> textual information extracted from reports of crime. [The application] is for use by police attempting to establish links between crimes committed in different parts of the country. An entry may include information about suspects, provided that names and other details do not allow identification of subjects without reference to other police information. Witnesses and victims must be clearly identified as such ...

The data is entered from crime reports, and will remain 'until the relevant crime has been cleared up'. The CPA is intended to be used, as its name implies, to compare crimes in different areas or at different times. This application was at the time of writing relatively lightly used, with some 11,500 records stored on the PNC and users limited to regional criminal intelligence offices. The CPA system uses free text retrieval software to retrieve and compare items of information.

The most recent PNC development has been the provision, in 1985, of an 'emulation' of the auto-index system software used on local police force computers (see page 220) to investigate major incidents. In their 1984 *Computer Policy* circular,[41] the Home Office referred to this project as creating for the PNC 'an upwards growth path [which] will have an effect on the facilities which need to be provided locally'.

In respect of future plans for the PNC, the *Computer Policy* circular noted:

> The possibility of adding further elements of the NIB microfiche to the criminal names/convictions files ... methods of data input to these applications are being studied.

> The police requirement for a national computerised property index is being investigated (in response to a request from the Central Conference Committee on Criminal Information Systems).

> Crime Pattern Analysis application used by Regional Criminal Intelligence Office is currently being studied.

Clever systems, in the form of artificial intelligence techniques such as pattern recognition, have been applied to PNC operations by Home Office scientists from the Police Scientific Research and Development branch laboratories at Sandridge, near St Albans – in the invention of an automatic numberplate scanner.

The numberplate scanner includes a high-quality television camera, the image from which is turned into digital information and then processed by computer. The computer – an adapted Digital Equipment Corporation PDP11 – is programmed for pattern recognition similar to that of the human retina and visual cortex. The computer has first to identify where in a 'snapshot' image of a moving or stationary car the numberplate is, and then process the correct part of the image so that the numbers and letters can be recognised and read. A task of this nature – simple for the human eye – is still highly advanced for a computer. Once the number has been read, it is checked against a list of registration numbers held inside the processing computer, which are fed in from the stolen/ suspect vehicles index. If the number is recognised, an alarm is sent to police headquarters and hence to patrol vehicles.

The first test of this scanner was conducted on the approaches to the Dartford tunnel, under the River Thames, in 1980. A TV camera was mounted on a gantry on the Kent side of the tunnel, where vehicles slowed and queued to pay the tunnel toll – presenting an ideal target for the prototype scanner. The purpose of the camera's presence was kept secret, and tunnel staff on occasion forcibly prevented photographers taking pictures of the apparatus. After initial tests were complete, the camera was used in 1982 to feed information to Essex and Kent Police. The experiment, described as 'non-operational and in the early stages of development' by the Home Office, continued until October 1982.

In a second phase starting in 1983, a more sophisticated scanner was assembled and installed on a bridge over the M1 motorway, just north of junction 9, at Flamstead, Herts. Conveniently close both to the Sandridge laboratories and to the Hertfordshire Police HQ at Welwyn Garden City, the new scanner tracked moving vehicles entering London, in three lanes. Three separate cameras were contained in a heavy box with 'high voltage' warnings and linked by thick cables to a computer and processing equipment in a portakabin out of view of the motorway. The cameras overlooked a long, straight motorway section, making the scanner's task as easy as possible when dealing with moving traffic. They were also designed to use infra-red light, enabling them to work at night, when target vehicles were illuminated by an invisible infra-red source. Three still pictures of each car would be taken in rapid succession, at slightly different exposures. The best image was then processed by the computer. Electronic sensors, video cameras, burglar alarms and other security devices guarded the portakabin, and police officers made frequent visits to keep vandals away.

After the presence of the M1 installation was first suspected, the Home Office deliberately misled Parliament when Michael Meacher MP enquired about the operation in 1983.[42] Meacher was referred only to the Dartford experiment, which had by then been removed, and notified of 'further development work'. But, nine months later, one of the authors fortuitously spotted the scanner installation,[43] and further questioned the Home Office about their intentions for the system. It was claimed that details of stolen vehicles only were being fed into the Flamstead scanner from the PNC. Official statements were ambiguous, however, about whether the computer was attempting to detect only stolen vehicles or all vehicles on the stolen and suspect vehicles index.

The Flamstead scanner ceased operation in 1985, after two years' 'successful' testing. The scanner worked, officials said, but was too expensive 'to justify its widespread operational use'. (In the magazine *Crime Prevention News*, the cost of a working system was quoted as £60,000.) It had also been hoped that the experiment might lead to the development of a more discreet and easily portable system, which might have been moved between locations to suit both security and operational purposes. The Home Office said that they were not ruling out the project for the future, should the electronics become cheaper – which is inevitable. The automatic vehicle scanner, for which prototype hardware and software has now been developed and proven, and for which a clear police rationale exists, is likely to be prominent in the future development of clever systems.

9 Policing Politics

Britain has four national intelligence organisations, and an intelligence section – the Special Branch – is attached to every police force in the country. Each of these organisations will, if challenged, claim that the Data Protection Act leaves their personal information records immune from registration or disclosure. The members of the security and intelligence community are also granted *carte blanche* to tap the records of other government departments and private organisations (to the extent that these bodies or their employees may be willing to permit) without breach of the Data Protection Act.

There are known to be at least two million personal records held by the intelligence and security services, most of which are now on computer. The information in such records may well have been obtained by the least acceptable and most intrusive of means, including paid informers, telephone taps, bugs, mail interception, and even burglaries. Whether accurate or not, such information may be, and often has been, used to the severe detriment of the data subject – typically, to prevent the person concerned gaining employment. Were it not for the 'national security' exemption (see page 304), the main computer systems to which the Data Protection Act would apply are:

The Special Branch 'nominal index', which is the major application of the Metropolitan Police's C Department computer, housed at New Scotland Yard. The Special Branch expected to have 1.5 million names on file by 1986. At least 600,000 of these files were expected to be computerised by 1985.

The Security Service (MI5)'s Joint Computer Bureau (JCB) at Curzon Street, Mayfair. This giant computer is at the hub of a network of smaller intelligence computers, and had, at the time it was installed, the greatest information-checking capacity of any in Britain. The JCB could hold an on-line nominal index covering 20 million people; however, only about 500,000 people are said to be the registered targets of MI5 surveillance (see Chapter 10).

Army computer systems in operation in the north of Ireland for anti-terrorist purposes. (However, the main computer known to be in operation in the North, codenamed 'Operation Vengeful', contains an index of vehicles of interest to security forces, rather than individuals as such.)

The Special Branch, MI5, and army intelligence staff (chiefly in Northern Ireland) are the agencies primarily involved in internal political surveillance in the UK. But personal data on British citizens, gathered either during external intelligence operations or for their own security purposes, is also held by the three other intelligence services, each of which has different tasks and responsibilities: the Secret Intelligence Service (SIS, popularly called MI6), Government Communications Headquarters (GCHQ), and the Defence Intelligence Staff (DIS), which is formally a part of the Ministry of Defence. A Joint Intelligence Staff in the Cabinet Office receives and assesses the reports from the producing agencies, for distribution to government departments and ministers.

To understand why and how the Special Branch has compiled well over a million personal records, many of an essentially political character, it is necessary to look closely at the origins and detailed functions of the agency itself. Contrary to official protestations, the Special Branch is a 'political' police. Some Special Branch duties, such as the supervision of ports or the provision of bodyguards for ministers, are straightforward enough, and relatively uncontroversial. But fewer than 50 per cent of Special Branch officers are employed on such duties. The rest, with a few exceptions, do not police crimes or make arrests; they police politics. Despite the convening, in 1984, of the first ever parliamentary inquiry into the work of the Special Branch, by the House of Commons Home Affairs Committee, government statements about the structure and work of Special Branch continue to be deeply misleading.

Until the 1960s, the Special Branch remained a London-based organisation with a total strength of around 200. The restructuring of police forces which accompanied the 1964 Police Act brought about, for the first time, the formation of provincial Special Branches. The realigned and radical political groupings that developed in the late 1960s brought with them a great increase in protest activity. The targets of the fifties and early sixties – relatively well-organised left-wing groups and trade unions, and a single-issue CND campaign – were now supplanted by diverse anarchist, Maoist, Trotskyist, environmentalist and anti-war groups. Many of these were seen as stemming from university campuses, which immediately became high-priority targets for Special Branch surveillance.

Changes followed during 1970. A specially appointed Committee on Protective Security, chaired by Lord Helsby, former head of the civil service, met in secret to review surveillance and vetting procedures. Their report went to the Official Committee on Security – M15's oversight body – in July that year. It outlined the dangers of subversion:[1]

> The Communist Party has a fundamental interest in subverting the State, and constitutes a threat to the security of protected information. Individual Trotskyists, Maoists or anarchists might use protected information in such a way that would further their political ends or would give such information publicity if they thought that this would embarrass or damage the reputation of the government.

Formal instructions from the Official Committee on Security were amended so as to include the new protest organisations within official criteria on 'subversion'; membership of such groups would no longer be acceptable for those who might take up vetted posts in the civil service or elsewhere. The new left joined the old as targets of surveillance – a change that soon dramatically and obviously widened the Special Branch's information-trawling activities. At the same time in 1970, the Association of Chief Police Officers (ACPO), in consultation with the Home Office and MI5, issued terms of reference for these new Special Branches. By 1975, every provincial force had established its own full-time Branch, with strengths ranging from two to over a hundred officers. A major priority for the Special Branches was to recruit informers on every student campus to report on (left-wing) political activity. The continual turnover of students made it difficult to sustain discreet recruitment procedures, and many instances were reported in which Special Branch officers had attempted to bribe or cajole students into becoming informers.

The 1970 ACPO terms of reference, which are said to 'guide the work of Special Branches in some detail',[2] still retain a confidential classification. On the instigation of the House of Commons inquiry into the Special Branch, however, the Home Office prepared revised guidelines for publication; they appeared in December 1984 under the title *Work of a Special Branch*, and clarified in particular the Branch's relationship with MI5. The new guidelines were claimed to be more exacting and detailed than before on the matter of Special Branch record-keeping.

The work of the Special Branch became increasingly controversial during the 1970s, and frequently provoked questions from MPs. In 1974 a parliamentary reply by Home Secretary Roy Jenkins asserted (in fact inaccurately) that 'It [the Special Branch] is interested only in subversion and possible subversion.'[3] Soon after this, Lord Harris, a Labour junior Home Office minister, revealed for the first time the criteria used to define 'subversive'. (This definition was drawn from the then current ACPO/MI5 terms of reference, although for the next ten years it was generally assumed that it had been constructed at the time of Harris's statement.) 'Subversive activities' were those:[4]

> which threaten the safety or well-being of the State and which are intended to undermine or overthrow Parliamentary democracy by political, industrial or violent means.

This definition, striking in its breadth, has provided a great deal of fuel for controversy. How are police officers, normally conservative individuals, meant to interpret the 'well-being' of the state? What is the distinction between those who seek to change government policy and those who 'undermine' it? Neither illegal plans nor violent intentions are required in order to come under Special Branch or Security Service surveillance. Writing in 1985, Home Secretary Leon Brittan commented, 'It is all too easy to use tactics which are not themselves unlawful for subversive ends.' He urged the Special Branch not to have scruples about 'those who for tactical or other reasons choose to keep either in the long or the short term within the letter of the law'.[5]

Critically, however, the remit of the Special Branch goes far wider than this. The guidelines say that the 'basic' role of the Special Branch 'arises from the chief officer's responsibility for the preservation of the Queen's Peace. Its work is to assist the chief officer in discharging this responsibility.'[6]

This duty is fulfilled by wholesale surveillance of all political or public activity which might, at some future date, give rise to public meetings or the like. The Metropolitan Police, in their Special Branch training syllabus, call this activity 'the acquisition of intelligence related to public order'.[7] The guidelines say:

A Special Branch gathers information about threats to public order. Such information will enable the Branch to provide assessments of whether marches, meetings, demonstrations and pickets pose any threat to public order and help the chief officer determine an appropriate level of policing.

The 'threat to public order' can be actual or potential. Home Secretary William Whitelaw explained in 1982 to Labour MP Robin Cook that the preservation of public order:[8]

may require information to be kept on individuals who are active in a political movement, not because of the views they hold, but because the activities of the group could be such as to encourage public disorder.

This part of the guidelines is a charter for unbridled political surveillance: it suggests that everyone who is in any way critical of the *status quo* and who acts in public in accordance with their beliefs is a legitimate Special Branch target. Special Branch tasks thus include information-gathering on people involved in every aspect of community life, including organisers of campaigns for better nurseries or bus routes, people who write letters to newspapers to express legitimate points of view, or those who organise meetings for any purpose, be they trades unionists, feminists, ecologists, liberals, communists,

humanists, gays, socialists, pacifists or peace campaigners.
Examples of surveillance of all these groups of people have
occurred in the recent past. The public can scarcely draw reassurance from the screen smugly drawn over such activity by
successive Home Secretaries, epitomised by Merlyn Rees's
notorious 1978 remark: 'The Special Branch collects information on those whom I think cause problems for the State.'[9]

In justifying Special Branch intelligence-gathering in this
area, ministers have drawn manifestly spurious and quite
meaningless distinctions between surveillance of individuals
on the one hand because of their personal political views and
on the other because of the public order consequences of
being in groups that hold such views. It is stressed that Special
Branch's surveillance of trade unions and trade disputes does
not involve taking a view on the merits of either side's case.
Nevertheless, it is only the actions of the employees that attract
surveillance. If the Special Branch was remotely even-handed
in its activities, its files would bulge with dossiers on company
directors and managers whose creation of redundancies have
often brought about real and serious threats to public order.
One has only to postulate such a situation to see how quaint it
would be. Former Devon and Cornwall Chief Constable John
Alderson told the 1984 House of Commons Home Affairs
Committee inquiry that in all industrial disputes:[10]

> The Special Branch have to report daily on the number of pickets
> ... a daily report on all industrial disputes is sent to police
> headquarters and in appropriate cases to the Home Office.

Separate, classified reports might be prepared on key activists
in a strike. But the Special Branch has no brief to report on
employers' activities.

Individual Special Branches are not formally part of the
Security Service, but on many occasions may act as MI5's
agents and take their direction in making enquiries about or
maintaining surveillance on 'subversives' or 'extremists'. The
Home Office guidelines describe Special Branch tasks in
relation to MI5:

> A Special Branch assists the Security Service in carrying out its
> tasks of defending the Realm against attempts at espionage and
> sabotage or from the actions of persons and organisations

whether directed from within or without the country which may be judged to be subversive to the State.

A Special Branch provides information about extremists and terrorist groups to the Security Service.

Nationally, there are over 1600 Special Branch officers, of whom about 400 are employed by the Metropolitan Police. There are also at least 200 civilian staff employed in support of police Special Branches, 120 of them in London. Over the last 25 years the growth in the burden of political surveillance in Britain has been intense.[11]

The Home Office carefully misled the House of Commons select committee by pointing out that the strength of the Special Branch in London had grown by 'only' 75 per cent since 1960, over a period of vastly increasing international passenger traffic and, latterly, terrorism. In fact, the Special Branch has undergone an eightfold increase since 1960, taken on a substantial civilian staff and shed many tasks to other organisations. Most of the growth – some 1400 new posts – has arisen in the new provincial Special Branches, who took over regional duties previously carried out by Branch officers detached from Scotland Yard.

Excluding the Royal Ulster Constabulary (RUC) Special Branch and the national ports organisation, the number of Special Branch officers and civilian support staff not engaged on either anti-terrorist, port-watching, or personal protection duties – and therefore concentrating on domestic intelligence-gathering – would appear to have multiplied roughly five- or sixfold since 1960 – from about 150 to 800–900 staff. At the same time, many former Special Branch duties, such as the protection of royalty and diplomatic staff, the actual investigation and prosecution of bombing offences or terrorist crimes, and immigration intelligence, have been handed over to new specialist squads. A National Joint Unit at Scotland Yard, staffed jointly with provincial Special Branches and the RUC, co-ordinates the use of detention and exclusion powers under the Prevention of Terrorism Act.

Late in 1973, the Metropolitan Police prepared proposals for computerising the main records of C Department – covering the work of both the CID (Criminal Investigation Department)

and specialist groups, including the then Drugs and Illegal
Immigration Intelligence Units. The largest contender for
computerisation was, however, the Special Branch. A document prepared for computer manufacturers who wished to
tender for the contract indicated that, as at January 1974, the
Special Branch had 1,150,000 files on individuals. By January
1985, they expected to hold 1,412,000 files. These files would be
used, it was predicted, more than 300,000 times every year (see
Table 11, opposite).

The existence of the C Department computer had first been
revealed in very guarded terms in the 1975 Home Office White
Paper *Computers: Safeguards for Privacy*.[12] But the information provided was sparse indeed, and the task of extracting
further details defeated both the Lindop committee and other
concerned MPs and groups. The White Paper stated:

> A computer system is being planned to handle information held
> by the Metropolitan Police about crime, criminals and their
> associates. The system will be internal to those branches of the
> force who now use this information in manually held records, and
> it will not be connected to any other system.

This description was at best disingenuous, as it deliberately
omitted any reference to the Special Branch. The project went
ahead and a contract for the computer equipment, worth just
under £1 million, was placed in 1976.

The truth was revealed in 1977, when the tender document
was leaked to *The Times* newspaper, which then published
detailed specifications for the new computer. At least 600,000
of the million-plus names held on the Special Branch nominal
index were to go on computer, according to police plans.[13] The
Metropolitan Police refused to comment on the articles,
asserting that 'the publication of any figures purporting to
indicate the total number of records in any part of the project
would amount to speculation'. This was rather less than the
truth; the police were well aware that *Times* reporter Stewart
Tendler had had access to accurate figures that they themselves had compiled.

The specification for the C Department computer system
listed some 35 manual index systems then in use by police
specialist squads. Only 12 of these indexes were concerned

with named individuals. Half of these were stated to be concerned with 'criminals', and held a total of 17,000 names. The remainder, holding (in 1974) 1.3 *million* names, covered merely 'persons', who had not necessarily committed any crime. Besides the main nominal indexes, there were subsidiary indexes concerning vehicles, boats, aircraft, telephone numbers, special addresses, and other details.

Table 11
Personal files planned for the C Department computer, January 1985[14] (Projection made in January 1974)*

Unit	Number of records	New records per annum	Enquiries per annum
Special Branch	1.414 m (1.15 m)	24,000	277,000 (228,000)
Drugs Intelligence	60,000 (13,000)	4,000	6,000 (1,000)
Immigration Intelligence	287,000 (76,000)	19,000	28,000 (7,000)
Serious Crimes	193,000 (62,000)	12,000	N/A N/A
Fraud Squad	73,000 (26,000)	4,000	10,000 (4,000)
TOTAL	2.027 m (1.198 m)	63,000	(more than) 321,000 (240,000)

* The figures for January 1974, given in brackets, are the actual totals of manual files held by each department at that time. The likely expansion of files was then projected forward 11 years (probably to avoid the unwelcome attention that a ten-year plan for 1984 might have attracted!). Totals are rounded to the nearest thousand. The immigration intelligence files were transferred in January 1984 to the Home Office Immigration Service intelligence unit computer (IVAN) at Harmondsworth.

The Special Branch operates a nominal index and a subjects index, both huge in size. In January 1974, the nominal index contained:[15]

about 1.15 million names filed in alphabetical order. About a third of the records have personal dockets. A feature of the Nominal Index is that each record has a number denoting an 'area of

interest' (of which there are 27) ... it is proposed that computerisation of only about 8 of these areas will be undertaken initially, in
an order to be determined by the section.

Each person's card would also 'contain references to bulk
subject files or to personal files'. Some 350,000 people were the
subject of special 'dockets', containing papers and extra
surveillance information. These were held as 'pink slips' in the
index. 'White slips' denoted those about whom only basic data
was available. (There were no plans to computerise the Special
Branch subjects index.) It was estimated that, by 1985, Special
Branch records would occupy some 226 megabytes of computer storage. But it was unlikely that all the Branch's nominal
records would be computerised:

> It may be assumed that only about 50 per cent of them will be
> computerised and that implementation will take place in stages
> over a 10 year period ... each stage involving, on average, about
> 50,000 records.

These would be 'of the highest priority from the operational
point of view'.

All C Department nominal files include such personal
descriptions and details as 'reason(s) of interest', passport
numbers, vehicles used, places frequented and names of
police officers to whom the subject is 'known'. There are cross
references to 'associates'. The Special Branch held (in 1974)
separate subsidiary indexes on 6100 addresses, 1300 telephone numbers and 2500 vehicles. There was then also 'an
index containing 7,600 records of special interest, which require a very rapid response to enquiries based on a name'. The
former records seem most likely to have concerned intercepted mail, tapped telephones, and vehicles under surveillance. The rapid-access index was (and is) probably for use at
Heathrow airport, where a terminal to the C Department
computer has been installed.

Details of the records placed on the C Department computer, given in Table 11, show that other units – the Serious
Crimes Squad, Drugs and Illegal Immigration Intelligence
Units and the Fraud Squad – share the computer with Special
Branch (although the intelligence compiled on illegal immigration has now been moved to the Immigration Service's IVAN
intelligence computer at Harmondsworth). But the files of

the Special Branch far outstrip in size those of all the other sections. Most files concern 'persons' of interest, not 'criminals'.

After the Special Branch, the next largest sections, according to the projections, were the 'new and fast growing' immigration intelligence section – 287,000 names by 1985; the drugs intelligence nominal index – 60,000 names, also described as 'new and fast growing'; and the Fraud Squad's files on 73,000 people, and 33,000 companies. Both the Drugs and Illegal Immigration Intelligence Units were relatively novel, having been established in 1972. One of the key intelligence methods that detectives wanted to expand was the development of networks of friends – or 'associates' – which might point to other drug dealers and users. The seizing of personal documents, letters and above all address books became, and has remained, a key feature of police raids, whether in the investigation of crime, or solely for gathering intelligence. The fifth section using the C Department computer, the Serious Crimes Squad, would, by 1985, have files on 193,000 people, with only two small indexes – containing 130 and 2500 files respectively – holding data on 'criminals' of 'major' or 'particular' interest.[16]

Further applications intended for the computer included recording an index of stolen fine arts materials, a stolen currency index, and a serious crimes information-collation system similar to that developed in the major incidents inquiry system discussed in Chapter 7. More ominously, it was noted that 'future developments will probably include ... behavioural pattern recognition'. The system would be operational '24 hours a day, 7 days a week'. Passwords and badge cards would be used to control access to the system's VDUs, and special encryption would be adopted for communications with terminals outside the building. Noting that 'this system will handle sensitive data', the specification added:

> [Special Branch] must have access to all records that belong to other sections, but access to [Special Branch] data is to be withheld from other sections.

The Special Branch registry and the C Department computer are located on the top floors of New Scotland Yard's tower block overlooking Victoria Street in Westminster. The computers were installed in 1978. Immediately below, on the 18th floor, are the headquarters and offices of the Special Branch itself. Unless it was an underground bunker, the location could scarcely be more secure. The computers and their terminals are electromagnetically shielded against the accidental emission of signals which could enable a snooper to tap into information displayed on the police VDUs by a costly process known as TEMPEST. Other precautions are equally intense: security and password checks are necessary before a terminal can access any records. Passwords are stored in cypher, and take 40 seconds to encrypt or decrypt for checking. Some security routines are said to take more than half a day to complete.

During 1980, MI5 and police technical specialists feared that the computer was vulnerable to sabotage by radio beams being transmitted towards it. This fairly fanciful threat was not thought to pose a problem as far as the TEMPEST-screened computer itself was concerned; but the magnetic tapes backing up its data store were in an unshielded room. The specialists sought advice and were told that it would be very unlikely that radio beams or other rays could effectively penetrate the top of the New Scotland Yard tower to damage the magnetic tapes.

During the late 1970s, while the computers went through final technical acceptance tests, many provincial Special Branch officers posted to the anti-terrorist National Joint Unit were to their irritation instructed to spend their time entering Special Branch paper records into the new computer. Not until 1979, however, did the police acknowledge that the major purpose of the computer was to hold Special Branch records, when Deputy Assistant Commissioner Jock Wilson confirmed this fact on a BBC programme, *Horizon*. Home Secretary Merlyn Rees was then closely questioned about five misleading answers he had given to MPs about the computer, and the official description was altered to refer to a system storing information 'about crime, criminals and their associates; *and matters connected with national security*'. (Our emphasis.)

In a Home Office answer in 1983 John Tilley MP was told that the C Department computer stored:[17]

separate data bases maintained by a number of central CID departments supporting the fraud squad; the central drugs intelligence unit; the Special Branch; the special intelligence section which has responsibility for collating intelligence relating to organised international crime; the south-east regional intelligence unit; and one of the four area analytical and targeting units set up to deal with burglary and street crime.

By 1983, according to a later answer, there were 152,000 records on the C Department computer – *excluding* the Special Branch records.[18] There were then about 600,000 searches a year (50,000 per month) against these records. But the Home Office refused to be drawn on 'a more detailed analysis of that data [or] information about the number and distribution of terminals, as this would indicate the scale of effort devoted to the various units and their location'. However, these figures suggest that the computer is holding far more Special Branch data than originally anticipated.

Technical details of the computer installation have been published in the ACPO list of police computers.[19] The list says that the computer 'stores, manipulates and retrieves information previously held in a number of card indexes'. A new application – a method (or 'modus operandi') index – went live in 1984. This is used by the regional and international criminal intelligence units. By 1985, the C Department network consisted of six British-made Computer Technology 8050 computers, connected to 15 printers and 74 VDU terminals – 50 per cent more terminals than originally planned; and uses Status software. Seven disc stores hold 1100 megabytes of information – considerably greater than the amount planned in 1974, when the size of the data store was, by 1985, not expected to exceed 335 megabytes. At the same time, the number of *non*-Special Branch records is, at 152,000, far fewer than the 600,000 planned for computer storage by 1985 (see Table 11, page 265). Although the Status free text retrieval system is a heavy user of additional storage space, it is striking that the C Department computer now has a data store three times larger than originally planned, yet holds only one quarter of the projected non-Special Branch records.

The nature and quality of personal information held on

Special Branch records has come to light on many occasions during the 1970s and 1980s. The best known official review of the records was carried out in 1981 by the then Devon and Cornwall Chief Constable John Alderson. He reported that of 'several hundred' Special Branch files compiled by his own force, which he inspected, 'about 20' were relevant to police purposes. The weeding operation unearthed files on the lawful activities of anti-nuclear activists, opponents of blood sports, and past activities of members of the anti-apartheid movement. One surveillance entry noted that the target 'had meal with [Tony] Wedgwood Benn'.[20] Alderson said later, 'A lot of it was rubbish by junior officers slipped into the files. The left were given disproportionate attention.'

Soon afterwards, by using the Special Branch telephone enquiry service provided for units stationed at ports, the *Observer* newspaper obtained information about the past political activity of an SDP local election candidate. Oxfam worker Hugh Geach was the subject of a Special Branch file started in 1969, after he became active in the 'Stop the 70s Tour' campaign (against that year's planned South African cricket team visit) while a student at Reading University.[21] There was no information in the file after 1972, but it had not been weeded.

In a controversial case, West Midlands Police Special Branch opened files and investigations on four women peace campaigners who wrote during 1981 to a Sutton Coldfield newspaper about the need to protest if Parliament could not get the information it needed on nuclear weapons policy. The women received hoax telephone calls, obviously intended to establish their identities. Three months later, a Special Branch inspector visited one of the women, Madeleine Haigh, telling her a cock and bull story about investigating a £20 fraud on the mail-order company Grattan's. The local police station told her that her visitors had not been police officers. Despite repeated enquiries, the police continued to deny all involvement – until a fifth enquiry from Mrs Haigh's MP, cabinet minister Norman Fowler, finally unearthed the Special Branch officer responsible. Despite his 'unprofessional' methods, he was not disciplined, nor identified, and remained in the Special Branch. In a report to his police committee, West Midlands Chief

Constable Sir Philip Knights defended the enquiry on the grounds that it 'fell within the terms of reference of the Special Branch':

> Mrs Haigh had written to a newspaper in terms which were interpreted as indicating that she might be a person prepared to support or get involved in public protests ... the responsibility of Special Branch [is] analysing and assessing information of that kind.

Other similar instances of Special Branch officers using false pretences to investigate overt peace movement activities have been recorded. After writing letters to official bodies enquiring about local civil defence plans, a Reading student, Guy Smith, was approached and accused of being the prime suspect for a bank robbery; following his complaint to the police, he was told that the pretext for approaching him was 'fictitious' and the approach 'misguided'.[22]

A leaked Special Branch report on anti-racist groups in Bradford illustrated how easily the Branch guidelines may be twisted to accommodate surveillance of and information-gathering on any form of resistance to government policy. In 1982, a Bradford community relations worker and a local reporter entered Special Branch files as 'subversives' after a Branch sergeant had copied a 'human interest' story from the *Bradford Telegraph and Argus* about an Asian family due to be deported. Interpreting the article as a dramatic act of conspiracy and subversion, he copied it to an inspector, noting:

> These [articles] have been appearing at an alarming rate ... there is little doubt that there is a concerted effort by Bradford Asian Youth Movement (left wing), other left wing groups, Tim — (senior Community Relations Officer) (left winger) and John — (Reporter) to overthrow the Home Office's policy on Deportations.

The Branch officer making the report had also made an undercover visit to the offices of the Bradford Community Relations Council. But the note of his investigations was leaked to Max Madden MP.[23]

Leaked Special Branch files have often illustrated a three-way traffic in personal information between employers, the Branch and MI5. In 1977, trade unionists sitting in at Reinforcement Steel Services of Greenwich, a subsidiary of the publicly

owned British Steel Corporation, found personnel files referring to two recently sacked men. Of one, Paul Lutener, it was
recorded that:[24]

> The Special Branch have a file on this man for his political
> activities. They have four complaints on file against him of: 1.
> Distributing National Socialist literature [*sic* – a reference to
> *International* Socialists]; 2. Disturbing the peace during demon-
> strations; 3. Taking part in illegal demonstrations. [There are no
> 'illegal demonstrations' in the UK.]

Lutener, a union representative, had also been 'checked
through the Economic League and found to have no record on
their file'. Of a colleague, Charlie Duffin, there was also 'no
history known through the Economic League'. The Economic
League, described in the next chapter, is an industrial vetting
organisation which has been closely linked to the security
services (page 288).

During their inquiry, the Lindop Data Protection Committee
was infuriated by the refusal of the Metropolitan Police to
provide details of the C Department computer. Forced to rely
almost entirely on two articles from *The Times*, and parliamentary statements, Lindop said:[25]

> The observations we make on applications are of value only to the
> extent that the information on which they are based is adequate;
> in the case of the Metropolitan Police, we have not been able to
> satisfy ourselves that this is so ...
> In relation to the Metropolitan Police, we do not have enough
> evidence to give a firm assurance ... that the public need [not] be
> unduly alarmed by the use of computers for police purposes.

The Lindop report outlined a number of dangers foreseen in
connection with the new computer. To illustrate their fears,
they quoted an Australian report on the records of the New
South Wales Special Branch, which had been subject to investigation by a supreme court judge, Mr Justic White, in 1977/78.
The NSW Special Branch had accumulated 40,000 entries in
their card index, in a state with a population of 1,250,000 – a
level of surveillance comparable to that exercised by the Metropolitan Police Special Branch. Justice White reported that the
index had been compiled on:

the unreasoned assumption that any persons who thought or acted less conservatively than suited the security forces were likely to be potential dangers to the security of the state.

Files were held on:

All politicians of the Australian Labor Party at State and Federal level; current and former State Governors; half the judges of the supreme court; magistrates; prominent demonstrators; most prominent union officials; prominent clergymen in the peace movement; homosexuals; members of the Women's Movement; divorce-law reform campaigners ...

All Australian Labor Party election candidates automatically 'came under notice' of the Special Branch; but the candidates of the Australian right-wing and centre parties did not. The NSW Special Branch had been modelled on its British counterpart; its relationship with the Australian internal security organisation, ASIO, was the same as that between the British Special Branch and MI5; their Chief Constable was a British police officer, from Yorkshire. Their files, White said, were 'scandalously inaccurate'. Following the report, the NSW Special Branch was disbanded, and all but a tiny number of files destroyed under judicial direction.

Lindop also guessed that a national security database would have facilities to carry out multi-factor searches, and would use FTR techniques. This was indeed desired; the police specification noted that the new system would provide users with 'facilities not previously available', making possible 'much more sophisticated manipulation of the information ... than is possible with the existing manual methods'. There might therefore be 'suppressed [previously unobserved] demand' for the new facilities, when they became available. There was also 'a need to search free text information on un-keyed criteria, such as descriptions'. Lindop concluded:[26]

In the context of variable and diverse items of personal, and possibly unrelated, information [such a search capacity] leads us to infer that this is a [FTR] system ... If so, it introduces a new dimension of unease.

10 National Security Surveillance

The most secret computer in Britain is the on-line databank used by MI5, known as the Joint Computer Bureau. The Bureau's ICL computers are located at the service's Curzon Street House headquarters in Mayfair, London. The storage capacity of the computer, a reported 20 gigabytes in 1978, was then sufficient to hold basic data on about 20 million people. About 200 terminals, and a network of micro- and mini-computers in other government departments, are linked to the Joint Computer Bureau. Reportedly, registered 'permanent security files' are held on about half a million people who are formally regarded and classified as targets for MI5 surveillance – although the files necessarily refer to many more individuals than just those on the target list. The Security Service works with more independence of government supervision than any other comparable organisation in the country; its formal terms of reference are specified in a charter, which has never been published. The charter, according to former employees, is expressed in broadly the same terms as the Maxwell-Fyffe Directive, issued to MI5 in 1952 by the then Home Secretary, Sir David Maxwell-Fyffe.

This directive was not published until the Profumo inquiry in 1962. It stated that:

> The Security Service is part of the Defence Forces of the country. Its task is the Defence of the Realm as a whole, from external and internal dangers arising from attempts of espionage and sabotage, or from actions of persons and organisations whether directed from within or without the country, which may be judged to be subversive of the State.

The task of ensuring the 'Defence of the Realm as a whole', it then stresses, should be 'kept absolutely free from any political bias or influence'. But there is copious evidence that, so far as subversion is concerned, MI5 surveillance is wholly slanted towards the left. Organisations such as CND or NCCL have been placed under intensive MI5 surveillance because of government directives or the whims of senior officials. The service's internal structure (see Table 12 pages 276–7) shows that, while left-wing organisations are generally under heavy surveillance, no comparable attention is given to the political right or those who might financially damage the country. This trend – and the willingness to use unorthodox methods – has hardened inside the Security Service during the last 15 years, partly because of the intensified surveillance of radical groups since 1970, and partly because of the intractable struggle in Northern Ireland.

MI5 is organised into six major divisions. All except the staff and personnel divisions are involved in gathering and analysing 'security intelligence'. K Branch deals with counterespionage, and is primarily concerned with the hostile intelligence activities of the Soviet Union, the Soviet bloc and China. F Branch deals with domestic subversion, and has separate sections for the Communist Party; trades unions, industry and the media; radical and Trotskyist groups.[1] Considerable effort is devoted to recruiting and running literally hundreds of agents and informers into these groups, according to former MI5 officials.[2]

A Branch, perhaps the most controversial part of the Security Service, specialises in surveillance work. A1E provides and operates bugs and electronic equipment; A1C provides safe houses from which bugs and other equipment can be monitored and operated; A1A specialises in breaking into houses to plant bugs, steal or copy documents; A1D provides locksmiths and carpenters to assist in break-ins and planting bugs. A2A transcribes the results of bugs and taps; A2B provides photography services. A4, based in London's Euston Tower building, provides the 'watcher service' for tailing suspects.[3] Another A Branch desk specialises in acquiring personal information to which MI5 is not entitled, from other government departments, banks and the like.

The main tasks of S Branch ('Support') are to run the computer centre and organise MI5's huge registry and library of paper files. C branch supervises the vetting of civil servants and outside contractors working on government contracts. Overseas, MI5 security liaison officers are posted to Washington, Melbourne, Ottawa, British forces in Germany, Hong Kong, Cyprus and in the Caribbean. Senior retiring police officers, usually ACPO members, are also appointed as regional 'police liaison officers' to co-ordinate MI5 supervision of Special Branch work. According to former Special Branch chief Colin Hewett, MI5 has 'national responsibility' for 'central processing' and the 'link-up' of files on subversives. At offices in Grosvenor Street, Mayfair, MI5 runs regular training courses on security and subversion for Special Branch officers.

MI5 began computerising its records in 1971. By 1980, they had established what was at the time the largest computer

Table 12
Security Service organisation

Director General	Deputy Director General		Secretary
Secretariat	Auditor	Legal adviser	Overseas Stations

A Branch	Intelligence resources and operations
A1	Operations (bugging, break-ins, safe houses, etc.)
A2	Technical support (tapping, photography, laboratory, GCHQ)
A4	Watcher service
A5	Scientific research and development
B Branch	Staff office, administration, finance
B1	Recruitment and security of MI5
B2	Personnel management and welfare
B3	Management services
B5	Finance
C Branch	Protective security
C1	Security policy in government
C2	Vetting and security of government contractors
C3	Vetting of government departments staff
C4	Counter-terrorism security
F Branch	Domestic subversion
FX	Agents and informers in subversive organisations
F1	Communist Party (CPGB)

centre in Europe (in terms of on-line data storage). The original centre of MI5's computing operations was a discreet modern building in a quiet Mayfair mews, Mount Row. Although the building bore no external signs of ownership, door-keepers told callers that it was in use by the 'Ministry of Defence'. In records held by the government Property Services Agency (PSA), however, Nos 27–28 Mount Row were listed, together with an extensive portfolio elsewhere in Mayfair, as belonging to 'MoD-X'. MoD-X – i.e., Department X of the MoD – is a transparent euphemism for the Security Service, which traditionally takes cover as being part of the Defence Ministry.

PSA records described Mount Row as the MoD-X computer centre. Behind an entrance hall, passage onto the ground floor of Mount Row was blocked by massive metal doors, behind which was installed an ICL 1907 computer. Although small by

F Branch	*Domestic subversion (continued)*
F2	Trade unions (including industry, education, media)
F3	Terrorism (excluding Irish)
F4	Agents and informers – trade unions and CPGB
F5	Irish terrorism
F6	Agents and informers in Trotskyist and radical organisations; agents and informers in terrorist organisations
F7	Trotskyist organisations; anarchists; feminists; pacifists; black power; nationalist and other radical groups; fascists
K Branch	*Counter-espionage*
K1	Counter-espionage in government departments
K2	Soviet intelligence service
K3	Soviet agent recruitment
K4	Soviet diplomats and nationals – surveillance
K5	Soviet Bloc, Chinese agent recruitment
K6	Hostile intelligence services
K7	Counter-espionage within UK intelligence services
K8	Non-Soviet diplomats and nationals – surveillance
S Branch	*Support services (registry, JCB, training offices)*
S1	Joint Computer Bureau
S2	Registry
S3	Training
S4	Supplies, travel, printing

contemporary standards, the 1907 was, in 1971, the largest British-made computer. According to ICL officials, the computer was then handed over in exceptional secrecy.

The computer had to be installed away from MI5's then headquarters, Leconfield House, since that building was being returned to its owners after 30 years' occupation. MI5 was to move into former Department of Education and Science offices at Curzon Street House, which in 1974–76 were extensively modernised and refitted to accommodate an enlarged staff and a plethora of new information retrieval equipment, including the new computer. Counter-espionage activities – the service's K division – continued to be run from a separate building at 140 Gower Street, WC1, near Euston station, with the watcher service nearby at the Euston Tower. The Mount Row offices closed after the original computer was shut down.

During 1977, MI5 moved. Extensive rebuilding work had taken place at the rear of Curzon Street House, evidently to accommodate computer-support equipment, such as air-conditioning plant and standby generators. The computer itself is located on the ground floor of the building, which is a fortress. Curzon Street House was constructed during the Second World War with its ground and basement floors consisting of a massive concrete 'citadel' able to protect over 100 staff from intense aerial bombardment. In 1942, the King and Royal Family sheltered in the building during severe episodes in the London Blitz.

Above the computer centre, on the first floor, a vast hall contains MI5's R3 registry and filing system. This uses an automated file storage and retrieval system, called Conservatrieves, made by Roneo Vickers. Twelve computer-controlled Conservatrieves, installed in 1976, automatically find and produce personal and information files, held in 400 capacious ceiling-high storage bays.

After MI5 moved into Curzon Street House, a curious series of recruitment advertisements started to appear in the specialist computer magazines, *Computing* and *Computer Weekly*. They came – ostensibly – from a private employment agency, EDP Systems. In fact, MI5 was taking on staff, the first time the service had ever been known openly to advertise! The advertisements never stated, of course, that the client was MI5 – but it was nevertheless possible, in retrospect, to learn a great deal about MI5 and its computer from details disclosed in the advertisements.

They began in April 1977, shortly before MI5 took delivery of the new computer. MI5 was then stated to be 'developing large scale, sophisticated information systems using major ICL 1900 and 2900 computers'. Later that year the computer was described as a 'real time' system. In December 1977, computer programmers who considered working for MI5 were promised 'sound prospects in a growth situation . . .'; there would also be 'creative analysis work at one of the most advanced installations in London . . . our clients have a considerable volume of new projects on hand . . .'

Identifying the MI5 computer in all but name, EDP's advertisements repeatedly referred to 'one of the most powerful and advanced installations in central London (located in Mayfair)' with a 'large ICL 2980 configuration . . . The installation is busy and there is ample software work of a varied nature'; applicants were told to expect 'a stimulating career in a well organised department'. The number of advertisements suggest that MI5 has recruited between 60 and 100 computer professionals to develop its computer centre and national network.

One applicant for an MI5 computer programming job was responsible for first alerting the public to the presence of the new computer. The person concerned, a lecturer, had applied routinely to the agency, and was then interviewed at the MI5's Great Marlborough Street administrative offices. The interviewers told him that he would have to be positively vetted, but did not tell him that the job was with MI5. But they did say that the computer was a dual ICL 2980, to which were connected no fewer than a hundred EDS 200 disc stores, the largest type then made by ICL. This was, even by the standards of an industry accustomed to superlatives, gargantuan. His suspicions about the nature of the installation were further aroused when he was told that, although he would be working for the civil service, he would get one grade higher pay than usual. He passed information about the new installation to *Computer Weekly*. The Defence Ministry admitted the purchase of the computer, but said that its task was to hold a 'classified database'. Nothing further could be said.

When the existence of the MI5 computer was first revealed in 1983, ICL admitted that a dual 2980 system had indeed been bought by a 'government department [which could not be identified] somewhere in the UK'. The Ministry of Defence admitted that the computer existed as described, and said that it was 'in use in the intelligence field. We can't say any more.'[4]

The main purpose of the computer was to hold a large database, using a software system called IDMS. The use of this system implied that MI5 intelligence information and reports were to be pooled in a single, comprehensive store, in order to facilitate intelligence officers' enquiries. Special applications programs were to be written in the standard business and text programming language, COBOL. According to advertisements, the MI5 computer was to stand at the heart of a network of mini- and microcomputers. Little indication of the scope or extent of the network was given, but EDP's recruiting campaign made repeated references to an 'on-line mini-computer system' network linked to the main computer. In February 1978, one advertisement specified that minicomputer specialists would have to give 'presentations to [unspecified] user departments'. During 1979, a special programming group was set up in MI5's administrative offices at Great Marlborough Street (now vacated).

At least one of the minicomputer sites connected to MI5 can be identified from EDP's 1978 advertisements. It was located 'near Waterloo station' – which is likely to refer to the offices there of the Secret Intelligence Service (MI6). The MI6 mini-computer would utilise a 'large-scale database, communications systems and transaction processing techniques … [with] a newly installed major computer'.

These references confirm private information to the authors from ICL sources that MI5 has attempted to develop a national communications network linking several large government computers. ICL began developing such a network – known as 'MoD-mult' – in 1972. The name suggests that it has always been planned to link the MI5 or 'MoD-X' computer to multiple sites elsewhere. ICL sources said in 1982 that a secret government network was still under active development and named the executive leading the development team, Mr Trevor Davies. Davies was approached by the authors, but refused to comment on the project, asserting that he was 'sworn to secrecy'.[5] Applicants for MI5 jobs in 1983 were told by Peter Hilditch, recruiter for EDP Systems, that there were 'piles of minicomputers' linked to the MI5 computer centre. A colleague told other applicants that, by 1983, the 'autonomous government department' using the system had by then established a 'nationwide' network of 200 computer access terminals.[6]

Information about an early plan for a central government computer network (with, it is presumed, secret links to MI5) have now partly become public. Known as GANNET – for general administrative network – it was developed jointly by ICL and the government's Central Computing Agency (now Central Computing and Telecommunications Agency). ICL computers at government centres across Britain were linked, using GANNET. The first GANNET experiment was concluded in 1976, but the programs were taken over by two other customers: a British north-western universities network; and the Ministry of Defence, who had been working on a similar project for a network of giant military computer centres, known as GRIDFEST, since 1972.

Going 'live' in 1979, the dual 2980 configuration achieved particularly high computing power because of direct connection of the central computers. Only three such dual processors have ever been made, two of them going abroad. A third computer – an ICL 2960 – was bought at the same time. This could be used as a back-up to the 2960s, to convert programs and data from the now abandoned 1907 computer, or as part of the intelligence computer communications network. The reason for the gigantic data store (five times larger than the Police National Computer, for example) has not been made clear – 20 gigabytes is equivalent to the information contained in a library of about 50,000 paperback books. Theoretically, it could store personal dossiers on some 20 million people, if these consisted of identifying particulars and about 150 descriptive words (similar to the Special Branch files). It is more likely, however, that the capacious storage and processing capacity of the Joint Computer Bureau is used to provide rapid analysis and processing facilities for MI5's intelligence reports, and to assemble a comprehensive security intelligence database.

Despite considerable parliamentary concern when the scale of MI5's computer operations was revealed, the government has repeatedly refused to provide any information about the data stored or the safeguards against its abuse. When the computer first came to public notice, the Prime Minister asserted that 'it is the practice – long hallowed by all parties – not to comment on matters of security'. In January 1984 new and more powerful ICL computers were ordered by the Ministry of Defence, on behalf of the Security Service.

New information about MI5's records and surveillance targets have shown that repeated claims about the service's attention to the 'Defence of the Realm as a whole' are not well founded. 'Box 500' reports on top trade unionists – although 'sanitised' of illegally obtained or sensitive data – have been known to have been circulated to ministers for more than 20 years.[7] And even if local activists in radical or peace groups do not fall within MI5's criteria of subversion, the Special Branch can open files on them, as we have seen in Chapter 9, as a 'threat to public order'. MPs, lawyers, journalists and teachers have all been put under MI5 surveillance on the flimsiest of pretexts. Journalists and others who investigate or write about the activities of British intelligence or security services automatically become the target of the K7 counter-espionage section, which specialises in putting MI5's critics under surveillance. To the embarrassment of the then Home Secretary, Leon Brittan, his own assurance about the strict limits of MI5 surveillance on subversives were shown to be worthless by a series of revelations in 1985 about the service's campaign against NCCL and CND. Questioned, for example, in January 1985 by the House of Commons Home Affairs Committee as to whether 'people who are members of CND ... are subversives within the definition as given in your guidelines' (for telephone tapping), Brittan repeated earlier assurances that:[8]

> There is no doubt that peaceful political campaigning to change the mind of the Government and of people generally about the validity of nuclear disarmament, whether unilateral or otherwise, is an entirely legitimate activity which does not fall within the very strict criteria.

It seems most unlikely that, before Brittan had reiterated this claim, Home Office officials would have failed to draw his attention to the fact that these words were untrue: his approval had been given, in August 1983, to a telephone tap warrant against a leading CND official, John Cox, in order that MI5 might provide more information about CND at government's request. Brittan was soon reminded of this case and other aspects of the 'counter-subversion' campaign that had been mounted against CND.

A few weeks after he spoke, a temporarily banned Channel 4 programme on MI5, *20/20 Vision*, revealed that concerted MI5 surveillance of CND had been launched in the spring of 1981, under government pressure. At that time Cathy Massiter, a Security Service intelligence officer, who had worked for MI5 for 14 years, was given charge of the CND investigations. According to Massiter, John Cox, although a communist, was 'not getting up to anything' in CND; he was not, as the government's telephone tapping rules required, engaged in 'major subversive activity'. But the tap went ahead nonetheless. In December 1983, after protesting unsuccessfully that the activities she had been asked to supervise were politically biased and in contravention of the Security Service's charter, Cathy Massiter resigned.

MI5's reports on CND were sought by the Ministry of Defence for a political campaign against the peace movement, launched in 1983. The campaign was co-ordinated by a hitherto secret cabinet committee, the Working Party on Nuclear Weapons and Public Opinion. Subsequently, although temporarily, the Defence Ministry set up a special organisation, Defence Secretariat 19 (DS 19) to campaign against CND. Ordinary civil servants protested that the DS19 proposal was against their rules of not engaging in party politics. But they were told to 'put up or get out' by junior minister Peter Blaker. DS19 demanded enhanced MI5 surveillance of CND. Information about leading members of CND was turned to political ends before the 1983 general election, when Defence Secretary Michael Heseltine used selected information from the MI5 report in a letter to Conservative election candidates.

The contravention of MI5's own rules could scarcely have been more flagrant. But it went further. An MI5 agent, Harry Newton, was directed to infiltrate CND. Files contrary to the terms of the charter were opened on leading CND members, including its chair, Joan Ruddock. 'It was fully recognised that she had no subversive affiliation,' Massiter said on 20/20 Vision, so MI5 invented one. Ruddock had chanced to give a press interview to a Soviet journalist in London, who actually worked undercover for the KGB; she thereupon went into MI5's files as a 'contact of a hostile intelligence service'. A Christian CND executive member, Cathy Ashton, went into the files as a 'communist sympathiser', since a communist happened to live in the same house as her. There was a report than CND vice-chair Roger Spillman had once belonged to the Young Communist League, which MI5 did not believe – but it enabled them to keep the file open on him, so the false record stayed.[9] While MI5 improperly opened files on a few key CND members, the Special Branch opened 'thousands' of files on local CND groups. Their reports were passed to Cathy Massiter.

Similar ruses have been widely used to get round the formal criteria for defining subversives. MI5 found difficulties in opening a file on one of the authors of this book, Duncan Campbell, in 1976, as he did not belong to and had no links with any of the officially registered 'subversive' organisations. An MI5 officer therefore branded him and others like him, such as journalists and solicitors connected with the NCCL, as '*unaffiliated* revolutionaries' (our emphasis).

MI5's charter (as it has been published in the form of the Maxwell-Fyffe directive) might indeed ask that the service 'be kept absolutely free from any political bias or influence'. But without outside supervision and inspection, the charter is worthless. Without whistleblowers like Cathy Massiter, no one would have known how bad the situation had become.

Besides getting information through illegal or unofficial contacts, MI5 appears to have formal access to all government records. Accessing National Insurance records, held at the DHSS Central Office in Newcastle, provides routine and important, if rudimentary, data (see pages 110–12). Despite half-hearted claims that DHSS computers and records are protected, it is difficult to see how, if they are, MI5 could have come to make normal use of the NI number as a personal identifier. More specific personal information can be obtained by MI5 from DHSS personal files through direct contact with a special liaison office at Newcastle (Special Section A, Records B), or by asking local Special Branch officers to make enquiries of a DHSS local office manager. In particularly difficult cases, where access may be refused (such as when attempting to obtain Inland Revenue information), the enquiry will be referred to the MI5 A Branch team, which specialises in obtaining confidential information by subterfuge.

Although, as already mentioned, MI5's full charter (as opposed to the Maxwell-Fyffe directive) has not been published, it is likely to contain the same provisions as the charter that MI5 chiefs prepared in 1952 for their antipodean counterpart, ASIO – the Australian Security Intelligence Organisation. The charter was signed by the Australian Prime Minister. Since MI5's own charter formed the basis of ASIO's, it is likely that similar rights are secretly granted to MI5. Thus, although much of the ASIO Charter repeats the terms of the Maxwell-Fyffe Directive, some additional sections appear, which are not contained in the directive. The ASIO Charter adds the instruction that their information system should be 'comprehensive'. Another section gives the Director General of ASIO power to inspect any government records whatsoever:[10]

> You will arrange to have such access to the records of Government Departments and agencies as you may deem necessary for the purposes of your work... You will establish a comprehensive set of security records. In order to do this you will arrange that all Government Departments and agencies submit to you for inclusion in your record all information bearing on security which may be, or come into, their possession.

In short, the security agency was granted a licence to obtain any government information, without legal obstruction or administrative difficulty. For the British Security Service, with the means and ability to acquire personal data from other government records by legal or illegal methods, the right to breach privacy wholesale now appears to have been enshrined in the Data Protection Act (see Chapter 11).

Leaked MI5 documents and other reports have also illustrated the nature and extent of national security surveillance. The surveillance of working-class political activity has always commanded considerable attention. In 1980, for example, MI5 ordered a Special Branch check on a Scottish food factory worker, James Hogg of Dumfries. Unfortunately, the Branch report went astray in the post and arrived instead at the offices of the London magazine *Time Out*. Like all correspondence with the Security Service, it was addressed to Box 500 in London SW1. The Special Branch detective reported that:

> Hogg has been described by a management contact as being more than normally active in union debates within the factory and is thought of as very left wing. Hogg is thought to be connected with the Socialist Workers Party also, although this cannot be verified at present and is based purely on hearsay information from within the Carnation Foods factory ... It is thought by management that he may well leave some time in the near future to take up some kind of full time employment with the Transport and General Workers Union. This situation will obviously be monitored and any further developments will be reported.

In fact Hogg – although an active shop steward and trade unionist – was a member of neither the Communist nor the Socialist Workers party.[11]

The Hogg case demonstrated the widespread use of NI numbers for personal identification; the report twice quoted his NI number as a confirmation of his identity. The MI5 reference – PF886214/F1C/25 – also indicated Hogg's permanent security file (PF) number in the MI5 registry (886214) and the MI5 'desk' which kept him under surveillance. F1C deals with the branch and district organisation of the Communist Party of Great Britain (see Table 12, page 277). One recent investigator has asserted, after consulting former Special Branch officers, that the branch and MI5:[12]

> [utilise] with great effect the National Insurance system ... By accessing the information relating to a person's contributions, it is possible to learn his place of work, if she or he has one, or the area in which the individual lives.

The use of NI numbers as an identifier on Security Service and Special Branch files was emphasised in the case of Jan Martin. Ms Martin worked for a private film company run by TV broadcaster Michael Barratt. In September 1978, Barratt had contracted to produce PR films for the building company Taylor Woodrow; after receiving details of his employees who would work on the film, the company said that one, Jan

Martin, was a 'security risk' and therefore would not be permitted on Taylor Woodrow premises. Barratt challenged this assertion and was told that 'there is a connection with terrorists in Europe, Baader–Meinhof. We can absolutely confirm this if you tell us [Ms Martin's] NI number.' When her NI number was provided, Taylor Woodrow somehow caused further enquiries to be made – and confirmed, they said, the 'security risk' description.

Why was Jan Martin said to be a security risk? And how was Taylor Woodrow able repeatedly to vet prospective staff against security files? Martin's father, fortuitously, was a former senior Scotland Yard policeman, and he approached the Special Branch for help. They confirmed that the information obtained by Taylor Woodrow was contained in their records. Uniquely, Jan Martin was able to check that she had a record on Branch files; discover what was in it; and have it corrected. Her opportunity to restore her good name, obtained by virtue of family connections, is not, however, available to the thousands of other people whose job opportunities and personal lives will have been blighted by the effect of such secret security records (whether accurate or not).

Following her father's intervention, Jan Martin was interviewed by Branch Detective Chief Superintendent Peter Phelan, and the source of the report on her identified within two days. She and her husband had been travelling through the Netherlands soon after a Baader–Meinhof attack. Her husband resembled terrorist Willi Stoll, whose photograph had been circulated after the attack. Someone spotted the likeness and took her car number. A report was passed back to Scotland Yard and MI5 that she had been escorting a known terrorist. The report was never taken further, but remained on file against her name – and NI number. But for her father's intervention, Jan Martin said, 'I could have spent the rest of my life in the shadow ... If one company could get that information, then every other company could get it.' She thought that her career was finished.[13]

Subsequently, in evidence to the House of Commons Home Affairs Committee, Special Branch chief Deputy Assistant Commissioner Colin Hewett admitted that, in the Martin case:[14]

There was information divulged which should not have been
divulged, and an inquiry showed that this was the case. This is one
of these cases which is very much regretted.

But Jan Martin is far from being the only case of gross error in
security files. In 1977, it was reported that MI5 had provided
Prime Minister Harold Wilson with adverse security reports on
two distinguished MPs, both future ministers, Judith Hart and
Dr David Owen. Owen had been confused with another MP,
the late Will Owen, who was accused (and acquitted) of Official
Secrets Act offences. Judith Hart may have been confused with
a communist called Tudor Hart; at any rate, MI5 are known to
have tried to block her appointment as a minister on grounds
of a 'security enquiry'. But their evidence was found inadequate or worse by two successive Prime Ministers, and
rejected.[15]

How and why did the information on Jan Martin reach
Taylor Woodrow? There is evidence that the Special Branch
may *not* have been to blame, although they chose to accept
responsibility. The Martin case was not an aberrant 'leakage';
the conduct of Taylor Woodrow made it quite clear that they
had routine and automatic access to security data, even to the
extent of being able to double check and seek confirmation.
This transaction in information on 'subversives' and the like
was probably one example of the then long-established
arrangement between the Security Service and the right-wing
employers' organisation, the Economic League.

Financed by private industry to the tune of about £800,000
a year, the Economic League provides a 'labour-vetting' service
to its subscribers – checking on hundreds of thousands of
employees or job applicants every year. Taylor Woodrow and
other large construction industry companies are prominent
supporters of the League, and make extensive use of its
services to check on building workers. In 1980, for example,
Taylor Woodrow paid the League £30,048. The existence of
the vetting service conducted by the League's 'research department' – although often denied by League officials – has
periodically been confirmed by press exposés, when journalists or trade unionists have obtained the ex-directory numbers
and client identity codes used to contact the League's
vetting service, operated at the time from headquarters in

Thornton Heath, Croydon.[16] To use the vetting service, an employer must supply the League with the name, date of birth – and NI number – of the person they wish checked.

Links between the Economic League and the Security Service have in the past been not merely close but intimate. Economic League officials work within MI5's premises, and lecture on training courses for military and Special Branch officers. This arrangement was discovered, and subsequently reported to the authors, by an RAF officer, who during his career was reponsible for the ground defence and security of several key British nuclear weapons bases. In 1970, he attended a joint services intelligence course organised by MI5 and held at their Gower Street offices. The lecture on 'Subversion in Industry' was given, not by an MI5 desk officer, but by an Economic League official. After the lecture, the officer was 'astonished' to discover and see that the Economic League official had a desk and filing cabinet within MI5's offices. The League has also published many leaflets and booklets describing alleged subversion in industry. During the early 1970s, League officials frequently lectured on the same topic at Ministry of Defence courses and civil defence meetings.

Many enquiries to the Economic League have produced information which could openly have been culled from Communist Party and left-wing publications. But – as in Jan Martin's case – there are occasions when information likely to have been passed on by the League could only have come from MI5 files. The League supplied Taylor Woodrow with their so-called research (i.e., vetting) service. The critical piece of information used to double-check her identity, *on a file containing information of a purely security nature*, was her NI number. This is established Economic League and MI5 practice – but is not usual for checking police (including Special Branch) records. After the Jan Martin case was revealed, the authors confirmed this arrangement by tape recording a conversation with League officials, in which we posed as potential industrial subscribers. A League area representative explained that:

> We normally just need to know the name of the person and his National Insurance number. Within a very short time ... usually the same day ... we will be able to advise you.

To avoid declaring payments on their accounts as 'political',
many companies who use the League's services describe them
as 'research'. The official also explained, 'If you want the sub-
scription paid anonymously, that can be arranged ... normally
the Inland Revenue will accept that [as tax deductible].'

The MI5 links with the League were confirmed by an internal
document leaked to *Labour Research* magazine in 1985, entitled *The need for a change in direction*.[17] The 'flow of information' to the League's Research (i.e., vetting) Department, it
noted, 'came from London Region [of the League]'s contact
with official sources ... London Region had four men who had
professional security or police backgrounds working in the
Research Department ...' But both the security links and the
vetting service had declined since the late 1970s, the document
noted, as the ex-police and MI5 staff who had operated the
liaison had departed: 'The official sources of information have
now virtually dried up, as they were confidential to the old
London Region professional staff.' In 1983, the League had
carried out 'only' 140,000 vettings, as against 400,000 five years
previously. There was no longer 'a single professionally trained
or counter-subversive member ... of the department'.

While the Economic League vetting service operated with
official blessing, vetting lists processed by the League were
presumably passed back to MI5, enhancing the Security
Service's industrial surveillance outside the public sector, and
enabling them to disrupt the careers and employment of their
targets. This was certainly the effect of the systematic and
unacknowledged use of MI5 information for political vetting
purposes inside the BBC. Arrangements made in 1937 for MI5
security checks on employees survived unchanged until 1985.
A secret office at the BBC has liaised with MI5 and holds political 'security files' on staff and prospective employees.[18]

To indicate that a BBC employee had a secret security file, it
was the practice to stamp a symbol resembling a Christmas
tree on their ordinary personnel file.[19] Candidates for internal
promotion would have their secret files checked; those
coming in from outside were checked with MI5's F Branch,
dealing with domestic subversion. MI5's spotlight on 'media
subversives' includes directors, film editors, journalists and
presenters, even actors and actresses. An exposé in the

Observer in 1985 illustrated half a dozen of the many cases where MI5 records were used to block employment. One of the most chilling of these concerned the 1981 appointment of the editor of the *Listener* magazine. After the selection panel had chosen their desired candidate, *Guardian* sub-editor Richard Gott, a security check – known obscurely as 'colleging' – produced allegations that Gott was an 'ultra-leftist' who 'digs with the wrong foot'. Gott was rejected on the basis of these vague assertions (which amounted to no more than a highly prejudicial way of describing his left-of-centre outlook). Another candidate was appointed.

The Irish 'troubles' have brought into being the most comprehensive population surveillance system in the United Kingdom. Virtually every member of the nationalist (Catholic) community in Northern Ireland is indexed in army intelligence records, either as a 'carded' subversive personality or in a system of 'house cards' (see below). During the 1970s, it was reported on several occasions that the population records amassed by the British army since they arrived in Northern Ireland had been placed on computer;[20] and in 1976 Prime Minister Harold Wilson announced that some records were to be computerised (see page 294): both these claims were inaccurate. At the time of writing, there is no evidence that any army nominal records – other than those relating to Operation Vengeful, which tracks vehicles – have been put on computer. Plans for computerising army intelligence data were still being 'reviewed' in 1980.[21] Whether some further computerisation has now been completed cannot definitively be established, as the Ministry of Defence affirmed in 1985 that they 'could not comment on questions about security matters', so far as these concerned the extent to which computers were in use in Northern Ireland.

The *Times* was the first newspaper to report prominently the widespread computerisation of army records. Journalist Robert Fisk claimed in 1974 that the 'army's computer has data on half the population of Ulster'.[22] Fisk had been given a demonstration of the efficiency of the (non-existent) computer system. An army sergeant had offered to tell him the colour of the sofa in the front room of the house in which the journalist lived. The correct answer was returned, by radio, in 30 seconds. But the information had not come from a computer but from the local index of house cards. A major purpose of the house cards, and related house search reports, was and is to provide information which army street patrols could use to check an individual's identity (by asking them to provide small domestic details about their home). The reporter's house had been included in the system, and so the cards revealed the colour of his sofa.

The card indexes were set up in Northern Ireland following the arrival of the first military units in 1969. The centrepiece of the system is a card personality index, maintaining details of all suspected subversives in each unit's operating area. The cards are called 'P' (for personality) cards; the people to whom they refer are generally described in army circles as being 'carded'. Standing army intelligence instructions say that 'a Personality card is to be opened on all persons who, because of their subversive or criminal activities, have come to notice of the intelligence office'. Apart from basic personal information, the cards also hold details of other family members, religion (which 'will probably indicate which side of the political divide the subject is on'), occupation, car details, lists of associates and any alleged membership of illegal organisations. If more than one family member is carded, a family card will usually be opened on the entire family, in a separate index.

Carded persons are periodically 'screened', a process which is disguised as routine checking, but is actually a planned updating of army records. Usually, one or more four-page personality files are then added to the basic P card. Photographs are taken, and filed for future reference. Each P card is given a number, prefixed by the first initial of the subject's surname by which it is indexed. The P cards are then interlinked with and cross referenced to house cards, street index sheets, 'organisation' cards (or files), 'job' cards and vehicle records. According to army intelligence training notes,[23] house cards are maintained 'in respect of all houses and small businesses within the Republican areas'; Protestant areas are not, apparently, included. House cards include a full description of the house, its telephone number if any, cars owned, a list of all occupants, their dates of birth, and schools attended by children. House cards are also opened on all business premises in Republican areas, listing all employees. So far as the Catholic community is concerned, the army's intelligence system is, in theory at least, total.

Street sheets are compiled from P cards and house cards, indicating suspected subversive activity or locations in the street or area. In country areas, where settlements are scattered, files are organised on a geographical grid index, rather than by streets. These are known, for reasons that remain obscure, as 'farmer's daughter files'. Job cards record terrorist or criminal incidents of interest to the army. Organisation files are held on any subversive organisation believed to be operating in a unit's area. These files usually include all local community groups in Republican areas, whether or not any terrorist involvement is suspected.

Many houses are the subject of even more detailed records, which are compiled when a house has been raided or searched by a military patrol. A 12-page Northern Ireland search report (NISR) is then filed as an annexe to the house cards. A NISR form lists comprehensive domestic details, including the number of telephone extensions, the type of television set, the colour of the front door, the colour of the furnishings, and the type of fire in the main room.

But the only part of this system which had gone on to computer, by 1974, were the vehicle cards. During the year, the army had constructed massive, fortified blockhouses on major border roads and at Belfast's Aldergrove airport, and erected less securely protected sites in towns and city centres. These vehicle check points, or VCPs, were part of the first, trial phase of the Operation Vengeful computer system. Based on a computer at Northern Ireland army headquarters at Lisburn, Vengeful is linked to 50 static or mobile VCPs throughout the North. A terminal operator types in registration numbers as the vehicles pass; an associated teleprinter rapidly prints out any information or warnings connected with the vehicle. Covert vehicle checkpoints can be connected to the computer by ordinary telephone or military radio. A vehicle may be listed as Stopchek (stop and search); Dontstop (do not let the persons inside realise they are under surveillance); Lookhard (search

extensively, the vehicle is suspected of being used by terrorists; Hardarea (owned or used by someone living in 'hard
Catholic or Protestant areas'). Hardarea lists are compiled for
the Vengeful computer at least once a year during periodic
'vehicle sweeps or trawls, which are usually done in the early
hours of the morning', according to official briefings. An army
patrol moves through the entire designated 'hard' area and
lists on a Vengeful data form every vehicle seen.

At first, Vengeful – like the Police National Computer – held
registration details of every vehicle in the North. But this
version of the system was notoriously unsuccessful. It answered queries very slowly, and too much information was
recorded to be useful. A former army area commander with 18
months' experience of the system said that he 'didn't know of a
single case' in which the first Vengeful system was helpful; it
was a 'disaster', with too much information being passed
about entirely innocent vehicles. A new version of Vengeful
began operating in 1977, with entries confined to *suspect*
vehicles.

The existence of Vengeful was admitted by Northern Ireland
Secretary Merlyn Rees in 1974, after the *Times* report stirred up
a parliamentary row. Rees stated, accurately, that there was
only a 'computer for vehicle checking'. Two years later,
however, following the terrorist murder of 12 Protestant
workers at Bessbrook, Harold Wilson – desperately searching
for a political response to the outrage – announced that the
SAS were to be sent to Ulster (they were there already) and that
the army *was* getting a new computer (they weren't getting
anything new). Wilson said:

> A new information system, based on automatic data processing, is
> to be introduced by the army to handle existing records so that
> information can be processed and acted on more quickly.

Defence Ministry officials stated that the computer held 'army
records, at present held in manual files and covering details of
suspects, weapons, incidents and vehicles'. In fact, they were
talking about nothing more than the modified and more
effective version of Vengeful.

Over 200 military intelligence specialists now gather data in
the North, together with about 280 RUC Special Branch officers.
Special military intelligence officers (MIOs) work as plain-

clothes officers inside Special Branch units, liaising on the operation of agents and informers, and exchanging intelligence with uniformed military staff. Before being detached to Special Branch jobs, army MIOs are instructed to 'try to achieve a position with access to all current intelligence and to gain the confidence and trust of the local officers'. But they themselves come 'under the direct command of the local head of Special Branch' to whom they are told to have 'primary allegiance'. The most important means of obtaining information for MIOs and Special Branch activity is said to be 'human sources' – i.e., informers. An annexe to the 'Northern Ireland Intelligence Environment' training course, however, lists a wide range of military and civilian 'agencies available ... from which information/intelligence can be obtained'. The civil sources which could be used included the Northern Ireland Housing Executive, the vehicle licensing and taxation offices, the registrar of births and deaths, and 'Newspaper Editors (for photographs) (direct)'.[24]

The Lindop committee faced as much difficulty getting information about computer systems in Northern Ireland as it had encountered with the Special Branch and MI5. Although they received evidence from the Northern Ireland Civil Rights Association about the scale and adverse effects of army surveillance and intelligence gathering, the committee reported that they were 'unsuccessful in obtaining any detailed information'. The future development of the Northern Ireland military intelligence system remains uncertain; the growing primacy of the civil police, the Royal Ulster Constabulary, may mean that efforts to develop further computer systems will centre on the RUC, rather than on the army.

The parallels between the Northern Ireland surveillance system described above and the index systems developed and used by civil police collators or local intelligence officers in the rest of Britain are evident. The differences between the two, in terms of basic data stored and indexing methods, are clearly quantitative rather than qualitative. But counter-terrorist operations are conducted with the aid of far more extensive legal powers and far greater resources than are yet available for orthodox police operations in Scotland, England and Wales.

*   *   *

All intelligence agencies report to government departments through a complex system of five committees, none of which involve regular supervision by ministers. Besides MI5, the other agencies all hold extensive computerised records, which will also attract exemption under Section 27 of the Data Protection Act (see Chapter 11). The Secret Intelligence Service (SIS) is only interested in British nationals in so far as they might become useful agents or observers overseas, or – in the UK – provide access or facilities enabling SIS to observe or recruit foreign nationals.

The Defence Intelligence Staff is primarily interested in military affairs, but they play a part in activities affecting the security of military bases in Britain and terrorism and counter-insurgency in Northern Ireland; they also receive MI5 briefings on aspects of home defence.

GCHQ (Government Communications Headquarters) is the largest British intelligence agency. Its tasks are sigint (signals intelligence) and comsec (communications security). Sigint is defined as intelligence obtained from the interception of electronic and communications signals – in short, electronic eavesdropping. Although GCHQ's prime targets are the military and diplomatic signals of foreign nations, and of the Warsaw Pact countries in particular, huge quantities of information are harvested from domestic and international communications channels; information on British persons and any other subjects identified as being of interest to MI5 or other departments will automatically be sieved from the huge volume of intercepted international communications traffic.

This work is done in co-operation with the United States National Security Agency (NSA). Personal information on such targets may be held at GCHQ's Cheltenham headquarters or passed into the Special Branch or MI5 computer systems. Because of the extreme sensitivity of sigint, it is closely protected; nevertheless, the authors have obtained from intelligence officials details of some individuals and organisations that have been targeted. One person identified as a named target on GCHQ's 'watch list' is leading Scots trade unionist Jimmy Milne, the Secretary of the Scottish Trades Union Congress.

Similar, and unconstitutional, sigint activities have been

revealed in the United States. During the Watergate investigations in the 1970s, NSA was found to have targeted for
interception the communications of such people as Dr
Benjamin Spock (prominent as an anti-war speaker), the
actress Jane Fonda, and black civil rights leaders Martin Luther
King and Eldridge Cleaver. Files were then assembled on a
computer network shared with the CIA and other agencies,
known as COINS (the [Intelligence] Community On-line Information Network System).

Besides MI5's Joint Computer Bureau, a number of other
specialised networks are used to transfer sensitive police or
security data. In 1975, the Home Office paid for police
headquarters to be supplied with telex connections to the
military TARE system, which is part of the UK defence
communications network. The TARE terminals were installed
in force operations rooms. Separately, provincial Special
Branches were supplied with teleprinters fitted with scram-
blers, to communicate between themselves, or with MI5, the
Defence Ministry or the Home Office. Within London, a
separate high-security network run by the Cabinet Office –
CODIN – links key ministries, the Metropolitan Police Special
Branch, MI5 and other intelligence departments.

The Lindop report addressed the problem of supervising
national security records in a well-considered and effective
manner. The committee suggested that:[25]

> A simple – and we believe satisfactory – solution ... would be to
> ensure that the DPA has at least one senior official with a security
> clearance sufficiently high for him to be able to operate as a
> privacy consultant to the Home Office and the Security Service,
> and to work out with them the appropriate rules and safeguards
> for their systems.

But the government was not interested; the idea was rejected
out of hand. Nor did ministers wish to undertake the job of
supervision themselves. Lindop also stressed that it was vital
that any exemptions allowed for national security reasons
should be 'strictly circumscribed'. In particular, the Data
Protection Committee said, there should be no exemption
from the rules prohibiting disclosure of data to unauthorised
third parties, 'even in the interests of national security'. But

these careful and balanced recommendations were completely disregarded in the drawing-up of the Data Protection
Act, along with so much else in the Lindop report. The result,
so far as data protection is concerned, has been to weaken still
further the restraints on national security surveillance at the
very time when the most compelling and authoritative evidence of abuse of power has become available to public and
Parliament.

11 Loopholes in the Law

The Data Protection Act received the Royal Assent in July 1984, but there remains a lengthy period – until November 1987 – before many of its provisions can be enforced. The two-year timescale for the introduction of the Act began in November 1985, with a six-month period for the registration of users of personal data on computer. From 11 May 1986, the operation of an unregistered databank became an offence; and compensation became available for some victims of inaccurate data. After November 1987, people who are the subject of computer data files will, finally, have a general right to see and challenge information which is held about them.

But the new Act is plagued with deficiencies and uncertainties, reflecting the uneasy compromise sought by the government between the concerns of official, institutional and commercial information processors and those of interest groups who place a higher value on personal privacy. In the legislation, the balance has almost always been drawn in favour of the information processors. Some of the Act's most informed critics, including former members of the Lindop committee, do not believe that the Act can survive much longer than two years before its many faults become glaringly obvious, and make clear a need for re-legislation.

Since the Act was passed, concern about data protection has been high amongst data users, on whom the burdens of registration, ensuring compliance with the data protection principles (see Table 1, page 32), and eventually of providing subject access, now fall. Public criticism has to some extent been muted by the impression that personal privacy has at last won some formal legal protection; and by the need to wait and see how the Act works in practice. But although some valuable protection has been provided (especially where the private sector is concerned), the new law will not necessarily curtail some of the most dangerous practices of the information-gatherers and information-swappers.

The power of sophisticated surveillance technology is changing qualitatively as well as quantitatively every few years. As public administration comes increasingly to rely on automatic data processing, as electronics continue to penetrate more and more areas of daily life, the information pool that the malign or merely curious may tap is growing. It is unlikely that either the Act or the Registrar will require any review of the privacy aspects of the central computer plans of the DHSS and the Inland Revenue – or of any other central databank plan still held in the dark recesses of the Central Computing and Telecommunications Agency.

To these regulatory problems may be added those presented by the new potential surveillance tools: scanners, character readers, vast text retrieval databanks, identity-card and passport monitors, telephone-call logging equipment, and much more – tools which would create grave enough difficulties for a law which had actually been designed to protect personal privacy. But the Data Protection Act was designed minimally to comply with the intentions of the European Convention on Data Protection, lest British business suffer from a prohibition on international electronic information processing.

Some – probably the vast majority – of data users will nonetheless meet their obligations under the 1984 Act. But for those who are not ready or willing to do this, the Act is replete with loopholes through which abuses of personal data may escape:

> It does not cover manual records, allowing information users to protect their most damaging data by retaining them or transferring them to paper.

> Information once held on a computer databank need not be disclosed to the data subject if it is later processed only on paper.

> Even if data users do not transfer their sensitive data to paper, they can evade the Act by processing it in a fashion contrived to avoid referring to individuals in their main records.

Sir Norman Lindop has christened such activities *extrusion* –
the process of moving personal data onto manual records, or
otherwise altering it radically, in order to evade data protection law. Other problems posed by the Act concern its
weakness so far as regulation or enforcement is concerned:

> There is no duty of supervision or inspection placed on the
> Registrar after data users have registered; violations of the
> Act will only be detected, in almost all cases, if the data
> subject happens to stumble across evidence of abuse (al-
> though the Registrar intends to 'monitor' the working of the
> Register).

> In consequence, data subjects have no chance of ensuring
> that damaging or unlawful processes are stopped before
> they cause actual harm; the harm must necessarily occur
> first.

> Data subjects have no right to have inaccurate data changed
> or removed. The Registrar can issue an 'enforcement notice',
> but such data may still remain if the user records the sub-
> ject's claim that the data is inaccurate alongside the data.
> Data subjects may, with difficulty, apply for a court order –
> but a court is not obliged to order that erroneous data be
> corrected.

> The Act does not allow government departments to be
> prosecuted for any offence, although private users are liable
> to criminal prosecution and penalties.

> The Act provides no safeguard against a data subject being
> forced to obtain access to sensitive personal data about
> themselves, and then pass it on to a third party (such as an
> interviewee being asked by a potential employer to produce
> a copy of their criminal record).

Further problems may arise from the special exemptions for
some data users, allowing them to hold data secretly or obtain
it from third parties:

> There are powers to make widespread exemptions from
> subject access for information about physical or mental
> health, or records concerned with social work – for which
> statutory regulations have yet to be written.

The Act grants ministers absolute power to exempt 'national security' databanks even from registration; other databanks are fully registered but partly or wholly exempt from subject access.

Information exempt from access for a purpose such as the 'prevention and detection of crime', the 'apprehension or prosecution of offenders' or the 'assessment or collection of any tax or duty', as well as for national security', will not be inspected or supervised by the Registrar.

Information gathered by or for these databanks need not be obtained or processed 'fairly or lawfully', as normally required by the Act.

The Act could become a tappers' charter for the exempt agencies, who could conceivably use the Data Protection Register itself as a guide to gathering further personal information.

All these pitfalls were pointed out to the government as the legislation went through Parliament, but the Home Office paid little attention.

So far as the exclusion of manual records from the Act is concerned, the government has circumvented the normal meaning of the terms of the European Convention by exempting from subject access 'mixed' records (i.e., those handled partly by computer, partly on paper). Article 2 of the convention requires ratifying states to legislate to control information processed by 'operations ... carried out in whole *or in part* by automated means' (our emphasis). In contrast, the Data Protection Act speaks only of 'information ... processed by equipment operated automatically'. Thus information of the most sensitive type, obtained or held in breach of the data protection principles, or even of the law, indexed but not 'held' on computer, need never be disclosed to the subject and therefore cannot be challenged.

Apart from Denmark, Britain is the only Western European country without a data commissioner whose duties include dealing either legislatively or administratively with complaints arising from the processing of manual records. The United States, too, has such a commissioner. Most commissioners have found that the majority of complaints from the public concern the handling of manual records; in Austria during 1983, for example, 80 per cent of complaints were of this kind.[1] Because of this serious flaw in the 1984 Act, MPs of all parties in 1985 launched an Access to Personal Files Bill, promoted by the Campaign for Freedom of Information, and intended to provide access to all personal files, whether computerised or on paper, held by official bodies. In order to retain wide backbench support, however, the bill's promoters excluded from their legislation the more contentious areas, such as police or national security files.

No tests of public interest are applied to the many special exemptions in the Data Protection Act, to limit their use to occasions of sufficient public importance. Nothing in the Act prohibits the police from provoking breaches of confidentiality for trivial purposes – for example, by obtaining and using computerised hospital records to see if someone who owns a vehicle has failed to notify a change of address to the Swansea computer. In Britain, such failure is a crime, punishable on detection and conviction by a £50 fine. Nor would DVLC staff be prohibited from access to hospital, clinic or benefit claimants' records, if they wanted the information thus sought in order to send someone a reminder to pay their vehicle excise duty (tax disc). The Act permits exemption to disclose such information for the purpose of the 'collection of any duty'. TV licence inspectors might similarly have access to social work records. Inland Revenue and VAT inspectors could decide that VD clinic records are relevant to their investigations, lawfully obtain them (although clients had been told that the records were confidential), and interview syphilis sufferers to establish whether prostitutes were evading personal taxation. The police could lawfully obtain from a family planning clinic a confidential list of all their clients, if their purpose was to discover the identities of 15-year-old girls who were pregnant (in the interests of 'the detection of crime' – in this case, statutory rape). Even if the police obtained this information unlawfully, for example by means of theft or blackmail of an employee, the unlawfully obtained data could be lawfully held on a police intelligence computer. The Act permits police information of this kind to be processed unfairly, or unlawfully, or both. For example, family planning clinic records could be processed to identify practising Catholics, with a view to using this information to recruit new police informers under duress of exposure. Under the Act, the police may lawfully conceal their access to such records, as may the clinic which handed them over, if both parties believe that their action might assist the prevention or detection of any crime. The police are then free to pass on the information gained to anyone else, as long as they believe it might help apprehend offenders. None of this information traffic need be registered or disclosed by the person passing on the data. Generally, the Act grants employees of organisations holding confidential personal data legal protection if they pass on information within the terms of these exemptions. It specifically grants them a discretion to breach confidentiality, and a defence against losing their jobs if they do.

The evil of these exemptions is not simply that they exist but that they are wholly permissive – unqualified by any weighing of the public interest between disclosure and the maintenance of confidentiality. Neither the Act nor the Registrar has any role in giving guidance in situations where a conflict of interests may arise (since the Act does not *compel* disclosure either). An individual employee asked for information must make a decision based on personal judgement, professional or institutional codes of conduct ... or nothing at all.

All privacy protection is put aside 'for the purpose of safeguarding national security'. These provisions set the UK aside from many other countries in which data protection rules – although not permitting subject access – allow independent checking and correction of records. For example, in Sweden and France external data protection agencies are permitted to check security records. But by citing a wide range of responsibilities, ranging from gathering information about possible threats to public order through to counter-espionage and counter-terrorism, ministers have sought to justify the wholesale accumulation of political and industrial intelligence, heedless of the effect this has on ordinary rights and liberties.

Section 27(1) of the Data Protection Act provides that personal data held 'for the purpose of safeguarding of national security' are exempt from all conditions of registration, regulation, supervision and access given in Parts II and III of the Act. The data protection principles cannot be enforced. Once again, data need not be obtained – or used – lawfully or fairly. Unlimited data can be held on political opinions or religious beliefs, physical or mental health, and sexual life – all topics which are otherwise subject to special protection, under Section 2(3) of the Act. The computers and databases concerned will not be registered, and not even the Data Protection Registrar – let alone members of the public – will find out about such installations or the personal records that they hold, except by accident.

Far greater potential damage, however, is threatened by the second provision of Section 27, which provides that, for national security purposes, information can secretly be passed out from any *registered* databank. Ordinarily, an entry in the Data Protection Register should contain a full list of persons or organisations to whom data may be disclosed. Once registration has taken place, this list is binding, and personal data may only be disclosed to authorised recipients. The third data protection principle also requires data users not to disclose data 'in any manner incompatible with [the] purposes' for which it is held. But national security is again an exception.

To claim 'national security' exemption, all that is necessary is for a cabinet minister (or the Attorney General) to sign a certificate. Sections 27(2) and 27(4) provide that:

> A certificate signed by a Minister of the Crown certifying that exemption is or was at any time so required [or ... that personal data are or have been disclosed for the purpose of safeguarding national security] shall be conclusive evidence of that fact.

In contrast to the exemptions allowed to police and tax authorities (see below), where national security is concerned no case can be taken to test the issue: the ministerial certificate is final and 'conclusive evidence'. If the security and intelligence services are able to convince a suitable minister – on the basis of arguments that may be arbitrary or untrue, inaccurate or incomplete – that exemption is required, then no challenge of that decision will be permissible. Parliament was told in 1984 that there were no provisions for the minister who signs

such a certificate to perform checks on the security, accuracy
and relevance of data stored on national security computer
systems.[2] And there is no obligation for national security
organisations to maintain accurate records. Furthermore,
according to parliamentary answers, there is no need for
government departments or ministers to notify the Home
Office when they have signed a certificate of authorisation.
Once the certificate is signed, it remains in force indefinitely,
without any obligation on the minister who signed it to check
its continuing validity.

Like the more restricted exemptions provided to the police
and taxation authorities, the dispensation to allow unregistered disclosures of personal data may well be deployed by
over-zealous security officials as though it were lawful authority to compel disclosure.

The Data Protection Register may itself threaten privacy,
turning the purposes of legislation on its head. By indicating to
security or police organisations where personal data of
interest is to be found, and providing the details which
facilitate an approach to the holder of the data, the Register
could even become an official snoopers' charter. There should
be particular concern that the National Insurance number,
used as a personal identifier in major central government
databanks and in employers' files, is also used by MI5 for the
same purpose. All data users, but especially such professional
interest groups as medical and social workers and their
authorities, should make it clear to the public and security
authorities alike that unregistered tapping of their databanks
will never be permitted; since the law provides no formal
safeguards, the remedy is in the hands of the databank
operators themselves.

The difficulties created by the exemptions were foreseen by
the Lindop committee, who warned that:[3]

> The security services [would be left] in a hermetic compartment
> where they can never discuss their problems with anyone outside
> their own tight community; thus they [would not be] open to the
> healthy – and often constructive – criticism and debate which
> assures for many public servants that they will not stray beyond
> their allotted functions.

*   *   *

The Act appears likely to be more effective in the case of the police than originally anticipated by critics. The PNC is registered as a computer bureau,[4] and individual police forces are registered as data users in respect of the PNC, as well as for their own computers. Detailed codes of practice are, at the time of writing, due to be issued in 1987, and will come into force late that year. The police are not generally immune either from registration or from subject access. Section 28 of the Act exempts specific items of information in police databanks from subject access – but only when such disclosure 'would be likely to prejudice ... the prevention or detection of crime [or] the apprehension or prosecution of offenders'. The databank itself must be registered. If access were refused by police forces or the PNC in any individual case, that refusal could be challenged either by complaint to the Registrar or by seeking a court order under the Act. Moreover, transfers of data to the police (or Inland Revenue) for allegedly exempt purposes can – *provided that they are discovered* – be tested in the courts. The onus would then be on the data users or computer bureaux concerned to show reasonable grounds for believing that the disclosure was made for an exempt purpose.

The Home Office first produced 'interim guidance' for the police on *Privacy Precautions for Computer Systems Handling Personal Information* in 1976. This was a few months before the Lindop committee visited the PNC. In the space of six pages, however, the interim notes had less than one sentence on the desirability of 'limiting data held to the minimum necessary', and nothing at all to say about testing the relevance or accuracy of personal data, or restricting its circulation within the police service to those who needed it. At that time, the guidance concentrated entirely on security matters.

At first, Home Office officials assumed that the PNC and all other police systems would be exempt from scrutiny by the (then proposed) Data Protection Authority. But the Lindop committee reported that any exemptions should be 'strictly limited' – and could not include the PNC. The government accepted this view. The first edition of a further code of conduct for the PNC itself (see Chapter 8) was issued in 1982.

Since then, further circulars have advised Chief Constables to improve precautions against abuses and leaks. Initially, the police did not keep a record of PNC transactions (an important safeguard against unauthorised use). Logs of varying formality were kept with each PNC terminal. Then, in 1980, a parliamentary answer revealed that the PNC itself had started keeping a record of 'each enquiry, including those related to motor vehicles, and the terminal involved. The record is kept one month ...'[5] Individual police forces were also asked to keep records of each enquiry and the name of the officer making the enquiry. The PNC code of conduct now prescribes that each force's use of the PNC will be checked by an officer of the rank of Assistant Chief Constable at least every six months.

So far as subject access is concerned, Home Office advice to police forces is that each item of data should be considered on a case by case basis.[6] That also applies to the PNC. It is therefore likely that most of the data on the PNC will be available to be checked by data subjects, should they so choose. It is unlikely that an attempt by the PNC to exempt entire indexes *en masse* would succeed. However, such a course of action might be considered in relation to the wanted/missing persons index, or to personal information on the stolen/suspect vehicle index.

In respect of the Special Branch, one important matter remains to be tested. When the Data Protection Act was passed, the government assumed – as did the Act's critics – that records held by the Special Branch, being 'matters connected with national security', would be fully exempt from registration. Since then, the House of Commons inquiry has shown that this is not the case. Special Branch records concern national security only when they are connected with assisting MI5 to deal with espionage, terrorism, subversion or sabotage. Public order intelligence does not fall within this definition; it may not even necessarily attract subject access exemption under Section 28, since it need not deal directly with either the 'prevention or detection of crime' or 'the apprehension or prosecution of offenders'. If that is so, then Special Branch personal files on computer which affect only public order might have to be disclosed under the Act. This might be a fruitful area for future legal exploration.

Other weaknesses in the Act affect, for example, major private sector organisations. In respect of the giant mail order/ electoral register databanks described in Chapter 3, it is obviously questionable whether such wholesale assembly of information from a wide variety of sources is in harmony with the data protection principles. The examination of these giant mailing list databases could be an important early test of the effectiveness of the Act. The principle that information should be used only for the purposes for which it was supplied ought to be the basis of judgement about the treatment of such population registers, once the Act is in force.

Although most people would see these private databanks as a substantial threat to privacy, the Data Protection Act may not be able to deal with them. The (computerised) electoral register, as originally compiled, is specially exempt from registration, because there is a statutory obligation to publish the register. There is no action that can be taken (even if judged appropriate) to ensure that the information in the register is not used by others for purposes for which it was not originally supplied. It is supplied (so far as the individual is concerned) *solely* in order to maintain the democratic right to vote – not to permit the commercial exploitation of information about who lives where by private or public bodies.

Given knowledge of what might happen to the information, many individuals might seriously consider not registering to vote. The Younger commission found, in their 1971 privacy survey, that some 40 per cent of respondents regarded the public display of a document listing the names of every adult who lived in every house in their neighbourhood as a breach of privacy. This was, of course, an exact description of the electoral register as it then was. The modern extension of the printed register to a computerised, on-line, nationwide network available to anyone able to afford to rent a Prestel terminal can only multiply such popular concern. (It should be said that members of the British Direct Mail Marketing Association – who operate databanks like those mentioned in Chapter 3 – have adopted a code of practice which includes agreeing to delete from their active mailing list files the names and addresses of customers who do not wanted unsolicited mail.)

Besides these specific problems, the Act and the data

protection principles pay no special heed to *scale*, to *linkage* of databanks, or to such critical and related issues as the use of personal identifiers or the carriage of identity cards. The Act also remains plagued by uncertainties over the definition of words like 'automatic', in the sense of automatic data processing.

There remain, too, many questions about whether the Act meets its task of complying with the European Convention. A legal opinion prepared for NCCL in March 1984 by Mr J.E.S. Fawcett, a member of the European Commission of Human Rights (although advising in a private capacity), found that the Act was inconsistent with the *European Convention for the Protection of Individuals with Respect to Automatic Processing of Personal Data* on three counts, and inconsistent with the *International Civil and Political Rights Covenant* on a further three counts. The practical significance of this is that, once the Convention comes into force, a signatory country could, if it so desired, refuse to send data to Britain, claiming that Britain was in breach.

Nor has the Data Protection Act been easy for many data users or commentators to understand. The same difficulty afflicts the Data Protection Registry itself. During 1985, Registrar Eric Howe's booklets, *Guidelines*, were twice cited as extreme examples of incomprehensible official prose by organisations such as the Plain English Campaign and the National Consumer Council. *Guidelines* was entered for the 'Golden Bull' award for official gobbledegook.

If the Act gives free rein to some and provides a multitude of loopholes for others, it is, nevertheless, absurdly *over-*regulatory and unnecessarily tough on many data users. The Act bites – and bites hard – on many users whose activities are little or no threat compared to the major databanks surveyed in this book. Under the Data Protection Act, a group of fifth-form schoolchildren who use a classroom computer out of school hours to survey other schoolmates' preferences for pop singers or sandwich fillings will become data users under the Act. They will have to designate one person as the legally responsible 'data user', and that person will have to register with the Data Protection Registry, and send off a £22 fee. If a printout of the information compiled is sent to the junior school down the road, and such a disclosure has not been registered, then the child chosen as the 'data user' is liable to prosecution and, on conviction, to pay an unlimited fine. If, meanwhile, the sixth form copy the databank and use it to issue questionnaires on career intentions, they will have to register anew, and pay another £22.

Similarly, a local newsagent who maintains anything more than the simplest customer accounts on a microcomputer may have to register, pay the fee, and provide subject access. He will be prohibited from passing information to anyone not identified in his Register entry. Few people would regard that newsagent as any threat to their privacy or liberty. Yet a police local intelligence officer (collator) working in the police station next door – whose computer may hold the most derogatory and potentially damaging information on hundreds or thousands of local people and their families – need neither provide access, nor arrange checks on accuracy, nor acknowledge in the Data Protection Register to whom such information may be disclosed, nor use the information lawfully – if this was judged to be in the interests of prevention and detection of crime. This is a serious injustice of the Act, for databank users as much as for those who are the subjects of computer data.

Not just newsagents, but solicitors and other professionals – including, dare one say, journalists, broadcasters and authors – have legitimate *and real* grounds for concern as to how the powerful might use the Act. In the film industry, for example, a piece of film might come under the Act if it was electronically time-coded; but not otherwise. One leading television editor has warned that the subjects of TV investigative journalism may use the Act to frustrate their work, if it is done on such time-coded equipment.[7] Similar problems could afflict public organisations like Citizens' Advice Bureaux (CABs). Landlords or employers might apply for subject access to computer files held at advice centres, or by trade unions or local authorities, to see what complaints had been made about them – perhaps in order to intimidate the complainants. Although there are restrictions on providing subject access to data which might breach the confidence of a third party, it may be difficult in practice to know when certain kinds of information on, say, a landlord's file might betray the identity of a complainant or informant. In practice, a CAB or local authority advice service operating such a computerised file could avoid having to provide access by not indexing the information about landlords by name (or not on computer anyway). But, as will immediately be apparent, others can also use this dodge to drive a coach and horses through the Act, by using obstructive indexing techniques.

The text of this book (which has been written and is stored as part of a computer word processing system) provides another example of these ambiguities. Should *On the Record* be registered under the Act? The answer to this question is a bit daft: yes, if it has an index on the same computer system as the text, but not otherwise. This bookful of computer data, being simply word processor text material, is normally exempt from the Act. If, however, the index is computerised and associated with the main body of text, information can then be processed automatically 'by reference to the data subject'. The authors, as data users in respect of the text of the book, would have to register under the Act, pay £22 and not sell the book to anyone not mentioned in the register entry (so our register entry would have to read 'data disclosed to anyone at all if the price is right'). After November 1987, the Home Secretary, or Sir Norman Lindop, or Mr Eric Howe himself, could write to us for subject access, enclose the prescribed fees and receive copies of the relevant few pages. But it would be quicker and cheaper to visit a good bookshop. So, if the computerised index is kept away from the text, or not used to process information about individuals, the book is exempt. But the information – and, more importantly, the uses to which it may be put – is unaffected.

The Act draws fine distinctions between information processed 'by reference to the data subject', and that which is processed 'only for the purpose of preparing the text of documents'. Already, these definitions have begun to cause severe difficulties. The Act provides data users with a tribunal, to which they may appeal to resolve any difficulties they have with the Registrar over the meaning of such phrases. But the tribunal is for data users alone; the same privilege is not available to data subjects, even though they may be far more in need of simple and cheap remedies than having to go to court.

Absurd distinctions abound in the Data Protection Act for two reasons. First, civil service administrators in general still make a virtue of their scientific and technical illiteracy; to many, computers remain outlandish technological mystery boxes, whose mysteries make them feel inadequate to the task of writing laws to govern their use. Second, this outlook very much suits their purposes. We cannot stress too much that the threat posed by computer databanks does not spring from the machines, but from administrators – and public sector administrators in particular. The threat lies in the information administrators gather and transact (whether in the form of computer data or paper files) and how they use the information. By portraying the mysterious computer as the villain of the piece, they let themselves off the hook. This artifice has also enabled them to exempt entirely manual records from privacy protection.

As to the question of the value of the Act in the protection of information privacy, there may be a short, simple and unkind answer. Small wonder that some users of sensitive data were rather pleased with the drafting of the Act. In 1981, a senior police officer responsible for one of the largest criminal intelligence computer systems in Britain confided in one of our colleagues his view that 'with this government ... we can expect more holes than Lindop had'.

Having considered the unnecessary difficulties some data users face, it is worth briefly considering the long obstacle course that a data subject will have to negotiate to use the Act effectively. (But neither this section, nor the book as a whole, can be or is intended to be a guide to the use of the subject access provisions of the Act. Many pamphlets on this and related subjects are available from the Data Protection Registrar's Office, and advice may also be had from bodies such as the National Consumer Council or local Citizens' Advice Bureaux.[8])

Suppose that it is 1992 and the Data Protection Act is fully in operation. An official of – let's call it the Administration Department – calls at your door, and asks a string of intimidating and highly offensive questions which are clearly based on a detailed accumulation of knowledge of your

personal life. Most of the information is very accurate, but
some of it is scandalously and damagingly inaccurate. You ask
where the information comes from and the official replies,
'From the computer.' He will say no more.

This is a clear case for concern. You have been reliably told
that inaccurate information about you is held on a computer,
and it has been disclosed to your obvious disadvantage. The
Data Protection Act is quite clear about your entitlement to
damages in these circumstances.

But where next? The local main public library holds the full
Data Protection Register, from which you discover that the
official's organisation doesn't have a computer. They must
have got the information from somebody else's computer. But
whose? You have no right to find out from the visiting official.
There are 300,000 entries in the Register. Somewhat pains-
takingly, you may establish that at least 5000 of those listed
make disclosures to official Administration Departments. But
the register will not tell you the size of any of these databanks,
and it may not indicate whether the people covered are
restricted to goat-owning crofters in Caithness or inhabitants
of your own home town. To make subject access enquiries to
them all would cost a fortune. At the time of writing, the
subject access fee had yet to be fixed, but was expected to be
set (by the Home Secretary) at several pounds.

In fact, even if the official's department did have a computer
databank registered, and you were able to exercise subject
access to your own records, you are not entitled to find out
where they got the inaccurate information from, or to whom
they may have subsequently disclosed it.

The information might have come from a 'national security'
databank, in which case you haven't got a hope. Or it might
have come from any one of the thousand databanks which
are covered by exemptions. None of them have registered
their intention to transfer information to the Administration
Departments. They don't have to. But an exhaustive check
of all the other databanks would be fruitless, if the information could have come from, say, a subject-access-exempt
police computer. Or the information might be exempted
from subject access for other reasons (such as its origin in
health or social work records), in which case you won't get

to see it anyway, and won't know where it originally came from.

There is no point in writing to the Registrar for help. He has no more powers than you to find out who might be passing on all this erroneous data, as he will have no reasonable grounds to suspect that any particular data user has committed an offence. And if he cannot swear on oath to a judge that he has such evidence, then he has no powers to go and inspect the data. He can write a letter asking them if they did it; but so can you. If the information had come from a government databank which was not exempted, disclosure of the transfer could become exempted if the Home Secretary decided that the information transferred was covered by the Official Secrets Act.

If, by good fortune, you find the right source, you have to pay a fee and wait 40 days. You will not receive any information which might identify third parties, or which is not processed by reference to yourself, or which is held on cross-linked manual records – or which has been deleted from the computer since you first asked to see it. It is an offence for a data user to 'specially process ... data to make it acceptable to the subject', including deleting or altering information, or dumping it to manual records. But it is very hard to envisage any means by which the data subject or the Registrar could find out if this had been done, or find sufficient evidence to prosecute if it had.

Suppose, however, that you both find the data user concerned and are provided with a copy of the inaccurate data being held. Even if you now show the user that the data was wrong, you have, in fact, no absolute right to get the data removed. You can ask, through the Registrar, for your correction to be recorded also – but if you want to enforce removal, you have no alternative but the courts. Nor can the Registrar determine that you are entitled to damages; only the courts can do that. Unlike the Parliamentary, Health Service or Local Government Ombudsmen, the Registrar has no powers to recommend settlements for damages, or to investigate disputes to assist the complainant or the court.

Going to court to enforce a right may sound fairly easy – to anyone who has never tried it. Only the very rich or very disgruntled may be able or willing to pursue a recalcitrant data user through the legal delays and complexities this involves. It could be an exceptionally costly process. Legal aid may be available – but many people of modest means do not qualify for it. The granting of legal aid is, in any case, not automatic, but is at the discretion of a legal aid committee. Since Clause 23 of the Data Protection Act puts the burden of proof of a damaging breach of privacy on the user, and since the Registrar has no investigative powers, that committee may be reluctant to grant legal aid for cases under the Act.

If a legally aided or privately paid for case does finally reach the courts, the data subject will still be going before a far less experienced or technically competent body than the Data Protection Tribunal, whose services are exclusively available to data users. But suppose that, at the end of this lengthy process, you have not only tracked down the offending databank but obtained an order for the data about you to be corrected. It is done. You will not, however, be able to find out the names of other parties to whom the inaccurate data may have been disclosed, or when, or to whom the information may then have been passed on. The erroneous data about you may by now have proliferated widely.

It is now 1995. The doorbell rings. It is an official of the Regulation Administration. He asks a string of intimidating and highly offensive questions which are clearly based on a detailed accumulation of knowledge of your personal life. Most of the information is very accurate, but some of it is scandalously and damagingly inaccurate; the same information as last time. You ask where the information came from and the official replies, 'From the computer.' He will say no more . . .

Before royal ink was even dry on the Act, attempts to defeat its already weak subject access provisions began. Some administrators and computer professionals responded to the spirit of the Act with an attempt to engineer further loopholes. A particularly disgraceful example of this activity was a booklet on the Act published during 1984 by the National Computing Centre (NCC) in Manchester. Its manual was entitled *Personal Data Protection*.[9] Section 8 of the manual listed a few devices that data users could use to protect personal data – from data subjects! The writer styled this 'mitigating the effects of legislation', and suggested that data users employ his three handy hints:

Keep records in a card index: 'you will be completely exempt' (the *extrusion* dodge).

Discourage data subjects from checking their entries by registering every different type of data held about them separately. The data user would thereby multiply the cost to anyone seeking subject access and 'require a separate fee for each request for access to information' (the *multiple file* dodge).

Attempt to dodge the letter *and* spirit of the law by having two databanks, one 'open' and one 'secret' – holding data the computer operator did not want to disclose (the *hidden file* dodge).

To use the third dodge, the open databank would hold only name and address and be linked to the separate, secret database using an identification code only. Subject access could then be restricted to name and address information. All other personal data would be connected only to the identification number, and could not be retrieved by reference to a person's name. A 'disk storage address' (an internal code generated by the computer) was suggested as the linking identifier, as this 'would do quite nicely'.

This wholesale violation of the purposes of the Act would, the NCC booklet claimed, enable non-registration, not require data transfers to be registered, avoid all disclosure and eliminate personal data 'from the application of the Data Protection Act altogether'. The entire booklet was written from the point of view of trying to avoid the Act to the greatest possible degree; even raising the rather unlikely spectre of dawn 'raids' on computer files by the 'Registrar's men'.

The booklet, published by the NCC with a note that author John Court was a member of the centre's panel of computer audit lecturers, but without any disclaimer as to the opinions he held, seems an improper publication for a publicly funded body. It was also published in apparent contravention of the goals of the National Computing Centre itself, since the booklet suggested the *abandonment* of computers in order to avoid

legal privacy controls. It was particularly ill advised that
guidance for law avoidance should be issued, and so rapidly,
by a body which was still employing the future Data Protection
Registrar. A similar guide to the Act, published by two senior
academics, in 1985, was equally forthright about evading the
new law. Authors Dr Nigel Savage and Professor Chris Edwards
suggested that 'to avoid the Act, the simplest thing to do is to
return [information] to the old-fashioned filing cabinet'.[10]
Their book, *A Guide to the Data Protection Act*, suggested that:

> Anyone wishing to use information 'for a variety of non-
> registered purposes ... may do so by transferring the data
> to manual files'.

> Data users can 'avoid giving access to sensitive data by
> careful use of language', and by seeking to 'disguise opinion
> as intentions'.

The latter dodge, it was suggested, could be used to conceal
data on a 'trade-union troublemaker', by saying, 'We intend to
select Mr Y for redundancy [given the opportunity] because of
trade-union activities'.

Such advice in these publications stood in squalid contrast
to many other high-quality guidance materials prepared about
the same time by City institutions (whose reputation for
placing personal rights above financial interests is not always
high).[11] After critical enquiries from the authors during the
writing of this book, the NCC booklet was rapidly withdrawn
in November 1985.

The new law leaves many key issues yet to be defined. After
so many years of study and struggle, there had been public
hopes for an Act that would be a powerful tool for privacy, one
that would give the public an understanding that information
privacy rights existed, and could effectively be enforced. These
hopes have been dashed. But the Act does create a new
climate, promoting the education of data users about their
responsibilities, and we may be grateful for that. Perhaps, too, a
battle lost by the Home Office after a 20-year struggle is *ipso
facto* worth celebrating.

Registrar Howe has said that 'what the Act means will
ultimately be defined by the courts; case law will define it'.[12]
Sadly, this is all too true. Recent British legislative history has

seen comparable major civil rights initiatives – on race relations and equal opportunities – picked apart, watered down, and all but annulled by the indifference of administrators and the conservatism of lawyers and judges. The Acts which created regulatory bodies such as the Equal Opportunities Commission and the Commission for Racial Equality left them without vital powers, and hemmed them about with 'safeguards' to curb their real effectiveness (on civil liberties grounds, it was occasionally claimed). The data protection situation is little different.

In many respects, the Data Protection Act is woolly, ambiguous and formless. The Act's supervisory body, the Data Protection Registry, is small, weak, burdened with some excessive regulation, constrained from entering the few real danger areas, and bereft of necessary powers of investigation, inspection and surveillance. Were the Registrar and Registry now to disappear in a sea of paper, never to be seen or heard of again in Whitehall, the mandarins might well exchange thin, reserved smiles over a morning's sherry, and reflect quietly that data protection was less of an impediment to efficient public administration than first they had feared. This is how the British establishment had always seen off and neutralised irritating civil rights reforms, they would later recall in their memoirs.

Notes

1: *The Politics of Information Privacy* (pages 19–38)

1. *Guardian*, 21 February 1980.
2. *Data Protection – Perspectives on Information Privacy*. Continuing Education Unit, University of Leicester, 1983.
3. Command 5012, July 1972.
4. Command 6353, December 1975.
5. We were informed privately that, in the event, the individual concerned played no significant role in the Data Protection Committee's deliberations on national security matters or other issues.
6. *Report of the Data Protection Committee*, Command 7341, December 1978. (The Lindop report.)
7. House of Commons Home Affairs Committee, First Report, Session 1979–80. House of Commons Paper 755, 1979–80 (evidence), and House of Commons Paper 23, 1980–81.
8. *Times*, 21 July 1980.
9. *Guardian*, 16 September 1981.
10. Command 8539, April 1982. The European Convention on data protection is reproduced as part of this White Paper, as are the OECD guidelines on privacy and the transborder flows of personal data.
11. *Data Protection – Perspectives on Information Privacy*. Continuing Education Unit, University of Leicester, 1983.
12. In Chapter 11, we deal in depth with the provisions of the Act, and summarise its inadequacies.
13. *Guardian*, 1 July 1983.
14. Reported in *Lindop and After*, by Professor F.M. Martin; proceedings of Social Research Association conference on Data Protection and Privacy, March 1982.

2: *Inside a Databank* (pages 39–52)

1. Lindop report, pages 16–17.
2. Lindop report, page 84.

References to *Hansard* are normally to answers to parliamentary written questions.

3. Command 6353, December 1975.
4. *Financial Times*, 17 July 1985.

3: The Threat *(pages 53–85)*

1. Command 8539.
2. Patricia Hewitt, *Privacy: the Information Gatherers*, NCCL, 1977; Campaign for Freedom of Information, *'I want to know what's in my file ...'*, 1985.
3. *Computing*, 1 May 1984.
4. *Daily Telegraph*, 12 February 1979.
5. *Time Out*, 13 July 1973.
6. Senate Report S402–17, 1975 (75–601684) – subtitled *Privacy Developments in Europe and Their Implications for US Policy*.
7. Lindop report, pages 260–64.
8. Lindop report, page xxiv.
9. Patricia Hewitt (ed.), *Computers, Records and the Right to Privacy*, page 175. Input Two Nine, 1979.
10. *Guardian*, 30 and 31 August 1985. See also note 9.
11. *Observer*, 13 May 1984.
12. *Guardian*, 6 March 1984.
13. *Rights*, 7/8, 1979.
14. Respectively, details of these nine incidents were reported by: *Western Morning News*, 19 May 1983; *Daily Telegraph*, 19 November 1975; *Computing*, 10 April 1975; NCCL files, 1980; *Times*, 15 July 1980; *Guardian*, 17 November 1980; private communications, NCCL files, 1981; *Newsnight* (BBC), 14 May 1982; *New Scientist*, 29 November 1979.
15. *Sun*, 9 February 1982.
16. These incidents of police computer leakage are described respectively in *Datalink*, 19 July 1979, and *Observer*, 11 October 1981; *Observer*, 8 November 1981; *Observer*, 30 August 1981; *Observer*, 4 October 1981; *Observer*, 18 October 1981; *New Statesman*, 23 and 30 October 1981; *New Statesman*, 6 November 1981; *Time Out*, 11 April 1980; *Observer*, 31 January 1982; *Computing*, 20 June 1985, and *Daily Telegraph*, 13 October 1985.
17. See also Hugo Cornwall, *The Hackers' Handbook*. Century Communications, 1979.

4: From the Cradle to the Grave *(pages 87–119)*

1. *Hansard*, 5 March 1984.
2. *Social Security Operational Strategy – a Framework for the Future*. HMSO, 1982.
3. *A Strategy for Social Security Operations*. DHSS, 1980.

4. *A Strategy for Social Security Operations.* DHSS, 1980.
5. *Computing,* 8 April 1982.
6. *Hansard,* 20 June 1984.
7. *Social Security Operational Strategy – a Framework for the Future.* HMSO, 1982.
8. Lindop report, page 263.
9. Lindop report, page 263.
10. DHSS briefing.
11. *Computing,* 26 March 1982.
12. House of Commons Public Accounts Committee, Thirtieth Report, Session 1984–85, *The Unemployment Benefit Service; and the Prevention and Detection of Fraud.* House of Commons Paper 434, 1984–85.
13. *Hansard,* 24 April 1985.
14. Lindop report, page 60.
15. *Social Security Operational Strategy – a Framework for the Future.* HMSO, 1982.
16. *Social Security Operational Strategy – a Framework for the Future.* HMSO, 1982.
17. *Social Security Operational Strategy. Report of a Seminar.* DHSS, 1981.
18. *Guardian,* 8 April 1982.
19. *Datalink* (magazine), 20 October 1982.
20. *Housing Benefit Review,* 1985. Command 9520.
21. Ros Franey, *Poor Law.* CPAG, 1983.
22. *Reform of Social Security,* Vol. 2, para. 2.107. DHSS, 1985 (Command 9158).
23. *State Research,* 24 June 1981. The information comes from an internal DHSS manual entitled *Specialist Claims Control.*
24. *Guardian,* 24 January 1985.
25. In practice, by 1985, there were a little more than half this number in post.
26. *Guardian,* 24 January 1984.
27. *Fraud Officer Assistance.* ICL proposal to DHSS, 1984.
28. Correspondence from the DHSS to one of the authors, 6 January 1982.
29. *Observer,* 13 May 1984.
30. Lindop report, page 60.
31. *Guardian,* 11 February 1984.
32. *New Statesman,* 10 May 1985.
33. *Hansard,* 20 June 1984.
34. House of Commons Public Accounts Committee, Thirtieth Report, Session 1984–85, *The Unemployment Benefit Service; and the Prevention and Detection of Fraud.* House of Commons Paper 434, 1984–85.
35. *Hansard,* 15 March 1984.
36. *Committee on the Enforcement Powers of the Revenue Departments,* (chaired by Lord Keith). HMSO, 1983 (Command 8822).
37. *Guardian,* 30 August 1985.
38. Alistair Hetherington, *Guardian Years.* Chatto and Windus, 1981.
39. DHSS background briefing note, January 1984.
40. *Computing,* 9 August 1984.

5: In Sickness and In Health (pages 120–50)

1. Office of Population Censuses and Surveys (OPCS), *Vital Registration in England and Wales*, 1985.
2. *Guardian*, 18 April 1984.
3. *Steering Group on Health Services Information*, supplement to First and Fourth Reports. DHSS, March 1985.
4. *Management in General Practice*. Oxford General Practice Series 8. OUP, 1984.
5. Lindop report, page 72.
6. *British Medical Journal*, 16 February 1985.
7. *New Scientist*, 8 August 1985.
8. Lindop report, page 66.
9. *Computing*, 22 April 1982.
10. *Computing*, 6 May 1982.
11. *Computing*, 4 May 1978.
12. *Computing*, 26 January 1978.
13. Lindop report, page 68.
14. ICL press release, 16 October 1985.
15. *Computing*, 26 September 1985.
16. *New Scientist*, 5 July 1973.
17. *Steering Group on Health Services Information*, First Report. HMSO, 1982.
18. *Health Services Information*. HMSO, 1982.
19. *Steering Group on Health Services Information*, supplement to First and Fourth Reports. DHSS, March 1985.
20. Lindop report, page 69.
21. British Medical Association, *Ethics and the Police* (public statement), 3 August 1979.
22. British Medical Association press release, 20 December 1982.
23. DHSS Circular DA(84)25, *Confidentiality of Personal Health Information*, October 1984.
24. *British Journal of Health Care Computing*, summer 1984.
25. *Data Protection Act Subject Access to Personal Health Data*. DHSS, 1985.

6: At Home and Abroad (pages 151-89)

1. *Guardian*, 21 March 1985.
2. *Guardian*, 3 October 1980.
3. Commission for Racial Equality, *Immigration Control Procedures: Report of a Formal Investigation*. CRE, 1985.
4. *Hansard*, 27 February 1984.
5. House of Commons Home Affairs Committee, Sixth Report, Session 1984–85, *Immigration and Nationality Department of the Home Office*. House of Commons Paper 277, 1984–85.
6. House of Commons Home Affairs Committee, Sixth Report, Session 1984–85, *Immigration and Nationality Department of the Home Office*. House of Commons Paper 277, 1984–85.

7. *Computing*, 10 February 1983.
8. *Times*, 2 May 1983.
9. *Hansard*, 27 February 1984.
10. House of Commons Foreign Affairs Committee, Third Report, Session 1981–82, *Supply Estimates*. House of Commons Paper 406, 1981–82.
11. *Hansard*, 11 April 1983.
12. Home Office Immigration and Nationality Department, *Machine-Readable Passport Experiment and Suspect Index Feasibility Study* (internal paper). Home Office, November 1980.
13. Home Office Immigration and Nationality Department, *Machine-Readable Passport Experiment and Suspect Index Feasibility Study* (internal paper). Home Office, November 1980.
14. *Hansard*, 26 January 1983.
15. International Civil Aviation Organisation, *A Passport with Machine-Readable Capability*, Document 9303, 1980.
16. *Guardian*, 5 July 1979.
17. House of Commons Home Affairs Committee, Sixth Report, Session 1984–85, *Immigration and Nationality Department of the Home Office*. House of Commons Paper 277, 1984–85.
18. *New Scientist*, 5 January 1984.
19. *Guardian*, 7 July 1978.
20. *Guardian*, 7 July 1978.
21. *Guardian*, 11 April 1979.
22. *Guardian*, 6 July 1978.
23. *Guardian*, 17 May 1978.
24. Tabone, *Report on Terrorism in Europe*. Council of Europe, 1978.
25. Council of Europe, *Establishment and Harmonisation of National Identity Cards*, Resolution (77) 26, 1977.
26. *Times*, 2 May 1983.
27. *Hansard*, 6 April 1978.
28. *Hansard*, 21 February 1983.
29. The name IVAN is not an acronym; the computer is said to have been named after one of its designers.
30. *Times*, 2 May 1983.
31. *Observer*, 24 February 1985.
32. House of Commons Foreign Affairs Committee, Third Report, Session 1981–82, *Supply Estimates*. House of Commons Paper 406, 1981–82.
33. *Hansard*, 29 March 1982.
34. *Guardian*, 16 August 1980.
35. For an extensive account of such cases, see Paul Gordon, *Policing Immigration*, Pluto Press, 1985.
36. *Hansard*, 22 February 1983.
37. House of Commons Home Affairs Committee, Sixth Report, Session 1984–85, *Immigration and Nationality Department of the Home Office*. House of Commons Paper 277, 1984–85.
38. *Hansard*, 12 June 1984.
39. *Hansard*, 6 July 1984.
40. *New Scientist*, 21 March 1985.
41. *Hansard*, 12 June 1984.
42. Home Office, *Tackling Drug Misuse*, March 1985.

43. Home Office press statement, 18 July 1985.
44. *Sunday Express*, 1 April 1979.
45. *Sunday Telegraph*, 26 August 1979.
46. OPCS, *Census Topics*, *1981*.
47. OPCS, *Monitor*, 1981.
48. Letter from Sir George Young to Michael Ancram MP, 15 April 1980.
49. *Computing*, 21 August 1980.
50. OPCS, *Efficiency Scrutiny Report*, February 1985.
51. *Computing*, 23 February 1978.
52. *Hansard*, 23 February 1984.
53. *Hansard*, 23 February 1984.
54. *Hansard*, 16 March 1984.
55. Letter from Department of Transport to Dr Chris Pounder, 23 December 1977.
56. Road Vehicle Registration and Licensing Regulations, 1971. See also *Hansard*, 23 February 1984.
57. House of Commons Public Accounts Committee, Fourth Report. Session 1975–76.
58. *Computing*, 19 October 1982.
59. *Computing*, 4 June 1981.
60. *New Scientist*, 19 May 1983.
61. *Computers: Safeguards for Privacy*, Command 6354, 1975.
62. *Where?*, 109, 1975.
63. *Computing*, 21 October 1982.

7: Coming to Notice (pages 190–225)

1. *Police Review*, 12 May 1972.
2. Carole F. Willis, *The Use, Effectiveness, and Impact of Police Stop and Search Powers*. Home Office Research and Planning Unit, Paper 15, 1983.
3. Policy Studies Institute, *Police and People in London*, Vol. IV, page 322.
4. *Hansard*, 3 December 1984.
5. Metropolitan Police *Standing Orders*, Chapter 6, Section 21(1).
6. Richard Kinsey and Robert Baldwin, *Police Powers and Politics*. Quartet, 1982.
7. *Observer*, 18 October 1981; a tape in which the Liverpool criminal records office gave the information out was broadcast on BBC *Newsnight*, 14 May 1982.
8. *New Statesman*, 2 April 1982.
9. *Time Out*, 20 July 1979.
10. *New Statesman*, 10 August 1979.
11. *Guardian*, 25 February 1984.
12. *New Scientist*, 23 April 1981.
13. *The Police Use of Computers*, page 19. Technical Authors Group (Scotland), 1982.

14. Richard Kinsey and Robert Baldwin, *Police Powers and Politics*. Quartet, 1982.
15. *Guardian*, 20 September 1979.
16. Metropolitan Police *Standing Orders*, Chapter 6, Section 21(3).
17. Information from New Scotland Yard press office, August 1979.
18. Lindop report, page 220.
19. *Datalink*, 24 October 1977.
20. Full details of the formats of Thames Valley Police local intelligence records are given in Duncan Campbell, *Policing the Police*, pages 123–28. John Calder, 1980.
21. *Computer Weekly*, 5 March 1981.
22. *Police Review*, 21 April 1978.
23. Home Office Scientific Research and Development Branch, Report no. 13/82. See *New Statesman*, 29 June 1984.
24. *New Statesman*, 13 January 1984.
25. *Datalink*, 4 July 1983.
26. *Datalink*, 30 July 1982.
27. *Computing*, 5 April 1984.
28. Information supplied by the Home Office, May 1985.
29. Lindop report, page 82.
30. *Hansard*, 28 February 1983.
31. Lindop report, pages 220–21.
32. *Guardian*, 20 February 1979.
33. Report by Dr Brian Leutchford, *Police Research Bulletin*, 38. Home Office, 1981.
34. *Guardian*, 21 November 1984.
35. *Guardian*, 22 January 1982.
36. *Guidelines for the Control of Computerised Personal Data Obtained During Major Crime Investigations*. Home Office, 1985.
37. Appendix 34, *Consolidated Circular to the Police on Crime and Kindred Matters*. Home Office, 1977 (most recently updated to January 1985).
38. *Hansard*, 18 May 1984.

8: PNC (pages 226–56)

1. *Computer Policy Circular*, COCPIT(84)8, Home Office 1984.
2. Duncan Campbell, *Policing the Police*, Vol. 2, 1979, page 94. John Calder, 1980.
3. Described personally to one of the authors by a former programmer on the Home Office Police National Computer Unit.
4. Lindop report, page 220.
5. This information was not given in subsequent years. There were then 22 Special Branch officers in North Wales Police. This type of detailed breakdown of PNC usage has only rarely been published.
6. Technical Authors Group (Scotland), *The Police Use of Computers*. Edinburgh, 1980, pages 14–17.
7. *Daily Telegraph*, 18 December 1982.

8. *Guardian,* 9 May 1972.
9. *Hansard,* 2 December 1977, 21 March 1983, 21 April 1983, 9 March 1984, 11 June 1985; information supplied directly to the authors by the Home Office in May and July 1985; and to Duncan Campbell for *Policing the Police,* Vol. 2 (John Calder, 1980). 1985 information provided directly by PNCU, for the week ending 18 May 1985.
10. Duncan Campbell, *War Plan UK,* page 135. Paladin, 1983.
11. 1983 information, *Hansard,* 21 April 1983, 21 July 1983, and 11 June 1985. (Information scaled from data for separate four-week periods, during March and June 1983.) Information for 1985 was provided directly by the Home Office and PNCU, for the single week ending 18 May 1985.
12. *Hansard,* 21 April 1983.
13. Full details of the data fields (the actual elements of information stored) on each then current application of the PNC were given in a series of parliamentary answers to Jeremy Corbyn MP in *Hansard,* 13 November 1984.
14. Merseyside Police *Standing Orders* ('confidential').
15. *Hansard,* 11 June 1985 (see also 21 March 1983). About 7 per cent of those covered have more than one index entry in the wanted/missing index.
16. *Hansard,* 13 November 1974.
17. *Police Review,* 8 April 1983, notes that the DRUGS warning signal might mean that 'the drugs could be possessed legally or illegally'.
18. Source: police form CRO74A.
19. Lindop report, page 80. In 1985, the Home Office refuted this allegation and stated that 'there is no Special Branch indicator in CN record'. Lindop may have been referring to an indicator that relevant information is held at NIB.
20. Under Section 6(3) of the Sexual Offences Act 1956 or Section 27(3) of the Theft Act 1968. Recordable offences are defined by the Home Office as those for which details of convictions may be held in national police records – that is to say, at the National Identification Bureau and on the PNC. They are usually offences in which the police are involved in prosecution, and for which a prison sentence could be imposed by magistrates (whether or not such a sentence is imposed). The full list, published from time to time in a Statutory Instrument, therefore includes very minor offences, such as trivial shoplifting offences.
21. *Computing,* 18 July 1985.
22. Source: police form CRO74A; code RC7 is sometimes used to denote 'half-caste' or 'unidentified'.
23. *Computing,* 1 June 1978.
24. *Hansard,* 21 March 1985.
25. *Hansard,* 22 March 1984.
26. *Hansard,* 21 July 1983.
27. *Code of Practice for Personal Data Held on the Police National Computer,* Home Office, March 1982 ('in confidence').
28. *Daily Telegraph,* 23 December 1979.
29. *Hansard,* 13 November 1984. The only such indicator which has been acknowledged to be included on all vehicles is a marker to show that the vehicle has been stolen (Lindop report, page 81).
30. J.R. Cubberley and D. Blakey, *The Police National Computer in the United*

Kingdom, Home Office conference on the use of computers in police operations; London, November 1976.

31. See, for example, *Guardian*, 3 and 19 March 1984.
32. *Hansard*, 20 June 1984.
33. Figures from *Hansard*, 21 March 1983; further information from the PNC *Code of Practice* (see note 27), and Merseyside Police *Standing Orders*. The actual number of vehicles recorded is less than the sum of those in individual categories, as some vehicles are entered in more than one category. The ratio between the two totals is approximately 1.054 (*Hansard*, 21 April 1983).
34. Merseyside Police *Standing Orders*, Section 6, July 1978.
35. *Listener*, 8 March 1979.
36. *Hansard*, 2 December 1977. Police officers admitted in court to routinely recording the numbers of cars parked at the Oxfordshire house of a member of the Hunt Saboteurs Association, and at other anti-hunt meetings. During an M6 motorway service station check in Cumbria, some time after these numbers had been noted, a patrol officer was told by the radio operator that a car checked in the car park 'belonged to a prominent member of the Anti Blood Sports League [sic]'. Sixty miles away, huntsman John Peel's grave had just been symbolically damaged; the occupants of the car were arrested. (See Duncan Campbell, *Policing the Police*, Vol. 2, pages 77–78. John Calder, 1980.)
37. *Daily Express*, 13 January 1982.
38. J.R. Cubberley and D. Blakey, *The Police National Computer in the United Kingdom*, Home Office Conference on the Use of Computers in Police Operations; London, November 1976.
39. The police 'modus operandi' (MO) reference system is a ten-point checklist for identifying the crimes and chosen targets of particular criminals. The ten points are 'classword' (the nature or type of property or person attacked), 'entry' (point of entry), 'means' (means of entry), 'object' (purpose of the entry), 'time', 'style' (type of criminal), 'tale' (excuse for being at the scene of the crime if apprehended), 'pal' (whether the crime was committed by a group, or 'solo'), 'transport' (vehicles used), and 'trade marks' (any special act by the criminal).
40. *Hansard*, 13 November 1984.
41. Home Office *Computer Policy Circular*, COCPIT(84)8, circulated to Chief Officers and Clerks of Police Authorities, 1984.
42. *Hansard*, 21 March 1983.
43. *New Scientist*, 12 January 1984, and 24 January 1985.

9: *Policing Politics* (pages 257–73)

1. *Leveller*, 16, June 1978.
2. House of Commons Home Affairs Committee, *Special Branch*, page 4. HMSO, May 1985.
3. *Hansard*, 20 June 1974.
4. *Hansard*, 26 February 1975.
5. House of Commons Home Affairs Committee, *Special Branch*, page 106.

6. House of Commons Home Affairs Committee, *Special Branch*; the Home Office guidelines appear on pages x–xiii.
7. House of Commons Home Affairs Committee, *Special Branch*, page 119.
8. Quoted in the *Observer*, 28 February 1982.
9. *Hansard*, 2 March 1978.
10. House of Commons Home Affairs Committee, *Special Branch*, page 63.
11. The approximate numbers of Special Branch officers were, in 1985: Metropolitan Police, 379; Merseyside Police, 108; other forces in England and Wales, 762; Scotland, 107; Ulster, 280.
12. Command 6354, December 1975.
13. *Times*, 14 February and 9 September 1977.
14. Source: *Summary of Operational Requirements for an Information Storage and Retrieval System for the MPO* (tender document distributed to manufacturers), Metropolitan Police, 1974.
15. Source: *Summary of Operational Requirements for an Information Storage and Retrieval System for the MPO* (tender document distributed to manufacturers), Metropolitan Police, 1974.
16. In the police tender document (see above), the individual squads using each part of the database were referred to as Section 1, Section 2, etc., and formal titles were not given. The Special Branch was Section 5. The identity of each squad could, however, be worked out by the type of data held; in 1979, the police confirmed this identification.
17. *Hansard*, 21 April 1983.
18. *Hansard*, 14 July 1983.
19. *Police Use of Computers* (5th edition), prepared by the Association of Chief Police Officers.
20. *Observer*, 10 January 1982.
21. *Observer*, 31 January 1981.
22. *New Statesman*, 20 October 1983.
23. *Policing London*. GLC, January–March 1985.
24. *Time Out*, 17 June 1977.
25. Lindop report, pages 79 and 84.
26. Lindop report, page 88.

10: National Security Surveillance (pages 274–98)

1. *New Statesman*, 26 November 1983.
2. *Guardian*, 17–19 April 1984.
3. *Guardian*, 17–19 April 1984.
4. *New Statesman*, 5 March 1982.
5. *New Statesman*, 5 March 1982.
6. *New Statesman*, 2 March 1984.
7. *Sunday Times*, 12 December 1976.
8. House of Commons Home Affairs Committee, *Special Branch*, page 113.
9. See, for example, *Observer*, 24 February 1985.
10. *New Statesman*, 5 March 1982.
11. *Time Out*, 25 July 1980.

12. Rupert Allason, *The Branch*. Secker and Warburg, 1983.
13. Details of the Jan Martin case were first revealed on BBC *Panorama*, 2 March 1981.
14. House of Commons Home Affairs Committee, *Special Branch*, page 85.
15. *Observer*, 17 July 1977; *Guardian*, 4 August 1977.
16. For example, *Guardian*, 26 July 1978; a summary of such incidents appeared in *State Research Bulletin* no 7, August–September 1978.
17. *Labour Research*, February 1985.
18. *New Statesman*, 27 February 1981.
19. *Observer*, 18 August 1985.
20. See, for example, *Sunday Times*, 7 September 1975.
21. *Computing*, 14 February 1980.
22. *Times*, 5 December 1974.
23. *Northern Ireland Precis* (summary of Northern Ireland Intelligence Environment course). Army Intelligence Wing, School of Service Intelligence, Ashford, Kent, 1977 ('restricted').
24. *Northern Ireland Precis* (summary of Northern Ireland Intelligence Environment course). Army Intelligence Wing, School of Service Intelligence, Ashford, Kent, 1977 ('restricted').
25. Lindop report, page 222.

11: *Loopholes in the Law* (pages 229–319)

1. National Council for Civil Liberties, *Briefing on the Data Protection Bill 1983*. NCCL, January 1983.
2. *Hansard*, 5 July 1984, 17 December 1984, and 25 February 1985.
3. Lindop report, page 222.
4. As stated by the Home Office at the time of writing.
5. *Hansard*, 14 January 1980.
6. *Data Protection Act 1984*, Home Office (Police) Circular 64/1984.
7. *Guardian*, 13 May 1985.
8. Office of the Data Protection Registrar, Springfield House, Water Lane, Wilmslow, Cheshire SK9 5AX (0625 535777). The National Consumer Council is at 18 Queen Anne's Gate, London SW1H 9AA (01 222 9501). Citizens' Advice Bureaux are listed in every local telephone directory.
9. J.M. Court, *Personal Data Protection – the 1984 Act and Its Implications*, National Computing Centre, 1984.
10. Dr Nigel Savage and Professor Chris Edwards, *A Guide to the Data Protection Act*, Financial Training Publications, 1984, 1985; see also *Computing*, 28 November 1985.
11. For example, that published by City accountants Ernst and Whinney.
12. *Informatics*, July 1985.

Index